DISPOSABLE PEOPLE

New Slavery in the Global Economy

KEVIN BALES

REVISED EDITION
WITH A NEW PREFACE

UNIVERSITY OF
CALIFORNIA PRESS

Berkeley / Los Angeles / London

University of California Press
Berkeley and Los Angeles, California

University of California Press, Ltd.
London, England

First Paperback Printing 2000

Library of Congress Cataloging-in-Publication Data

Bales, Kevin.

   Disposable people : new slavery in the global economy /
Kevin Bales. — Rev. ed.
       p.   cm.
   Includes bibliographical references and index.
   ISBN 0-520-24384-6 (alk. paper)
   1. Slavery.   2. Slaver labor.   3. Poor—Employment.
4. Prostitution.   I. Title.
HT867.B35   2004
306.3'62—dc22   2004008180

Manufactured in the United States of America
13   12   11   10   09   08   07   06   05
10   9   8   7   6   5   4   3

The paper used in this publication is both acid-free
and totally chlorine-free (TCF). It meets the minimum
requirements of ANSI/NISO Z39.48-1992 (R 1997)
(*Permanence of Paper*). ∞

CONTENTS

PREFACE TO THE REVISED EDITION

"I spoke of these people as captives. I talked about the harsh conditions they found in New York. They were malnourished, diseased. Infant mortality was high."

Dr. Michael Blakey heads up the African Burial Ground Project[1] in New York City. More than four hundred slaves are buried in Lower Manhattan, and Blakey, a physical anthropologist, is drawing out the stories their bones tell. Blakey described how the remains of one young man show that he was probably trafficked from Africa to the United States:

> *He has evidence of treponemal disease, probably yaws. So he's been exposed to a tropical disease. He has evidence of hard work and some healed fractures in his spine. He also has the most subtle and elegantly filed teeth.*

This man's bones bear witness to the destructive nature of slavery: he was no more than thirty-five when he died. There are also a very large number of small children buried in the cemetery. The impact of slavery on these families was enormous: *"When children die in large numbers,"* Blakey notes *"people feel a significant sense of loss."*

Blakey's work ties us to slavery in the past. It shows us the reality of slavery's pernicious and ugly damage to human life. The slaves buried in Manhattan also help us to understand something very important:

slavery has been, is, and will be part of our lives until we make it stop.

The slaves of Lower Manhattan and the slaves of today share many forms of suffering, among them the abuse and death of their children, the damage to their bodies through trauma and untreated disease, the theft of their lives and work, the destruction of their dignity, and the fat profits others make from their sweat. Slavery still exists in New York and around the world. Today it is often hard to see, but it is there. And like the slaves of the African Burial Ground in New York, the slaves all around us today have waited a long time for us and our governments to come awake to their existence.

When *Disposable People* was first published in 1999, many found its story shocking and unbelievable. Like the African Burial Ground Project, the research needed for the book was difficult to finance. But as the book's message about slavery began to sink in, it opened up new areas of study and action. As the first work in decades to show the extent of slavery around the world, *Disposable People* became a lightning rod, drawing both the energy of activists and the anger of governments trying to conceal slavery within their borders. I was amazed and humbled by the hundreds of people who after reading the book declared themselves new abolitionists and dedicated themselves to work against modern slavery. As the book was translated into more and more languages (nine, so far, in addition to English), the expanding knowledge of new slavery triggered off more and more reactions in individuals, groups, churches, schools, and governments. When I was writing *Disposable People* I had dreams of how it might stir people to action, but my dreams were too small. The reality has been great and rapid change in the last five years, change that seems to be growing in its momentum and reach.

Underlying this momentous growth is the decision made in thousands of minds that slavery must end. The outcomes of this decision have been as various as imagination can make them. A film based in part on *Disposable People* opened up new areas of slavery to the public view and won two Emmys and a Peabody award. As awareness of modern slavery expanded, other films, books, scripts, poems, articles, law reviews, photo essays, theses and dissertations, songs, even a dance program, expressed people's deeply felt desire to end slavery. For me, the growth in interest led to hundreds of interviews on television and radio, and in magazines and newspapers. The explosion of concern is being felt at the local, national, and international levels.

In the United States an important new law affecting slavery was passed at the end of 2000. Known as the Trafficking Victims Protection Act, it increased the penalties for human traffickers, brought new protections to victims, and ordered government departments to take action. This law has led to many initiatives and increased support for groups helping people who have been trafficked into the United States. Also in late 2000, the United Nations set out an agreement to fight trafficking in persons as part of a new Convention against Transnational Organized Crime. This protocol became international law on Christmas Day 2003, but has not yet been ratified by the United States. It will help bring national laws into agreement, which, since human trafficking is a crime that crosses borders, is crucial for successful prosecutions. Other countries too have written new laws. Now, as is the case for almost all laws against slavery around the world, the problem is getting those laws enforced.

One of the most exciting outcomes of this period followed the film that exposed slavery on cocoa farms in West Africa. The idea that the chocolate we feed our children, the chocolate we enjoy so much, could be tainted by slavery was disturbing. To their credit, chocolate companies in the United States and Europe moved quickly to address slavery in their product chain. Joining together, they made an agreement with anti-slavery groups, child labor organizations, and labor unions to take slavery and child labor out of cocoa for good. Now a well-funded new foundation has workers building programs in West Africa, and a system for inspecting and certifying cocoa is under construction. While some of the work has been held back by civil unrest in West Africa, the commitment and resources are there. For the first time since anti-

slavery groups called for it 150 years ago, an industry is taking full responsibility for its product chain. It is a historic breakthrough, one that
is serving as a model for other industries.

But what of the countries that made up the key stories of *Disposable
People?* Here there is news, but much of it is not good. In Thailand,
girls are still sold into brothels. Today these teenagers are more likely
to come from neighboring countries like Burma, Laos or Cambodia,
but their enslavement and destruction are the same. Since I first traveled to Thailand, the government there has made remarkable progress
with a campaign against HIV infection, but since the program relies
on condom use, and since enslaved teenage prostitutes have no choice
in that matter, they still are very likely to die of AIDS. The UN and
other organizations have given the Thai government help in designing
programs to fight slavery, but there is little will and fewer resources.
Police and government officials are still involved and profiting directly
from slavery. In the understated words of the U.S. State Department,[2]
"Official complicity in trafficking remains an area of concern."

Mauritania remains enigmatic. The government there has never
allowed free access to any researcher or monitor. Local anti-slavery
groups are still hounded and persecuted, their leaders arrested and
locked up to prevent them from talking to journalists. False-fronted
government agencies assure any listeners that slavery is all but gone.
Meanwhile, slaves continue to escape. One of these ex-slaves, who escaped in the late 1990s, told me some of her story:

> *I was born a slave. I was born in Mauritania in 1956. My mother and
> father were slaves for one family, and their parents were slaves of the
> same family. Ever since I was old enough to walk, I was forced to work for
> this family all day, every day. We never had days off. We hardly knew
> that it was Saturday or Sunday, because we had to work every day. Even
> if we were sick, we had to work. . . . In Mauritania, I didn't dare go to
> the government, because they wouldn't listen. Because for them, slavery is
> normal. It doesn't matter what the laws say there, because there they don't
> apply the laws. Maybe it's written that there is no slavery, but it's not*

true. Even in front of the president of Mauritania I can say in full voice that there is slavery in Mauritania, because now I'm as free as he is.

This woman had to escape and then bring her children out of bondage. Her courage is staggering. Today she lives in the United States and is building a new life, but behind her in Mauritania are thousands upon thousands of slaves.

Without a doubt the best news comes from Brazil. A new government under President da Silva (popularly known as "Lula") has dramatically increased the number of police officers assigned to slavery cases and given them more money and equipment. After his inauguration, Lula came out strongly against the slavery that destroys the lives of many Brazilians and is also a key element in the destruction of the country's natural environment. There is a long way to go in Brazil— thugs and slaveholders still control much of Amazonia and the west— but with a government that is facing up to the problem there is room for optimism.

Pakistan has been rocked by revolution and the American invasion of Afghanistan. Hundreds of thousands of Afghan refugees have poured across the border, creating the confusion and disorder that generate enslavement and trafficking. Recent observers report hundreds of enslaved children in camps near the Afghan border, working in quarries and crushing stone by hand. The current leader of Pakistan has called for stronger enforcement of anti-slavery laws, but he is hampered by a myriad of other problems. In the flurry of anti-terrorist campaigns, the hunt for Osama bin Laden, assassination attempts, threats of war with India, and a teetering economy, the bonded laborers of Pakistan are easy to forget.

India continues to be a mixed bag. With one of the best anti-slavery laws in the world, it still has more slaves than any other country. Millions of people throughout the country live in debt bondage. Some are trapped in the traditional forms of slavery that enslave generation after generation, others in new types of bondage emerging as India's economy modernizes and globalizes. But though they may only be drops in the ocean, I have seen amazing moments of liberation in India. In Northern India, groups like Sankalp and the Bal Vikas Ashram[3] have brought hundreds out of slavery and helped them to build new lives. They have done this on the slimmest of shoestrings, helping families achieve freedom and a safe and productive life for around thirty-five dollars. They do this not by buying them out of slavery, but by helping them learn their rights and standing by them when they fight for those rights. These groups show us how slavery will come to an end.

Around the world we still face the terrible frozen face of ignorance. The awareness that there are twenty-seven million slaves in the world has not yet fully penetrated the public mind, but the sparks and fires of committed people are beginning to melt that icy apathy. Traveling the world and speaking about slavery, I see how awareness leads quickly to action. This action can have enormous results. No one wants to live in a world with slavery, and today we are, in many ways, closer to its final eradication than ever. This could be the generation that brings slavery, after five thousand years, to an end. To do so we have to join together. Slavery is too big a problem to solve as individuals.

I've saved the best news for last. Of all the outcomes of the publication of *Disposable People*, the most exciting is the establishment of Free the Slaves, the first broad-based anti-slavery organization in modern America. Set up in late 2000, Free the Slaves is based in Washington, D.C. and has been joined by thousands of Americans who want to end slavery. In its very short life Free the Slaves has achieved breakthrough after breakthrough, from the agreement with the chocolate companies, to supporting the liberation of child slaves in India and West Africa, to educating the public, and bringing together clubs, churches, schools, universities, and individuals to fight slavery. Free the Slaves works against human trafficking and slavery in the United States and across the globe. Sometimes it does so by advising governments, but its most important work is backing up those grassroots groups that are literally kicking in doors and bringing slaves to freedom. Imagine my joy when I get an email like this one from India:

We had a rescue operation and rescued seven children from a carpet loom in Allahabad. All seven children are aged between ten and twelve years. Two of them are very sick, suffering from jaundice, and the others look malnourished. . . . after medical check ups they will be sent to Bal Vikas Ashram for rehabilitation. Their parents have been contacted.

Slave children in the carpet looms are often kidnapped at the age of seven or eight; these desperate parents won't have seen their children for years. Americans helped bring these children out of slavery by joining and supporting Free the Slaves, which in turn helps fund rescue and rehabilitation for slaves in India and other countries. As a father and a son, when I think about how these lost children are found and returned to their families, I have to admit I can't help but cry.

I hope that this new revised edition of *Disposable People* speaks to you. I've tried to update it where needed without changing the story it has to tell. I've been helped by the thousands of people who have read this book and talked to me about it. There are still likely to be errors, and these are all mine.

April 2004
Oxford, Mississippi

Contact Free the Slaves at:
info@freetheslaves.net
www.freetheslaves.net
Free the Slaves
1326 14th Street NW
Washington, D.C. 20005
202–588–1865

1. "Return to the African Burial Ground: An interview with physical anthropologist Michael L. Blakey," *Archeology Magazine*, online edition, January 2004, www.archeology.org.

2. U.S. State Dept. *Trafficking in Persons Report 2003*, pg. 149.

3. To learn more about these groups visit www.freetheslaves.net.

1

————— ✦ —————

THE NEW SLAVERY

THE FRENCH COUNTRYSIDE IN SUMMER lives up to its reputation. As we sit outdoors in a little village about one hundred miles from Paris, the breeze
brings us the scent of apples from the orchard next door. I have come
here to meet Seba, a newly freed slave. She is a handsome and animated young woman of twenty-two, but as she tells me her story she
draws into herself, smoking furiously, trembling, and then the tears
come.

> I was raised by my grandmother in Mali, and when I was still a little
> girl a woman my family knew came and asked her if she could take me
> to Paris to care for her children. She told my grandmother that she would
> put me in school and that I would learn French. But when I came to Paris
> I was not sent to school, I had to work every day. In their house I did all
> the work; I cleaned the house, cooked the meals, cared for the children,
> and washed and fed the baby. Every day I started work before 7 A.M. and
> finished about 11 P.M.; I never had a day off. My mistress did nothing;
> she slept late and then watched television or went out.
>
> One day I told her that I wanted to go to school. She replied that she
> had not brought me to France to go to school but to take care of her chil-
> dren. I was so tired and run-down. I had problems with my teeth; some-
> times my cheek would swell and the pain would be terrible. Sometimes

1

I had stomachaches, but when I was ill I still had to work. Sometimes when I was in pain I would cry, but my mistress would shout at me.

I slept on the floor in one of the children's bedrooms; my food was their leftovers. I was not allowed to take food from the refrigerator like the children. If I took food she would beat me. She often beat me. She would slap me all the time. She beat me with the broom, with kitchen tools, or whipped me with electric cable. Sometimes I would bleed; I still have marks on my body.

Once in 1992 I was late going to get the children from school; my mistress and her husband were furious with me and beat and then threw me out on the street. I had nowhere to go; I didn't understand anything, and I wandered on the streets. After some time her husband found me and took me back to their house. There they stripped me naked, tied my hands behind my back, and began to whip me with a wire attached to a broomstick. Both of them were beating me at the same time. I was bleeding a lot and screaming, but they continued to beat me. Then she rubbed chili pepper into my wounds and stuck it in my vagina. I lost consciousness.

Sometime later one of the children came and untied me. I lay on the floor where they had left me for several days. The pain was terrible but no one treated my wounds. When I was able to stand I had to start work again, but after this I was always locked in the apartment. They continued to beat me.

Seba was finally freed when a neighbor, after hearing the sounds of abuse and beating, managed to talk to her. Seeing her scars and wounds, the neighbor called the police and the French Committee against Modern Slavery (CCEM), who brought a case and took Seba into their care. Medical examinations confirmed that she had been tortured.

Today Seba is well cared for, living with a volunteer family. She is receiving counseling and is learning to read and write. Recovery will take years, but she is a remarkably strong young woman. What amazed me was how far Seba still needs to go. As we talked I realized that though she was twenty-two and intelligent, her understanding of the world was less developed than the average five-year-old's. For example, until she was freed she had little understanding of time—no knowledge of weeks, months, or years. For Seba there was only the endless round of work and sleep. She knew that there were hot days and cold days, but never learned that the seasons follow a pattern. If she ever knew her birthday she had forgotten it, and she did not know her age. She is baffled by the idea of "choice." Her volunteer family tries to help her make choices, but she still can't grasp it. I asked Seba to draw the best picture of a person that she could. She told me it was the first time she had ever tried to draw a person. This was the result:

If Seba's case were unique it would be shocking enough, but Seba is one of perhaps 3,000 household slaves in Paris. Nor is such slavery unique to that city. In London, New York, Zurich, Los Angeles, and across the world, children are brutalized as household slaves. And they are just one small group of the world's slaves.

Slavery is not a horror safely consigned to the past; it continues to exist throughout the world, even in developed countries like France and the United States. Across the world slaves work and sweat and build and suffer. Slaves in Pakistan may have made the shoes you are wearing and the carpet you stand on. Slaves in the Caribbean may have put sugar in your kitchen and toys in the hands of your children. In India they may have sewn the shirt on your back and polished the ring on your finger. They are paid nothing.

Slaves touch your life indirectly as well. They made the bricks for the factory that made the TV you watch. In Brazil slaves made the charcoal that tempered the steel that made the springs in your car and the blade on your lawnmower. Slaves grew the rice that fed the woman that wove the lovely cloth you've put up as curtains. Your investment portfolio and your mutual fund pension own stock in companies using slave labor in the developing world. Slaves keep your costs low and returns on your investments high.

Slavery is a booming business and the number of slaves is increasing. People get rich by using slaves. And when they've finished with their slaves, they just throw these people away. This is the new slavery, which focuses on big profits and cheap lives. It is not about owning people in the traditional sense of the old slavery, but about controlling them completely. People become completely disposable tools for making money.

On more than ten occasions I woke early in the morning to find the corpse of a young girl floating in the water by the barge. Nobody bothered to bury the girls. They just threw their bodies in the river to be eaten by the fish.[1]

This was the fate of young girls enslaved as prostitutes in the gold mining towns of the Amazon, explained Antonia Pinto, who worked there as a cook and a procurer. While the developed world bemoans the destruction of the rain forests, few people realize that slave labor is used to destroy them. Men are lured to the region by promises of riches in gold dust, and girls as young as eleven are offered jobs in the offices and restaurants that serve the mines. When they arrive in the remote mining areas, the men are locked up and forced to work in the mines; the girls are beaten, raped, and put to work as prostitutes. Their "recruitment agents" are paid a small amount for each body, perhaps $150. The "recruits" have become slaves—not through legal ownership, but through the final authority of violence. The local police act as enforcers to control the slaves. As one young woman explained, "Here the brothel owners send the police to beat us . . . if we flee they go after us, if they find us they kill us, or if they don't kill us they beat us all the way back to the brothel."[2]

The brothels are incredibly lucrative. The girl who "cost" $150 can be sold for sex up to ten times a night and bring in $10,000 per month. The only expenses are payments to the police and a pittance for food. If a girl is a troublemaker, runs away, or gets sick, she is easy to get rid of and replace. Antonia Pinto described what happened to an eleven-year-old girl when she refused to have sex with a miner: "After decapitating her with his machete, the miner drove around in his speedboat, showing off her head to the other miners, who clapped and shouted their approval."[3]

As the story of these girls shows, slavery has not, as most of us have been led to believe, ended. To be sure, the word *slavery* continues to be used to mean all sorts of things,[4] and all too often it has been applied as an easy metaphor. Having just enough money to get by, receiving wages that barely keep you alive, may be called wage slavery, but it is not slavery. Sharecroppers have a hard life, but they are not slaves. Child labor is terrible, but it is not necessarily slavery.

We might think slavery is a matter of ownership, but that depends on what we mean by *ownership*. In the past, slavery entailed one person legally owning another person, but modern slavery is different. Today slavery is illegal everywhere, and there is no more *legal* ownership of human beings. When people buy slaves today they don't ask for a receipt or ownership papers, but they do gain *control*—and they use violence to maintain this control. Slaveholders have all of the benefits of ownership without the legalities. Indeed, for the slaveholders, not having legal ownership is an improvement because they get total control without any responsibility for what they own. For that reason I tend to use the term slave*holder* instead of slave*owner*.

In spite of this difference between the new and the old slavery, I think everyone would agree that what I am talking about is slavery: the total control of one person by another for the purpose of economic exploitation. Modern slavery hides behind different masks, using clever lawyers and legal smoke screens, but when we strip away the lies, we find someone controlled by violence and denied all of their personal freedom to make money for someone else. As I traveled around the world to study the new slavery, I looked behind the legal masks and I saw people in chains. Of course, many people think there is no such thing as slavery anymore, and I was one of those people just a few years ago.

First Come, First Served

I first encountered the vestiges of the old slavery when I was four years old. What happened is one of my strongest memories. It was the 1950s in the American South and my family was having dinner in a cafeteria. As we started down the serving line I saw another family standing behind a chain, waiting as others moved through with their trays. With the certainty of a four-year-old, I knew that they had arrived first and should be ahead of us. The *fairness* of first come, first served had been drummed into me. So I unhooked the chain and said, "You were here first, you should go ahead." The father of this African American family looked down at me with eyes full of feeling, just as my own father came up and put his hand on my shoulder. Suddenly the atmosphere was thick with unspoken emotion. Tension mixed with bittersweet approval as both fathers grappled with the innocent ignorance of a child who had never heard of segregation. No one spoke, until finally the black father said, "That's OK, we're waiting on someone; go ahead."

My parents were not radicals, but they had taught me the value of fairness and equal treatment. They believed that the idea of our equality was one of the best things about America, and they never approved of the racism of segregation. But sometimes it takes a child's simplicity to cut through the weight of custom. The intensity of that moment stayed with me, though it was years before I began to understand what those two sets of parents were feeling. As I grew up I was glad to see such blatant segregation coming to an end. The idea that there might still be actual slavery—quite apart from segregation—never crossed my mind. Everyone knew that in the United States slavery had ended in 1865.

Of course, the gross inequalities in American society brought the slavery of the past to mind. I realized that the United States, once a large-scale slave society, was still suffering from a botched emancipation program. Soon after Abraham Lincoln's celebrated proclamation, Jim Crow laws and oppression took over to keep ex-slaves from economic and political power. I came to understand that emancipation was a *process*, not an event—a process that still had a way to go. As a young social researcher, I generally held jobs concerned with the residue of this unfinished process: I studied bad housing, health differences between the races, problems in integrated schools, and racism in the legal system. But I still saw all this as the vestiges of slavery, as problems that were tough but not intractable.

It was only after I moved to England in the early 1980s that I became aware of real slavery. At a large public event I came across a small table set up by Anti-Slavery International. I picked up some leaflets in passing, and I was amazed by what I read. There was no flash-of-light experience, but I developed a gnawing desire to find out more. I was perplexed that this most fundamental human right was still not assured—and that no one seemed to know or care about it. Millions of people were actively working against the nuclear threat, against apartheid in South Africa, against famine in Ethiopia, yet *slavery* wasn't even on the map. The more this realization dug into me, the more I knew I had to do something. Slavery is an obscenity. It is not just stealing someone's labor; it is the theft of an entire life. It is more closely related to the concentration camp than to questions of bad working conditions.

There seems nothing to debate about slavery: it must stop. My question became: What can I do to bring an end to slavery? I decided to use my skills as a social researcher, and I embarked on the project that led to this book.

How Many Slaves?

For several years I collected every scrap of information I could find about modern slavery. I went to the United Nations and the British Library; I trawled through the International Labour Office and visited human rights organizations and charities. I talked to anthropologists and economists. Getting useful, reliable information on slavery is very difficult. Even when shown photographs and affidavits, nations' officials deny its existence. Human rights organizations, in contrast, want to expose the existence of slavery. They report what they are told by the victims of slavery, and it is their business to counter government denials with evidence of widespread slavery. Who and what can we believe?

My approach was to pull together all the evidence I could find, country by country. When someone gave reasons why a number of people were in slavery, I took note. When two people independently stated they had good reasons to think that there was a certain amount of slavery, I began to feel more convinced. Sometimes I found that researchers were working on slavery in two different parts of the same country without knowing about each other. I looked at every report I could find and asked, "What can I feel sure about? Which numbers do I trust?" Then I added up what I had found, taking care to be conservative. If I had any doubts about a report, I left it out of my calculations. It's important to remember that slavery is a shadowy, illegal enterprise, so statistics are hard to come by. I can only make a good guess at the numbers.

My best estimate of the number of slaves in the world today is 27 million.

This number is much smaller than the estimates put forward by some activists, who give a range as high as 200 million, but it is the number I feel I can trust; it is also the number that fits my strict definition of slavery. The biggest part of that 27 million, perhaps 15 to 20 million, is represented by *bonded labor* in India, Pakistan, Bangladesh, and Nepal. Bonded labor or debt bondage happens when people give themselves into slavery as security against a loan or when they inherit a debt from a relative (we'll look at this more closely later). Otherwise slavery tends to be concentrated in Southeast Asia, northern and western Africa, and parts of South America (but there are some slaves in almost every country in the world, including the United States, Japan, and many European countries). There are more slaves alive today than all the people stolen from Africa in the time of the transatlantic slave trade. Put another way, today's slave population is greater than the population of Canada, and six times greater than the population of Israel.

These slaves tend to be used in simple, nontechnological, and traditional work. The largest group work in agriculture. But slaves are used in many other kinds of labor: brickmaking, mining or quarrying, prostitution, gem working and jewelry making, cloth and carpet making, and domestic service; they clear forests, make charcoal, and work in shops. Much of this work is aimed at local sale and consumption, but slave-made goods reach into homes around the world. Carpets, fireworks, jewelry, and metal goods made by slave labor, as well as grains, sugar, and other foods harvested by slaves, are imported directly to North America and Europe. In addition, large international corporations, acting in ignorance through subsidiaries in the developing world, take advantage of slave labor to improve their bottom line and increase the dividends to their shareholders.

But the value of slaves lies not so much in the particular products they make as in their sweat, in the volume of work squeezed out of them. Slaves are often forced to sleep next to their looms or brick kilns; some are even chained to their work tables. All their waking hours may be turned into working hours. In our global economy one of the standard explanations that multinational corporations give for closing factories in the "first world" and opening them in the "third world" is the lower labor cost. Slavery can constitute a significant part of these savings. No paid workers, no matter how efficient, can compete economically with unpaid workers—slaves.

What Does Race Have to Do with It?

In the new slavery race means little. In the past, ethnic and racial differences were used to explain and excuse slavery. These differences allowed slaveholders to make up reasons why slavery was acceptable, or even a good thing for the slaves. The *otherness* of the slaves made it easier to employ the violence and cruelty necessary for total control. This otherness could be defined in almost any way—a different religion, tribe, skin color, language, custom, or economic class. Any of these differences could be and were used to separate the slaves from the slaveholders. Maintaining these differences required tremendous investment in some very irrational ideas—and the crazier the justifying idea, the more vehemently it was insisted upon. The American Founding Fathers had to go through moral, linguistic, and political contortions to explain why their "land of the free" was only for white people.[5] Many of them knew that by allowing slavery they were betraying their most cherished ideals. They were driven to it because slavery was worth a lot of money to a lot of people in North America at the time. But they went to the trouble of devising legal and political excuses because they felt they had to morally justify their economic decisions.

Today the hunger for money overrides other concerns. Most slaveholders feel no need to explain or defend their chosen method of labor recruitment and management. Slavery is a very profitable business, and a good bottom line is justification enough. Freed of ideas that restrict the status of slave to *others*, modern slaveholders use other criteria to choose slaves. Indeed, they enjoy a great advantage: being able to enslave people from one's own country helps keep costs down. Slaves in the American South in the nineteenth century were very expensive, in part because they originally had to be shipped thousands of miles from Africa. When slaves can be acquired from the next town or region, transportation costs fall. The question isn't "Are they the right color to be slaves?" but "Are they vulnerable enough to be enslaved?" The criteria of enslavement today do not concern color, tribe, or religion; they focus on weakness, gullibility, and deprivation.

It is true that in some countries there are ethnic or religious differences between slaves and slaveholders. In Pakistan, for example, many enslaved brickmakers are Christians while the slaveholders are Muslim. In India slave and slaveholder may be from different castes. In Thailand slaves may come from rural parts of the country and are much more likely to be women. But in Pakistan there are Christians who are not slaves, in India members of the same caste who are free. Their caste or religion simply reflects their vulnerability to enslavement; it doesn't cause it. Only in one country, Mauritania, does the racism of the old slavery persist—there black slaves are held by Arab slaveholders, and race is a key division. To be sure, some cultures are more divided along racial lines than others. Japanese culture strongly distinguishes the Japanese as different from everyone else, and so enslaved prostitutes in Japan are more likely to be Thai, Philippine, or European women—rarely, they may be Japanese. Even here, the key difference is not racial but economic: Japanese women are not nearly so vulnerable and desperate as Thais or Filipinas. And the Thai women are available for shipment to Japan because Thais are enslaving Thais. The same pattern occurs in the oil-rich states of Saudi Arabia and Kuwait, where Muslim Arabs promiscuously enslave Sri Lankan Hindus, Filipino Christians, and Nigerian Muslims. The common denominator is poverty, not color. Behind every assertion of ethnic difference is the reality of economic disparity. If all left-handed people in the world became destitute tomorrow, there would soon be slaveholders taking advantage of them. Modern slaveholders are predators keenly aware of weakness; they are rapidly adapting an ancient practice to the new global economy.

The Rise of the New Slavery

For thousands of years people have been enslaved. Slavery echoes through the great epics of the distant past. Ancient Egypt, ancient Greece, and the Roman Empire all made slavery integral to their social systems.[6] Right through the American and Brazilian slave economies of the last century, legal, old-style slavery persisted in what is now called the developed world. But slavery never disappeared; instead, it took a different form. The basic fact of one person totally controlling another remains the same, but slavery has changed in some crucial ways.

Two factors are critical in the shift from the old slavery to the explosive spread of the new. The first is the dramatic increase in world population following World War II. Since 1945 the world population has tripled, increasing from about 2 billion people to more than 6 billion. The greatest growth has been in exactly those countries where slavery is most prevalent today. Across Southeast Asia, South America, the Indian subcontinent, Africa, and the Arab countries, populations have exploded, flooding these countries with children. Over half the population in some of these countries is under the age of fifteen. In countries that were already poor, the sheer weight of numbers overwhelms the resources at hand. Without work and with increasing fear as resources diminish, people become desperate and life becomes cheap. Especially in those areas where slavery had persisted or was part of the historical culture, the population explosion radically produced a glut of potential slaves and drove down their price.

The second crucial factor is that at the same time that the population was exploding, these countries were undergoing rapid social and economic change. In many developing countries modernization brought immense wealth to the elite and continued or increased the impoverishment of the poor majority. Throughout Africa and Asia the last fifty years have been scarred by civil war and the wholesale looting of resources by home-grown dictators, often supported by one of the superpowers. To hold on to power, the ruling kleptocrats have paid enormous sums for weaponry, money raised by mortgaging their countries. Meanwhile traditional ways of life and subsistence have been sacrificed to the cash crop and quick profit. Poor families have lost their old ways of meeting a crisis. Traditional societies, while sometimes oppressive, generally relied on ties of responsibility and kinship that could usually carry people through a crisis such as the death of the breadwinner, serious illness, or a bad harvest. Modernization and the globalization of the world economy have shattered these traditional families and the small-scale subsistence farming that supported them. The forced shift from subsistence to cash-crop agriculture, the loss of common land, and government policies that suppress farm income in favor of cheap food for the cities have all helped bankrupt millions of peasants and drive them from their land—sometimes into slavery.

Although modernization can have good effects, bringing improvements in health care and education, the concentration of land in the hands of an elite and its use of land to produce cash crops for export have made the poor more vulnerable. Because the political elites in the developing world focus on economic growth, which is not just in their collective self-interest but required by global financial institutions, little attention is paid to sustainable livelihoods for the majority. So while the rich of the developing world have grown richer, the poor have fewer and fewer options. Amid the disruption of rapid social change, one of those options is slavery.

The end of the cold war only made matters worse. William Greider explains it well:

> One of the striking qualities of the post–Cold War globalization is how easily business and government in the capitalist democracies have abandoned the values they putatively espoused for forty years during the struggle against communism—individual liberties and political legitimacy based on free elections. Concern for human rights, including freedom of assembly for workers wishing to speak for themselves, has been pushed aside by commercial opportunity. Multinationals plunge confidently into new markets, from Vietnam

to China, where governments routinely control and abuse their own citizens.[7]

In fact, some of these countries *enslave* their own citizens, and others turn a blind eye to the slavery that generates such enormous profits.

THE OLD SLAVERY VERSUS THE NEW SLAVERY Government corruption, plus the vast increase in the number of people and their ongoing impoverishment, has led to the new slavery. For the first time in human history there is an absolute glut of potential slaves. It is a dramatic illustration of the laws of supply and demand: with so many possible slaves, their value has plummeted. Slaves are now so cheap that they have become cost-effective in many new kinds of work, completely changing how they are seen and used. Think about computers. Forty years ago there were only a handful of computers, and they cost hundreds of thousands of dollars; only big companies and the government could afford them. Today there are millions of personal computers. Anyone can buy a used, but quite serviceable, model for $100. Use that $100 computer for a year or two, and when it breaks down, don't bother to fix it—just throw it away.

The same thing happens in the new slavery. Buying a slave is no longer a major investment, like buying a car or a house (as it was in the old slavery); it is more like buying an inexpensive bicycle or a cheap computer. Slaveholders get all the work they can out of their slaves, and then throw them away. The nature of the relationship between slaves and slaveholders has fundamentally altered. The new disposability has dramatically increased the amount of profit to be made from a slave, decreased the length of time a person would normally be enslaved, and made the question of legal ownership less important. When slaves cost a great deal of money, that investment had to be safeguarded through clear and legally documented ownership. Slaves of the past were worth stealing and worth chasing down if they escaped. Today slaves cost so little that it is not worth the hassle of securing permanent, "legal" ownership. Slaves are disposable.

Around the world today the length of time a slave spends in bondage varies enormously. Where old-style slavery is still practiced, bondage lasts forever. A Mauritanian woman born into slavery has a good chance of remaining so for the rest of her life. Her children, if she has any, will also be slaves, and so on down the generations. But today most slaves are temporary; some are enslaved for only a few months. It is simply not profitable to keep them when they are not immediately useful. Under these circumstances, there is no reason to invest heavily in their upkeep and indeed little reason to ensure that they survive their enslavement. While slaves in the American South were often horribly treated, there was nevertheless a strong incentive to keep them alive for many years. Slaves were like valuable livestock: the plantation owner needed to make back his investment. There was also pressure to breed them and produce more slaves, since it was usually cheaper to raise new slaves oneself than to buy adults. Today no slaveholder wants to spend money supporting useless infants, so female slaves, especially those forced into prostitution, suffer violent, involuntary abortions. And there is no reason to protect slaves from disease or injury—medicine costs money, and it's cheaper to let them die.

The key differences between the old and new slavery break down like this:

Old Slavery	New Slavery
Legal ownership asserted	Legal ownership avoided
High purchase cost	Very low purchase cost
Low profits	Very high profits
Shortage of potential slaves	Glut of potential slaves
Long-term relationship	Short-term relationship
Slaves maintained	Slaves disposable
Ethnic differences important	Ethnic differences not important

Looking at a specific example will clarify these differences. Perhaps the best studied and best understood form of old slavery was the system in the American South before 1860.[8] Slaves were at a premium, and the demand for them was high because European immigrants were able to find other work or even start their own farms in the ever-expanding West. This demand for slaves was reflected in their price. By 1850 an average field laborer sold for $1,000 to $1,800. This was three to six times the average yearly wage of an American worker at the time, a cost equivalent to around $40,000 to $80,000 today. Despite their high price, slaves generated, on average, profits of only about 5 percent each year. If the cotton market went up, a plantation owner might make a very good return on his slaves, but if the price of cotton fell, he might be forced to sell slaves to stay in business. Ownership was clearly demonstrated by bills of sale and titles of ownership, and slaves could be used as collateral for loans or used to pay off debts. Slaves were often brutalized to keep them under control, but they were also recognized and treated as sizable investments. A final distinctive element was the extreme racial differentiation between slaveholder and slave, so strong that a very small genetic difference—normally set at being only one-eighth black—still meant lifelong enslavement.[9]

In comparison, consider the agricultural slave in debt bondage in India now. There land rather than labor is at a premium today. India's population has boomed, currently totaling three times that of the United States in a country with one-third the space. The glut of potential workers means that free labor must regularly compete with slave, and the resulting pressure on agricultural wages pushes free laborers toward bondage. When free farmers run out of money, when a crop fails or a member of the family becomes ill and needs medicine, they have few choices. Faced with a crisis, they borrow enough money from a local landowner to meet the crisis, but having no other possessions, they must use their own lives as collateral. The debt against which a person is bonded—that is, the price of a laborer—might be 500 to 1,000 rupees (about $12 to $23). The bond is completely open-ended; the slave must work for the slaveholder until the slaveholder decides the debt is repaid. It may carry over into a second and third generation, growing under fraudulent accounting by the slaveholder, who may also seize and sell the children of the bonded laborer against the debt. The functional reality is one of slavery, but its differences from the old slavery reflect five of the seven points listed in the table above.

First, no one tries to assert legal ownership of the bonded laborer. The slave is held under threat of violence, and often physically locked up, but no one asserts that he or she is in fact "property." Second, the bonded laborer is made responsible for his or her own upkeep, thus lowering the slaveholder's costs. The slaves may scrape together their subsistence in a number of ways: eking it out from the foodstuffs produced for the slaveholder, using their "spare time" to do whatever is necessary to bring in food, or receiving some foodstuffs or money from the slaveholder. The slaveholders save by providing no regular maintenance, and they can cut off food and all support when the bonded laborer is unable to work or is no longer needed.

Third, if a bonded laborer is not able to work, perhaps because of illness or injury, or is not needed for work, he or she can be abandoned or disposed of by the slaveholder, who bears no responsibility for the slave's upkeep. Often the slaveholder keeps an entirely fraudulent legal document, which the bonded laborer has "signed" under duress. This document violates several current Indian laws and relies on others that either never existed or have not existed for decades, yet it is normally used to justify holding the bonded laborer. It also excuses the abandonment of ill or injured slaves, for it specifies responsibilities only on the part of the bonded laborer; there are none on the part of the slaveholder. Fourth, the ethnic differentiation is not nearly so rigid as that of the old slavery. As already noted, bonded laborers may well belong to a lower caste than the slaveholder—but this is not always the case. The key distinction lies in wealth and power, not caste.

Finally, a major difference between the old and new slavery is in the profits produced by an enslaved laborer. Agricultural bonded laborers in India generate not 5 percent, as did slaves in the American South, but over 50 percent profit per year for the slaveholder. This high profit is due, in part, to the low cost of the slave (i.e., the small loan advanced), but even so it reflects the low returns on old-fashioned small-scale agriculture: indeed, almost all other forms of modern slavery are much more profitable.

Agricultural debt bondage in India still has some characteristics of the old slavery, such as the holding of slaves for long periods. A better example of the new slavery is provided by the young women lured into "contract" slavery and put to work in prostitution in Thailand. A population explosion in Thailand has ensured a surplus of potential slaves, while rapid economic change has led to new poverty and desperation. The girls are often initially drawn from rural areas with the promise of work in restaurants or factories. There is no ethnic difference—these are Thai girls enslaved by Thai brothel owners; the distinction between them, if any, is that the former are rural and the latter urban. The girls might be sold by their parents to a broker, or tricked by an agent; once away from their homes they are brutalized and enslaved, then sold to a brothel owner. The brothel owners place the girls in debt bondage and tell them they must pay back their purchase price, plus interest, through prostitution. They might use the legal ruse of a contract—which often specifies some completely unrelated job, such as factory work—but that isn't usually necessary. The calculation of the debt and the interest is, of course, completely in the hands of the brothel owners and so is manipulated to show whatever they like. Using that trick, they can keep a girl as long as they want, and they don't need to demonstrate any legal ownership. The brothel does have to feed the girl and keep her presentable, but if she becomes ill or injured or too old, she is disposed of. In Thailand today, the girl is often discarded when she tests positive for HIV.

This form of contract debt bondage is extremely profitable. A girl between twelve and fifteen years old can be purchased for $800 to $2,000, and the costs of running a brothel and feeding the girls are relatively low. The profit is often as high as 800 percent a year. This kind of return can be made on a girl for three to six years. After that, especially if she becomes ill or HIV-positive, the girl is dumped.

THE FORMS OF THE NEW SLAVERY Charted on paper in neat categories, the new slavery seems to be very clear and distinct. In fact, it is as inconveniently sloppy, dynamic, changeable, and confusing as any other kind of relation between humans. We can no more expect there to be one kind of slavery than we can expect there to be one kind of marriage. People are inventive and flexible, and the permutations of human violence and exploitation are infinite. The best we can do with slavery is to set down its dimensions and then test any particular example against them.

One critical dimension is violence—all types of slavery depend on violence, which holds the slave in place. Yet, for one slave, there may be only the threat of violence while, with another, threats may escalate into terrible abuse. Another dimension is the length of enslavement. Short-term enslavement is typical of the new slavery, but "short" may mean ten weeks or ten years. Still another aspect is the slave's loss of control over his or her life and ongoing "obligation" to the slaveholder. The actual way in which this obligation is enforced varies a great deal, yet it is possible to use this dimension to outline three basic forms of slavery:

1. *Chattel slavery* is the form closest to the old slavery. A person is captured, born, or sold into permanent servitude, and ownership might be asserted. The slave's children are normally treated as property as well and can be sold by the slaveholder. Occasionally, these slaves are kept as items of conspicuous consumption. This form is most often found in northern and western Africa and some Arab countries, but it represents a very small proportion of slaves in the modern world. We will look at chattel slavery in Mauritania in chapter 3.

2. *Debt bondage* is the most common form of slavery in the world. A

person pledges him- or herself against a loan of money, but the length and nature of the service are not defined and the labor does not reduce the original debt. The debt can be passed down to subsequent generations, thus enslaving offspring; moreover, "defaulting" can be punished by seizing or selling children into further debt bonds. Ownership is not normally asserted, but there is complete physical control of the bonded laborer. Debt bondage is most common on the Indian subcontinent. We will look at it in Pakistan and India in chapters 5 and 6.

3. *Contract slavery* shows how modern labor relations are used to hide the new slavery. Contracts are offered that guarantee employment, perhaps in a workshop or factory, but when the workers are taken to their place of work they find themselves enslaved. The contract is used as an enticement to trick an individual into slavery, as well as a way of making the slavery look legitimate. If legal questions are raised, the contract can be produced, but the reality is that the "contract worker" is a slave, threatened by violence, lacking any freedom of movement, and paid nothing. The most rapidly growing form of slavery, this is the second-largest form today. Contract slavery is most often found in Southeast Asia, Brazil, some Arab states, and some parts of the Indian subcontinent. We will look at contract slavery in Thailand and Brazil in chapters 2 and 4.

These types are not mutually exclusive. Contracts may be issued to chattel slaves in order to conceal their enslavement. Girls trapped into prostitution by debt bondage will sometimes have contracts that specify their obligations. The important thing to remember is that *people are enslaved by violence and held against their wills for purposes of exploitation.* The categories just outlined are simply a way to help us track the patterns of enslavement, to clarify how slavery might be attacked.

A small percentage of slaves fall into a number of other readily identifiable kinds of slavery. These tend to be specific to particular geographical regions or political situations. A good example of slavery linked to politics is what is often called *war slavery*; this includes government-sponsored slavery. In Burma today, there is widespread capture and enslavement of civilians by the government and the army. Tens of thousands of men, women, and children have been used as laborers or bearers in military campaigns against ethnic groups or on construction projects. The Burmese military dictatorship doesn't suggest that it owns the people it has enslaved—in fact, it denies enslaving anyone—but the U.S. State Department and human rights organizations confirm that violence is used to hold a large number of people in bondage. Once again, the motive is economic gain: not to generate profits but to save transportation or production costs in the war effort, or labor costs in construction projects. One major project was the natural gas pipeline that Burma's dictatorship built in partnership with the U.S. oil company Unocal, the French oil company Total, and the Thai company PTT Exploration and Production. These three companies have often featured in international and global mutual investment funds. The Thai company, which is owned in part by the Thai government, is recommended by one mutual fund as a "family" investment. In the pipeline project thousands of enslaved workers, including old men, pregnant women, and children, were forced at gunpoint to clear land and build a railway next to the pipeline.[10] War slavery is unique: this is slavery committed *by* the government, whereas most slavery happens because government officials are on the take.

In some parts of the Caribbean and in western Africa, children are given or sold into domestic service. They are sometimes called "restavecs." Ownership is not asserted, but strict control, enforced by violence, is maintained over the child. The domestic services performed by the enslaved child provide a sizable return on the investment in "upkeep." It is a culturally approved way of dealing with "extra" children; some are treated well, but for most it is a kind of slavery that lasts until adulthood.[11]

Slavery can also be linked to religion, as with the Indian *devadasi* women we will meet in chapter 6, or the children who are ritual slaves in Ghana.[12] Several thousand girls and young women are given by their families as slaves to local fetish priests in southeastern Ghana, Togo, Benin, and southwestern Nigeria. In a custom very alien to Western sensibilities the girls are enslaved in order to atone for sins committed by members of their families, often rape. The girls may, in fact, be the products of rape, and their slavery is seen as a way of appeasing the gods for that or other crimes committed by their male relatives. A girl, who *must* be a virgin, is given to the local priest as a slave when she is about ten years old. The girl then stays with the priest—cooking, cleaning, farming, and serving him sexually—until he frees her, usually after she has borne several children. At that point the slave's family must provide another young girl to replace her. Ghana's constitution forbids slavery, but the practice is justified on religious grounds by villagers and priests.

As can be seen from these cases, slavery comes in many forms. Moreover, slavery can be found in virtually every country. A recent investigation in Great Britain found young girls held in slavery and forced to be prostitutes in Birmingham and Manchester.[13] Enslaved domestic workers have been found and freed in London and Paris. In the United States farmworkers have been found locked inside barracks and working under armed guards as field slaves. Enslaved Thai and Philippine women have been freed from brothels in New York, Seattle, and Los Angeles.[14] This list could go on and on. Almost all of the countries where slavery "cannot" exist have slaves inside their borders—but, it must be said, in very small numbers compared to the Indian subcontinent and the Far East. The important point is that slaves constitute a vast workforce supporting the global economy we all depend upon.

The New Slavery and the Global Economy

Just how much does slave labor contribute to the global economy? Inevitably, determining the exact contribution of slaves to the world economy is very difficult because no reliable information is available for most types of slavery. Nevertheless, a few rough calculations are possible.

Agricultural bonded laborers, after an initial loan (think of this as the purchase price) of around $50, generate up to 100 percent net profit for the slaveholders. If there are an estimated 18 million such workers, the annual profit generated would be on the order of $860 million, though this might be distributed to as many as 5 million slave-holders. If 200,000 women and children are enslaved as prostitutes, probably an underestimate, and if the financial breakdown found in Thai prostitution is used as a guide, then these slaves would generate a total annual profit of $10.5 billion.

If these sums are averaged to reflect a world population of 27 million slaves, the total yearly profit generated by slaves would be on the order of $13 billion. This is a very rough estimate. But we might put this sum into global perspective by noting that $13 billion is approximately equal to the amount Americans spend each year on jeans, or substantially less than the personal worth of Microsoft founder Bill Gates.

Although the direct value of slave labor in the world economy may seem relatively small, the indirect value is much greater. For example, slave-produced charcoal is crucial to making steel in Brazil. Much of this steel is then made into the cars, car parts, and other metal goods that make up a quarter of all Brazil's exports. Britain alone imports $1.6 billion in goods from Brazil each year, the United States signifi-cantly more.[15] Slavery lowers a factory's production costs; these sav-ings can be passed up the economic stream, ultimately reaching shops of Europe and North America as lower prices or higher profits for re-tailers. Goods directly produced by slaves are also exported, and follow the same pattern. It is most likely that slave-produced goods and goods assembled from slave-made components have the effect of increasing profits rather than just lowering consumer prices, as they are mixed into the flow of other products. I'd like to believe that most Western consumers, if they could identify slave-produced goods, would avoid them despite their lower price. But consumers do look for bargains, and they don't usually stop to ask why a product is so cheap. We have to face facts: by always looking for the best deal, we may be choosing slave-made goods without knowing what we are buying. And the impact of slavery reverberates through the world economy in ways even harder to escape. Workers making computer parts or televisions in India can be paid low wages in part because food produced by slave labor is so cheap. This lowers the cost of the goods they make, and factories unable to compete with their prices close in North America and Europe. Slave labor anywhere threatens real jobs everywhere.

That slavery is an international economic activity suggests something about the way it is, and the way it isn't, being combated: there are almost no economic controls on slaveholding and the slave trade. Consider, in contrast, the pursuit of Colombian cocaine barons. Rarely are these men arrested for making or distributing drugs. Time after time they are caught for financial wrongdoing—tax avoidance, money laundering, or fraud and the falsification of records. In late 1996 one drug cartel lost $36 million, which was confiscated on money-laundering charges by the U.S. Justice Department. Bringing down criminals by investigating their finances and enforcing economic sanctions has been shown to be effective, yet these techniques are rarely applied to the crime of slavery. The power of a great range of organizations—the World Bank, national regulatory agencies, trade organizations, regional customs and excise units, individual companies, consumer groups—could be harnessed to break the profits of slavers. We will look more closely at this potential in the final chapter. But we need to understand how the new slavery works if we are going to do anything to stop it.

WHY BUY THE COW?—CONTROL WITHOUT OWNERSHIP One of the drawbacks of the old slavery was the cost of maintaining slaves who were too young or too old. Careful analysis of both American cotton plantations and Brazilian coffee farms in the 1800s shows that the productivity of slaves was linked to their age.[16] Children did not bring in more than they cost until the age of ten or twelve, though they were put to work as early as possible. Productivity and profits to be made from a slave peaked at about age thirty and fell off sharply when a slave was fifty or more. Slavery was profitable, but the profitability was diminished by the cost of keeping infants, small children, and unproductive old people. The new slavery avoids this extra cost and so increases its profits.

The new slavery mimics the world economy by shifting away from ownership and fixed asset management, concentrating instead on control and use of resources or processes. Put another way, it is like the shift from the "ownership" of colonies in the last century to the economic exploitation of those same countries today without the cost and trouble of maintaining colonies. Transnational companies today do what European empires did in the last century—exploit natural resources and take advantage of low-cost labor—but without needing to take over and govern the entire country. Similarly, the new slavery appropriates the economic value of individuals while keeping them under complete coercive control—but without asserting ownership or accepting responsibility for their survival. The result is much greater economic efficiency: useless and unprofitable infants, the elderly, and the sick or injured are dumped. Seasonal tasks are met with seasonal enslavement, as in the case of Haitian sugarcane cutters.[17] In the new slavery, the slave is a consumable item, added to the production process when needed, but no longer carrying a high capital cost.

This shift from ownership to control and appropriation applies to virtually all modern slavery across national or cultural boundaries, whether the slave is cutting cane in the Caribbean, making bricks in the Punjab, mining in Brazil, or being kept as a prostitute in Thailand. Mirroring modern economic practice, slavery in this respect is being transformed from culturally specific forms to an emerging standardized or globalized form. The world shrinks through increasingly easy communication. The slaveholders in Pakistan or Brazil watch television just like everyone else. When they see that industries in many countries are switching to a "just in time" system for the delivery of raw materials or necessary labor, they draw the same conclusions about profitability as did those corporations. As jobs for life disappear from the world economy, so too does slavery for life. The economic advantages of short-term enslavement far outweigh the costs of buying new slaves when needed.

LEGAL FICTIONS Today accepted systems of labor relations are used to legitimate and conceal slavery. Much modern slavery is hidden behind a mask of fraudulent labor contracts, which are most common in the fastest-growing areas of slavery. The contracts have two main uses for the slaveholder—entrapment and concealment. The use of false contracts is part of the globalization of slavery; the basic process of recruitment into slavery by fraudulent contract is the same from Brazil to Thailand. It allows slaves to be taken both into countries where their enslavement is relatively easily achieved (e.g., Filipinas taken to Saudi Arabia) and into countries where their enslavement would not normally be allowed. It is estimated, for example, that there are up to 1,000 domestic slaves in London,[18] all of whom are covered by a contract of employment and, until recently, by the recognition of that contract by British immigration control staff on their arrival.

False contracts work on several levels. Shown to people desperate for paid work, these contracts are a powerful incentive to get into the back of the truck that carries them into slavery. Among the rural poor of many countries, the well-spoken and well-dressed recruitment agent with the official and legal-looking document commands attention. Assured that the contract guarantees good treatment, that it sets clear legal rights and wages for the worker, the potential slave signs happily and places him- or herself in the hands of the slaver. After being used to entice workers into slavery, after bringing them far enough from their homes that violence can be used to control them, the contract can be thrown away. But it is more likely that it will be kept, for it has other uses for the slaveholder.

Since slavery is illegal in all countries, it must be concealed. Even in places where the police work hand in hand with the slaveholders and share in their profits, no one wants to advertise the fact that he or she is a slaveholder. It may be that local custom and culture support slavery and that most of the population knows of its existence, but admitting it is something else again. Here false contracts conceal slavery. Slaveholders can easily force their slaves to sign anything: mortgages, loan agreements, indentures, or labor contracts. If questions are raised, signed contracts are produced and corrupt law enforcement looks the other way. Even in countries with mostly honest and conscientious police, the contracts hide slavery. Until 1998 in Britain, domestic servants brought into the country depended for their livelihood and status on their employer, whose name was added to their passport when they entered the country; the law reinforced the dependence of the servant on the master. Under a concession in British immigration law, foreigners moving to or visiting the United Kingdom as well as returning British nationals had been allowed to bring their domestic servants. Immigration staff are supposed to make sure that these servants are at least seventeen years old and have been employed as servants for at least a year. Yet the system can readily be abused. Most of the servants do not speak English and are told how and what they must answer if questioned by immigration officials. False contracts can be shown that date employment to more than a year previous. But most important, none of the existing checks can uncover a slave of long standing, brought as a servant with a family group. Neither do they protect a servant once he or she is in the country. The story of Laxmi Swami, taken from Bridget Anderson's *Britain's Secret Slaves*, is typical:

> Born in India, Laxmi Swami came to Britain via Kuwait under
> the Home Office Concession as the servant to two half-sisters of
> the Emir of Kuwait. The princesses regularly spent six months
> of the year in Bayswater, central London, taking their servants with
> them. They subjected these women to extreme cruelty, both physi-
> cal and mental: beatings, whether with a broomstick, a knotted elec-
> tric flex or a horsewhip, were routine; Laxmi's eyes were damaged
> when they threw a bunch of keys at her face; they yanked out two

gold teeth. They told her that one of her four children had been killed in a motorcycle accident, and beat her when she broke down and cried. It was only years later that she discovered they were lying.

While in London the princesses frequently went out at 8pm and returned home at two or three o'clock in the morning. While they were away Laxmi had to stand by the door exactly where they had left her. On their return she had to massage their hands and feet and, should they be in a bad mood, suffer kicks while she did so. She slept, rarely for more than two hours a night, on the floor outside the locked kitchen, drinking forbidden water from the bath tap. She was permanently hungry and often denied food altogether for days at a time. There was plenty of food, but it was in the dustbin and deliberately spoiled so that she could not eat it even if she managed to put her hands between the bars on the windows and reach it.[19]

One day, by chance, the front door was left unlocked and Laxmi managed to escape. When she reached the Indian High Commission they sent her back to the princesses because she could not afford the airfare home. To add legal insult to her injuries, as soon as Laxmi ran away from her "employers" she was in violation of the immigration rules that tied her to them, and she was liable for immediate deportation. An investigation by Anti-Slavery International held "the effects of the Immigration Acts as they touch upon overseas domestic workers, the non-issuance of work permits to these workers, and the effective treatment of these workers as appendages of the employer rather than individuals in their own right, to be responsible for the servitude these domestics suffer in Britain. The Home Office, however inadvertently, is supporting slavery."[20]

If governments in countries such as Britain that abjure slavery can be duped, imagine how easily those who profit from slavery can be convinced to ignore it. In Thailand the government has always been ambivalent about the commercial sex trade and not particularly interested in making those involved with it comply with laws that would markedly reduce the incomes of many police officials. The extreme profitability of slavery means that slaveholders can buy political power and acceptance. In Thailand, Pakistan, India, and Brazil, local police act as enforcers of the "contracts" that conceal slavery. These police are the muscle for hire that can be sent after a runaway slave. Their availability and use by slaveholders point to another central theme in the new slavery: its emergence when the social order breaks down.

THE WILD WEST SYNDROME It is the hallmark of a civilized society that the government has a monopoly over armed violence. That is not to say that violence does not occur in advanced democracies, but when it does the force of the state is brought to bear and attempts are made to lock up the violent person. In our minds, lawlessness means fearing violence at every moment, as chaos and brutality reign. Order and safety mean that there are laws that most people obey most of the time, and legal force backs up those laws. For those who have always lived in a society where the police are usually honest, where criminals are usually locked up, where disagreements end in bad feelings and not death, it is hard to imagine the lawlessness in much of the developing world. The old Wild West has the reputation of having been lawless, in a dusty past when gunslingers could terrorize whole towns, but even then a sheriff or a U.S. marshal was ready to clean up Deadwood come morning. The reality in parts of the developing world today is much, much worse.

In Europe and North America the police fight organized crime; in Thailand the police *are* organized crime. The same holds true for many parts of Africa and Asia: the state's monopoly on violence, the monopoly that should protect citizens, has been turned against them. This disintegration of civil order often occurs in times of rapid social and political change. A community under stress, whether caused by disease, natural disaster, economic depression, or war, can break up and descend into the horror of "might makes right." These are the conditions found in areas of rapid development such as the frontier areas of Brazil or at the rural/urban interface in Thailand. There, transitional economies drive farming families off the land and leave them destitute, while fostering a demand for unskilled labor in the cities. With destitution, traditional systems of family or community support for the vulnerable collapse—and in these countries they are not replaced with any effective state welfare measures. Without protection or alternatives, the poor become powerless, and the violent, without state intervention, become supremely powerful.

Slavery blossoms in these circumstances. To control their slaves, slaveholders must be able to use violence as much and as often as they choose. Without permanent access to violence, they are impotent. The old slavery often regulated the violence a master could use against a slave. Though often ignored, the slave codes of the American South, which prohibited the teaching of reading and writing and recommended a program of strict discipline, also protected slaves from murder and mutilation and set minimum standards of food and clothing.[21] However, the codes gave the master, as his legal right, a complete monopoly on violence short of murder. If the master needed it, the law and the power of the state would back him up, for the state *was* allowed to murder (execute) slaves. Today, the monopoly of violence is often decentralized. It resides not in national law but in the hands and weapons of local police or soldiers. In fact, we can say that this transfer of the monopoly of violence from central government to local thugs is essential if the new slavery is to take root and flourish. What normally brings it about is the head-on collision of the modern and traditional ways of life.

Transition zones where the world's industrial economy meets the traditional culture of peasant farming are found throughout the developing world. At the interface there are often bloody struggles over the control of natural resources. In the Amazon a small but terrible war continues over the region's mineral wealth and timber as the line of exploitation advances. The Amazonian Indians have little to fight with, and they are pushed back repeatedly, killed wholesale, and sometimes enslaved. The new open mines ripped from the forests are hundreds of miles from direct government control. Here those with the most fire-power run the show, and those without weapons obey orders or disappear. The few local police have a choice: cooperate with the thugs and make a profit, or attempt to enforce the law and die. The result is the lawlessness and terror that Antonia Pinto described at the beginning of this chapter. In a mining village that does not expect the government to interfere anytime soon, the choice is clear and a brutal social order asserts itself. The situation in Brazil is dramatic, but the same trend appears from rural Ghana to the slums of Bangkok, from the highlands of Pakistan to the villages of the Philippines—and this Wild West syndrome strongly affects what can be done to end slavery.

From Knowledge to Freedom

Looking at the nature of the new slavery we see obvious themes: slaves are cheap and disposable; control continues without legal ownership; slavery is hidden behind contracts; and slavery flourishes in communities under stress. Those social conditions have to exist side by side with an economy that fosters slavery. Order sometimes breaks down in European or American communities, but slavery doesn't take hold. This is because very, very few people live in the kind of destitution that makes them good candidates for slavery. In most Western countries the extreme differential in power needed to enslave doesn't exist, and the idea of slavery is abhorrent. When most of the population has a reasonable standard of living and some financial security (whether their own or assured by government safety nets), slavery can't thrive.

Slavery grows best in extreme poverty, so we can identify its *economic* as well as social preconditions. Most obviously, there have to be people, perhaps nonnative to an area, who can be enslaved as well as a demand for slave labor. Slaveholders must have the resources to fund the purchase, capture, or enticement of slaves and the power to control them after enslavement. The cost of keeping a slave has to be less than or equal to the cost of hiring free labor. And there must be a demand for slave products at a price that makes slaveholding profitable. More-over, the potential slave must lack perceived alternatives to enslave-ment. Being poor, homeless, a refugee, or abandoned can all lead to the desperation that opens the door to slavery, making it easy for the slaver to lay an attractive trap. And when slaves are kidnapped, they must lack sufficient power to defend themselves against that violent enslavement.

It may seem that I am too insistent on setting out these conditions and themes in the new slavery. But the new slavery is like a new disease for which no vaccine exists. Until we really understand it, until we really know what makes it work, we have little chance of stopping it. And this disease is spreading. As the new slavery increases, the num-ber of people enslaved grows every day. We're facing an epidemic of slavery that is tied through the global economy to our own lives.

These conditions also suggest why some of the current strategies might not stop the new slavery. Legal remedies that enforce prohibi-tions against ownership are ineffective, since enslavement and control are achieved without ownership.[22] When ownership is not required for slavery, it can be concealed or legitimated within normal labor con-tracts. For laws against slavery to work, there must be clear violations that can be prosecuted. To be sure, other laws make it a violation to take away basic human rights, to restrict movement, to take labor with-out pay, or to force people to work in dangerous conditions. Slavery is unquestionably the ultimate human rights violation short of murder, but to uncover such violations requires two things: political will and an ability to protect the victim. If a government has no motivation to guarantee human rights within its borders, those rights can disappear. If those whose rights are violated cannot find protection, they are un-likely to accuse and fight those with guns and power. Such is the case in many of the countries where slavery exists today.

This lack of protection is the main problem in trying to stop the new slavery. The United Nations calls on national governments to protect their citizens and enforce their laws. But if the governments choose to ignore the UN, there is little that the UN can do. In 1986 the United Nations received reports of families being kidnapped into slavery in Sudan. In 1996, ten years after being asked to address the problem, the government of Sudan finally announced that it would undertake an official inquiry. Its deadline for announcing the results of the inquiry, August 1996, passed without any comment. Not until 2004 did a cease-fire agreement seem to bring an end to kidnapping and enslavement by government-backed militias. If slavery continues because national governments turn a blind eye, cooperate with slaveholders, or even enslave people themselves, then the diplomatic approach will have little impact.

That is why it is necessary to ask two questions: What can make (or help) these governments protect their own citizens? And what do we know about the new slavery that can help us put a stop to it, if national governments won't? Both have economic answers. If we have learned one thing from the end of apartheid in South Africa, it is that hitting a government in the pocketbook hard enough can make it change its ways. If slavery stops being profitable, there is little motivation to enslave. But what do we really know about the economics of the new slavery? The answer, I'm afraid, is almost nothing. That is the reason I began this journey. In Thailand, Mauritania, Brazil, Pakistan, and India (all countries that have signed the United Nations agreements on slavery and bonded labor), I investigated local slavery. In each case I looked hard into how slavery worked as a *business*, and how the surrounding community protected slavery by custom or ignored it in fear. When you have met the slaves I met and come to understand their lives, when you have heard the justifications of the slaveholders and the government officials, then you will know the new slavery and, I hope, how we can work to stop it.

2

—————✦✦✦—————

THAILAND
Because She Looks Like a Child

WHEN SIRI WAKES IT IS ABOUT NOON. In the instant of waking she knows exactly who and what she has become. As she explained to me, the soreness in her genitals reminds her of the fifteen men she had sex with the night before. Siri is fifteen years old. Sold by her parents a year ago, her resistance and her desire to escape the brothel are breaking down and acceptance and resignation are taking their place.

In the provincial city of Ubon Ratchitani in northeastern Thailand, Siri works and lives in a brothel. About ten brothels and bars, dilapidated and dusty buildings, line the side street just around the corner from a new Western-style shopping mall. Food and noodle vendors are scattered between the brothels. The woman working behind the noodle stall outside Siri's brothel is also spy, warder, watchdog, procurer, and dinner-lady to Siri and the other twenty-four girls and women in the brothel.

The brothel is surrounded by a wall with iron gates meeting the street. Within the wall is a dusty yard, a concrete picnic table, and the ubiquitous spirit house, a small shrine that stands outside all Thai buildings. A low door leads into a windowless concrete room that is thick with the smell of cigarettes, stale beer, vomit, and sweat. This is the "selection" room (*hong du*). On one side of the room are stained and collapsing tables and booths; on the other side is a narrow elevated platform with a bench that runs the length of the room. Spotlights pick out this bench, and at night the girls and women sit here under the glare while the men at the tables drink and choose the one they want.

Passing through a door at the far end of the bench, the man follows the girl past a window where a bookkeeper takes his money and records which girl he has taken. From there he is led to the girl's room. Behind its concrete front room the brothel degenerates even further into a haphazard shanty warren of tiny cubicles where the girls live and work. A makeshift ladder leads up to what may have once been a barn. The upper level is now lined with doors about five feet apart opening into rooms of about five by seven feet that hold a bed and little else.

Scraps of wood and cardboard separate one room from the next, and Siri has plastered her walls with pictures and posters of teenage pop stars cut from magazines. Over her bed, as in most rooms, there also hangs a framed portrait of the king of Thailand; a single bare light bulb hangs above. Next to the bed a large tin can holds water; there is a hook nearby for rags and towels. At the foot of the bed next to the door some clothes are folded on a ledge. The walls are very thin and everything can be heard from the surrounding rooms: a shout from the bookkeeper downstairs echoes through them all whether their doors are open or not.

After rising at midday, Siri washes herself in cold water from the single concrete trough that serves the twenty-five women of the brothel. Then, dressed in a T-shirt and skirt, she goes to the noodle stand for the hot soup that is a Thai breakfast. Through the afternoon, if she does not have any clients, she chats with the other girls and women as they drink beer and play cards or make decorative handicrafts together. If the pimp is away the girls will joke around, but if not they must be constantly deferential and aware of his presence, for he can harm them or use them as he pleases. Men coming in the afternoon are the exception, but those that do tend to have more money and can buy a girl for several hours if they like. A few will even make appointments a few days ahead.

At about five, Siri and the other girls are told to dress, put on their makeup, and prepare for the night's work. By seven the men are coming in, purchasing drinks and choosing girls, and Siri will have been chosen by one or two of the ten to eighteen men who will buy her that night. Many men choose Siri because she looks much younger than her fifteen years. Slight and round faced, dressed to accentuate her youth, she might be eleven or twelve. Because she looks like a child she can be sold as a "new" girl at a higher price, about $15, which is more than twice that charged for the other girls.

Siri is very frightened that she will get AIDS. Long before she understood prostitution she knew about HIV, as many girls from her village returned home to die from AIDS after being sold into the brothels. Every day she prays to Buddha, trying to earn the merit that will preserve her from the disease. She also tries to insist that her clients use condoms, and in most cases she is successful as the pimp backs her up. But when policemen use her, or the pimp himself, they will do as they please; if she tries to insist, she will be beaten and raped. She also fears pregnancy, and like the other girls she receives injections of the contraceptive drug Depo-Provera. Once a month she has an HIV test, and so far it has been negative. She knows that if she tests positive she will be thrown out of the brothel to starve.

Though she is only fifteen Siri is now resigned to being a prostitute. After she was sold and taken to the brothel, she discovered that the work was not what she thought it would be. Like many rural Thais, Siri had a sheltered childhood and she was ignorant of what it meant to work in a brothel. Her first client hurt her and at the first opportunity she ran away. On the street with no money she was quickly caught, dragged back, beaten, and raped. That night she was forced to take on a chain of clients until the early morning. The beatings and the work continued night after night until her will was broken. Now she is sure that she is a bad person, very bad to have deserved what has happened to her. When I commented on how pretty she looked in a photograph, how like a pop star, she replied, "I'm no star; I'm just a whore, that's all." She copes as best she can. She takes a dark pride in her higher price and in the large number of men who choose her. It is the adjustment of the concentration camp, an effort to make sense of horror.

In Thailand prostitution is illegal, yet girls like Siri are sold into sex slavery by the thousands. The brothels that hold these girls are but a small part of a much wider sex industry. How can this wholesale trade in girls continue? What keeps it working? The answer is more complicated than we might think; Thailand's economic boom, its macho culture, and its social acceptance of prostitution all contribute to it. Money, culture, and society blend in new and powerful ways to enslave girls like Siri.[1]

Rice in the Field, Fish in the River, Daughters in the Brothel

Thailand is a country blessed with natural resources and sufficient food. The climate is mild to hot, there is dependable rain, and most of the country is a great plain, well-watered and fertile. The reliable production of rice has for centuries made Thailand a large exporter of grains, as it is today. Starvation is exceedingly rare in its history and social stability very much the norm. An old and often-repeated saying in Thai is "There is always rice in the fields and fish in the river." And anyone who has tried the imaginative Thai cuisine knows the remarkable things that can be done with those two ingredients and the local chili peppers.

If there is one part of Thailand not so rich in the necessities of life, it is the mountainous north. In fact, that area is not Thailand proper; originally the kingdom of Lanna, it was integrated into Thailand only in the late nineteenth century. The influence of Burma here is very strong—as are the cultures of the seven main hill tribes, which are distinctly foreign to the dominant Thai society. Only about a tenth of the land of the north can be used for agriculture, though what can be used is the most fertile in the country. The result is that those who control good land are well-off; those who live in the higher elevations, in the forests, are not. In another part of the world this last group might be called hillbillies, and they share the hardscrabble life of mountain dwellers everywhere.

The harshness of this life stands in sharp contrast to that on the great plain of rice and fish. Customs and culture differ markedly as well, and one of those differences is a key to the sexual slavery practiced throughout Thailand today. For hundreds of years many people in the north, struggling for life, have been forced to view their own children as commodities. A failed harvest, the death of a key breadwinner, or any serious debt incurred by a family might lead to the sale of a daughter (never a son) as a slave or servant. In the culture of the north it was a life choice not preferred but acceptable, and one that was used regularly. In the past these sales fed a small, steady flow of servants, workers, and prostitutes south into Thai society.

Religion helped provide two important justifications for sales of daughters. Within the type of Buddhism followed in Thailand, women are regarded as distinctly inferior to men. A woman cannot, for example, attain enlightenment, which is the ultimate goal of the devout. On the ladder of existence women are well below men, and only if she is especially careful might a woman hope to be reborn as a man in her next life. Indeed, to enter this incarnation as a woman might indicate a particularly disastrous and sinful previous life. In the advice recorded as his own words, Buddha warns his disciples about the danger of women: they are impure, carnal, and corrupting. Within these Buddhist writings prostitution is sanctioned; the *vibaya*, or rules for monks, lists ten kinds of wives, the first three of which are "those bought for money, those living together voluntarily, those to be enjoyed or used occasionally."[2] Within these beliefs is no notion of sex as a sin; instead, sex is seen as an attachment to the physical and natural world, the world of suffering and ignorance. The implication is that if you must have sex, have it as impersonally as possible.

Thai Buddhism also carries a central message of acceptance and resignation in the face of life's pain and suffering. The terrible things that happen to a person are, after all, of an individual's own making, recompense for the sins of this life or previous lives. Whatever happens is a person's fixed destiny, his or her karma. To achieve the tranquillity necessary for enlightenment, a person must learn to accept quietly and completely the pain of this life. For some Thai children the pain of this life includes forced prostitution. They may struggle against the abuse they suffer, but most come to resign themselves, living out a psychology of slavery that we will explore in this chapter.

A religious belief in the inferiority of girls is not the only cultural rule pressing them into slavery. Thai children, especially girls, owe their parents a profound debt, an obligation both cosmic and physical. Simply to be born is a great gift, then to be fed and raised another; and both require a lifetime of repayment. Girls in Thailand have always been expected to contribute fully to their family's income and to service their debt of obligation. In extreme cases this means being sold into slavery, being sacrificed for the good of their family. At the same time some parents have been quick to recognize the money to be realized from the sale of their children.

The small number of children sold into slavery in the past has become a flood today. This increase reflects the enormous changes in Thailand in the past fifty years as the country goes through the great transformation of industrialization—the same process that tore Europe apart over a century ago. If we are to understand slavery in Thailand we must understand these changes as well, for like so many other parts of the world, Thailand has always had slavery, but never before on this scale and never before as the new slavery.

One Girl Equals One Television

The boom and bust of Thailand's cyclical economic miracle has had a dramatic impact on northern villages. While the center of the country, around Bangkok, rapidly industrialized, the north was left be-hind. Prices of food, land, and tools all increased as the economy grew, but the returns for rice growing and other agricultural work were stag-nant, held down by government policies guaranteeing cheap food for factory workers in Bangkok. Yet visible everywhere in the north is a flood of consumer goods—refrigerators, televisions, cars and trucks, rice cookers, air conditioners—all of which are extremely tempting. Demand for these goods is high as families try to join the ranks of the prosperous. As it happens, the cost of participating in this consumer boom can be met from an old source, one that has also become much more profitable: the sale of children.

In the past, daughters were sold in response to a serious family fi-nancial crisis. Under the threat of losing their mortgaged rice fields and faced with destitution, a family might sell a daughter to redeem its debt, but for the most part daughters were worth about as much at home as workers as they would realize when sold. Modernization and economic growth have changed all that. Now parents feel a great pres-sure to buy consumer goods that were unknown even twenty years ago; the sale of a daughter might easily finance a new television set. A recent survey in the northern provinces found that of the families who sold their daughters, two-thirds could afford not to do so but "instead pre-ferred to buy color televisions and video equipment."[3] And from the perspective of parents who are willing to sell their children, there has never been a better market.

The brothels' demand for prostitutes is rapidly increasing. The same economic boom that feeds consumer demand in northern villages lines the pockets of laborers and workers of the central plain. Poor eco-nomic migrants from the rice fields now work on building sites or in new factories earning many times what they did on the land. Possibly for the first time in their lives, these laborers can do what more well-off Thai men have always done: go to a brothel. The purchasing power of this increasing number of brothel users strengthens the call for north-ern girls and supports a growing business in procurement and traffick-ing in girls.

Siri's story was typical. A broker, a woman herself from a northern village, approached the families in Siri's village with assurances of well-paid work for their daughters. Siri's parents probably understood that the work would be as a prostitute—since they knew that other girls from their village had gone south to brothels. After some negotiation they were paid 50,000 baht ($2,000) for Siri, a very significant sum for this family of rice farmers.[4] This exchange began the process of debt bondage that is used to enslave the girls. The contractual arrangement between the broker and parents requires that this money be repaid by the daughter's labor before she is free to leave or is allowed to send money home. Sometimes the money is treated as a loan to the parents, the girl being both the collateral and the means of repayment. In such cases the exorbitant interest charged on the loan means there is little chance that a girl's sexual slavery will ever repay the debt.

Siri's debt of 50,000 baht rapidly escalated. Taken south by the broker, Siri was sold for 100,000 baht to the brothel where she now works. After her rape and beating Siri was informed that the debt she must repay, now to the brothel, equaled 200,000 baht. In addition, Siri learned of the other payments she would be required to make, including rent for her room at 30,000 baht per month as well as charges for food and drink, fees for medicine, and fines if she did not work hard enough or displeased a customer.

The total debt is virtually impossible to repay, even at Siri's higher rate of 400 baht. About 100 baht from each client is supposed to be credited to Siri to reduce her debt and pay her rent and other expenses; 200 goes to the pimp and the remaining 100 to the brothel. By this reckoning, Siri must have sex with 300 men a month just to pay her rent, and what is left over after other expenses barely reduces her original debt. For girls who can charge only 100 to 200 baht per client, the debt grows even faster. This debt bondage keeps the girls under complete control as long as they seem to the brothel owner and pimp worth having. Violence reinforces the control and any resistance earns a beating as well as an increase in the debt. Over time, if the girl becomes a good and cooperative prostitute, the pimp may tell her she has paid off the debt and allow her to send small sums home. This "paying off" of the debt usually has nothing to do with an actual accounting of earnings but is declared at the discretion of the pimp, as a means to extend the profits to be made by making the girl more pliable. Together with rare visits home, money sent back to the family operates to keep her at her job.

Most girls are purchased from parents as Siri was, but for others the enslavement is much more direct. Throughout Thailand agents travel to villages offering work in factories or as domestics. Sometimes they bribe local officials to vouch for them or they befriend the monks at the local temple to gain introductions. Lured by the promise of good jobs and the money that the daughters will send back to the village, the deceived families send their girls with the agent, often paying for the privilege. Once they arrive in a city, the girls are sold to brothels where they are raped, beaten, and locked in. Still other girls are simply kidnapped. This is especially true of women and children who have come to visit relatives in Thailand from Burma or Laos. At bus and train stations gangs watch for women and children that can be snatched or drugged for shipment to brothels.

Direct enslavement by trickery or kidnapping is not really in the economic interest of the brothel owners. The steadily growing market for prostitutes, the loss of girls due to HIV infection, and the especially strong demand for younger and younger girls make it necessary for brokers and brothel owners to cultivate village families so that they might buy more daughters as they come of age. In Siri's case this meant letting her maintain ties with her family and ensuring that after a year or so she sent a monthly postal order for 10,000 baht to her parents. The monthly payment is a good investment, since it encourages Siri's parents to place their other daughters in the brothel as well. Moreover, the young girls themselves become willing to go, when older sisters and relatives returning for holidays bring stories of the rich life to be lived in the cities of the central plain. Village girls lead a sheltered life, and the appearance of women only a little older than themselves with money and nice clothes is tremendously appealing. They admire the results of this thing called prostitution with only the vaguest notion of what it is. Recent research found that young girls know that their sisters and neighbors have become prostitutes, but when asked what it means to be a prostitute their most common answer was "wearing Western clothes in a restaurant."[5] Drawn by this glamorous life, they put up little opposition to being sent away with the brokers to swell an already booming sex industry.

By my own conservative estimate there are perhaps 35,000 girls like Siri enslaved in Thailand. Remarkably, this is only a small proportion of all prostitutes. The actual number of prostitutes, while unknown, is certainly much higher. The government states that there are 81,384 prostitutes in Thailand—but that official number is calculated from the number of registered (though still illegal) brothels, massage parlors, and sex establishments. Every brothel, bar, or massage parlor we visited in Thailand was unregistered, and no one working with prostitutes believes the government figures. At the other end of the spectrum are the estimates put forward by activist organizations such as the Center for the Protection of Children's Rights. These groups assert that there are over 2 million prostitutes. I suspect that this number is too high in a national population of 60 million. My own reckoning, based on information gathered by AIDS workers in different cities, is that there are between half a million and one million prostitutes.

Of this number only about one in twenty is enslaved. Most become prostitutes "voluntarily," though some start out in debt bondage. Sex is sold everywhere in Thailand—barber shops, massage parlors, coffee shops and cafés, bars and restaurants, nightclubs and karaoke bars, brothels, hotels, and even temples traffic in sex. Prostitutes range from the high-earning "professional" women who work with some autonomy, through the women working by choice as call girls or in massage parlors, to the enslaved rural girls like Siri. Many women work semi-independently in bars, restaurants, and nightclubs—paying a fee to the owner, working when they choose, and having the power to decide whom to take as a customer. Most bars or clubs could not use an enslaved prostitute like Siri, as the women are often sent out on call and their clients expect a certain amount of cooperation and friendliness. Enslaved girls service the lowest end of the market: the laborers, students, and workers who can afford only the 100 baht per half hour rate. It is low-cost sex in volume, and the demand is always there. For Thai men, buying a woman is much like buying a round of drinks. But the reasons that such large numbers of Thai men use prostitutes are much more complicated and grow out of their culture, their history, and a rapidly changing economy.

"I Don't Want to Waste It, So I Take Her"

Thais worship and imitate their royal family even more than the English do theirs. The current King Bhumibol is also known as Rama the Ninth, demonstrating the stability of a royal house that has governed the country since the eighteenth century. For much of Thailand's history this was an absolute monarchy, having life-and-death power over all of society. In the fifteenth century a Law of Civil Hierarchy codified the existing rigid and all-pervasive social structure. The law assigned every male of any rank a number of imaginary rice fields, from 25 for an ordinary freeman to 10,000 for ministers of state. This established a notional and measurable worth for every person in society; even the peasants, serfs, and slaves who made up the bulk of society were allotted 15 fields each (not that they ever got to own them). And while the law's official measurement of worth was in rice fields, an equally good measure of a man's status was in wives, mistresses, and concubines. Until it was officially disbanded in 1910 the king maintained a harem of hundreds of concubines, a few of whom might be elevated to the rank of Royal Mother or Minor Wife. This form of polygamy was closely imitated by status-hungry nobles and the emerging rich merchants of the nineteenth century. Virtually all men of any substance kept at least a mistress or a "minor wife." For those with less resources, prostitution was a perfectly acceptable option, as renting took the place of out-and-out ownership.

Even today everyone in Thailand knows their place within a very elaborate and precise status system. Mistresses and minor wives continue to enhance any man's social standing,[6] but the consumption of commercial sex has increased dramatically. If an economic boom is a tide that raises all boats, then vast numbers of Thai men have now been raised to a financial position from which they can regularly buy sex. Nothing like the economic growth in Thailand was ever experienced in the West, but a few facts show its scale: in a country the size of Britain, one-tenth of the workforce moved from the land to industry in just the three years from 1993 to 1995; the number of factory workers doubled from less than 2 million to more than 4 million in the eight years from 1988 to 1995; and urban wages doubled from 1986 to 1996. Thailand is now the world's largest importer of motorcycles and the second-largest importer of pickup trucks after the United States (these two types of vehicles being best suited to Thailand's warm climate and dubious roads). Between 1985 and 1995 the gross national product doubled and the gross domestic product tripled. Until the economic downturn of late 1997, money flooded Thailand, transforming poor rice farmers into wage laborers and fueling consumer demand.

With this newfound wealth Thai men go to brothels in increasing numbers. Several recent studies show that between 80 and 87 percent of Thai men have had sex with a prostitute. Up to 90 percent report that their first sexual experience was with a prostitute. Somewhere between 10 and 40 percent of married men paid for commercial sex within the past twelve months, as have up to 50 percent of single men. Though it is difficult to measure, these reports suggest something like 3 to 5 million regular customers for commercial sex. But it would be wrong to imagine millions of Thai men sneaking furtively on their own along dark streets lined with brothels: commercial sex is a social event, part of a good night out with friends. Ninety-five percent of men going to a brothel do so with their friends, usually at the end of a night spent drinking. Groups go out for recreation and entertainment, and especially to get drunk together. That is a strictly male pursuit, as Thai women usually abstain from alcohol. All-male groups out for a night on the town are considered normal in any Thai city, and whole neighborhoods are devoted to serving them. Most Thais, men and women, feel that commercial sex is an acceptable part of an ordinary outing for single men, and about two-thirds of men and one-third of women feel the same about married men.[7]

For most married women, having their husbands go to prostitutes is preferable to other forms of extramarital sex. Most wives accept that men naturally want multiple partners, and prostitutes are seen as less threatening to the stability of the family.[8] Prostitutes require no long-term commitment or emotional involvement. When a husband uses a prostitute he is thought to be fulfilling a male role, but when he takes a minor wife or mistress, his wife is thought to have failed. Minor wives are usually bigamous second wives, often married by law in a district different than that of the first marriage (easily done, since no national records are kept). As wives, they require upkeep, housing, and regular support, and their offspring have a claim on inheritance; so they present a significant danger to the well-being of the major wife and her children. The relationship may not be formalized (polygamy *is* illegal) but it nevertheless will be regarded as binding, and the children still have legal claims for support. For the minor wife from a poor background, attachment to a well-heeled older man is a proven avenue to upward social mobility. The potential disaster for the first wife is a minor wife who convinces the man to leave his first family, and this happens often enough to keep first wives worried and watchful.

Given that sex is for sale everywhere, and that noncommercial sex threatens the family more gravely, it is little wonder that Thai wives maintain a "don't ask—don't tell" policy about prostitution. As greater spending power means their husbands can buy sex at will, most Thai women are resigned to it, simply hoping that his interest doesn't shift to a minor wife.[9] Within this context, their husbands' occasional visits to brothels with the boys are overlooked by wives. Because it is part of a normal outing, most men feel little or no shame in buying sex. Certainly any hesitation they might feel is quickly melted by alcohol and peer pressure. Not all nights out lead to the brothel, of course, but a promotion, pay raise, or any sort of celebration makes a visit more likely. Not all groups of friends will go to brothels on their night out. Some groups of married men never do, but others will go often, their drinking parties naturally evolving into trips to the brothel. And once Thai men are out drinking, it is normal for one reveler to pay for the group, thereby hosting the party; picking up the tab is also a form of conspicuous consumption, deployed to impress one's colleagues. This carries over to the brothel as well and often makes the difference in whether a man will use a prostitute. Interviewed in a recent study one man explained, "When we arrive at the brothel, my friends take one and pay for me to take another. It costs them money; I don't want to waste it, so I take her."[10] Having one's prostitute paid for also brings an informal obligation to repay in kind at a later date. It is something many men would avoid because of the expense, if sober, but in the inebriated moment of celebration most men go along for the ride.

Buying prostitutes for someone else happens for other reasons as well. Businessmen in negotiations will provide or expect sex as part of the bargaining process. For most Thais this is a perfectly unremarkable part of business practice and necessary if one's firm or job is to continue and prosper. Men who travel on business are also more likely to use prostitutes, taking advantage of being away from their hometown or village. Government officials touring rural areas are offered local "flowers" as hospitality, and there is a saying that a man has not really been to a place until he has had a "taste" of it. Even first-year university students will be taken en masse to brothels in their first week as part of an initiation by upperclassmen. All of this behavior is made easier by the assumption that men are not responsible when they are drunk, and groups of friends egg each other on in heavy drinking—an opened whiskey bottle can never be resealed. In the macho

Thai culture, drunken accusations that a reluctant man is afraid of his wife almost always push him to accept an offered prostitute. Thai culture also emphasizes group solidarity and conflict avoidance, so acquiescence in commercial sex is often seen as better than disagreement or embarrassment. And whatever happens, men keep their secrets. Friends never admit to their wives or others what happens when the group is out drinking.

For most Thai men, commercial sex is a legitimate form of entertainment and sexual release. It is not just acceptable: it is a clear statement of status and economic power. Women in Thailand are *things*, markers in a male game of status and prestige. It is thus no surprise that some women are treated as livestock—kidnapped, abused, held like animals, bought and sold, and dumped when their usefulness is gone. When this customary treatment is combined with the relentless profit-making of the new economy, the result for women is horrific. Thousands more must be found to feed men's status needs, thousands more must be locked into sexual slavery to feed the profits of investors. And what are the police, government, and local authorities doing about slavery? Every case of sex slavery involves many crimes—fraud, kidnap, assault, rape, sometimes murder. These crimes are not rare or random; they are systematic and repeated in brothels thousands of times each month. Yet those with the power to stop this terror instead help it grow and grow in the very lucrative world of the modern slaveholder.

Millionaire Tigers and Billionaire Geese

Who are these modern slaveholders? The answer is anyone and everyone: anyone, that is, with a little capital to invest. The people that *appear* to own the enslaved prostitutes—the pimps, madams, and brothel keepers—are in fact usually just employees. As hired muscle, pimps and their helpers provide the brutality that controls women and makes possible their commercial exploitation. Although they are just employees, the pimps do rather well for themselves. Often living in the brothel, they receive a salary and add to that income from a number of scams; for example, food and drink are sold to customers at inflated prices and the pimps pocket the difference. Much more lucrative is their control of the price of sex. While each woman has a basic price, the pimps size up each customer and pitch the fee accordingly. In this way a client may pay two or three times more than the normal rate and all of the surplus goes to the pimp. In league with the bookkeeper, the pimp systematically cheats the prostitutes of the little that is supposed to be credited against their debt. If they manage the sex slaves well and play all of the angles, pimps will easily make ten times their basic wage—a great income for an ex-peasant whose main skills are violence and intimidation, but nothing compared to the riches to be made by the brokers and the real slaveholders.

The brokers and agents that buy girls in the villages and sell them to brothels are only short-term slaveholders. Their business is part recruiting agency, part shipping company, part public relations, and part kidnapping gang. They aim to buy low and sell high, while maintaining a good flow of girls from the villages. Brokers are equally likely to be men or women and usually come from the regions in which they recruit. Some will be local people dealing in girls in addition to their jobs as police officers, government bureaucrats, or even schoolteachers. Positions of public trust are excellent starting points for buying young girls. In spite of the character of their work they are well respected. Seen as job providers and sources of large cash payments to parents, they are well known in their communities. Many of the women brokers were once sold themselves, spent some years as prostitutes, and now, in their middle age, make a living by supplying girls to the brothels. These women are walking advertisements for sexual slavery. Their lifestyle and income, their Western clothes and glamorous sophisticated ways, point to a rosy economic future for the girls they buy. That they have physically survived their years in the brothel may be the exception—many more young women come back to the villages to die of AIDS—but the parents tend to be optimistic. Whether these dealers are local people or traveling agents, they combine the business of procuring with other economic pursuits. A returned prostitute may live with her family, look after her parents, own a rice field or two, and buy and sell girls on the side. Like the pimps, they are in a good business, doubling their money on each girl within two or three weeks, but like the pimps, their profits are small compared to those of the long-term slaveholders.

The real slaveowners tend to be middle-aged businessmen. They fit seamlessly into the community, and they suffer no social discrimination for what they do. If anything, they are admired as successful, diversified capitalists. Brothel ownership is normally only one of many business interests for the slaveholder. To be sure, a brothel owner may have some ties to organized crime, but in Thailand organized crime includes the police and much of the government. Indeed, the work of the modern slaveholder is best seen not as aberrant criminality but as a perfect example of disinterested capitalism. Owning the brothel that holds young girls in bondage is simply a business matter. The investors would say that they are creating jobs and wealth. There is no hypocrisy in their actions, for they obey an important social norm: earning a lot of money is a good enough reason for anything. Of course, the slaveholder living in a middle-class neighborhood would display no outward sign of his work. His neighbors would know that he was a businessman, a successful one, and respect him for that. To look too closely into someone else's affairs is a serious affront in Thai culture: "mind your own business" (*yaa suek*) is one of the strongest retorts in the Thai language. So the slaveholder gains all of the benefits of exploiting and abusing young girls with no social repercussions.

The slaveholder may in fact be a partnership, company, or corporation. From the 1980s, Japanese investment poured into Thailand, in an enormous migration of capital that was called "Flying Geese."[11] The strong yen led to buying and building across the country, and while electronics firms built television factories, other investors found there was much, much more money to be made in the sex industry. In the footsteps of the Japanese came investment by the so-called Four Ti-gers (South Korea, Hong Kong, Taiwan, and Singapore) who also found marvelous opportunities in commercial sex. (All five of these countries also proved to be strong import markets for enslaved Thai girls, as dis-cussed below.) The Geese and the Tigers had the resources to buy the local criminals, police, administrators, and property needed to set up commercial sex businesses. Indigenous Thais also invested in brothels as the sex industry boomed; with less capital, they were more likely to open poorer, working-class outlets.

While young prostitutes have regular contact with the police, they may never meet the person who effectively owns them. The relation-ship between slaveholder and slave in modern Thailand is a model of arm's-length capitalism. Brothel owners, whether individuals or com-panies, need have little contact with prostitutes. It is possible that some co-owners do not even know they are slaveholders, only that they em-ploy commercial sex workers. The promise of high returns is a power-ful incentive to invest in a friend's new enterprise, and most Thais in-vest in businesses run by friends or relatives rather than in stocks and shares. Diversified capital investment is a new thing in Thailand, but it has caught on quickly. The ways of Western markets and economics are avidly imitated by the new businesspeople throughout Thailand. Looking to the developed countries they see investors putting their money into stock-market mutual funds on the basis of returns above all else—and that the portfolio might include firms making land mines or instruments of torture need not concern anyone. But the amount of distance needed to plead ignorance doesn't have to be so great; a single step is enough to separate an investor from his or her conscience.

Whether they be individual Thais, partnerships, or foreign investors, the slaveholders share many characteristics and well exemplify today's new slavers. There is little or no racial or ethnic difference between them and the slaves they own (with the exception of Japanese investors). They feel no need to rationalize their slaveholding on racial grounds. Nor are they linked in any sort of hereditary ownership of slaves or of the children of their slaves. They are not really interested in their slaves at all, just in the bottom line on their investment. If they weren't slaveholders they would put their money into other businesses, but there is little incentive to do so since brothels are such solid investments, much more stable than the stock market. Contributing to the economy is a strong *moral* argument in Thailand, and these slaveholders might be proud of their contribution—they see themselves as providing jobs, and even as lifting the debt-bonded girls out of rural poverty. Not that these moral questions matter, since the slaveholders never need think about the women in their brothels, where they come from, or what will happen to them.

To understand the business of slavery today we have to know something about the economy in which it operates. In spite of the economic boom, the average Thai's income is very low by Western standards. Within an industrializing country, millions still live in rural poverty. If a rural family owns its house and has a rice field, it might survive on as little as 500 baht ($20) per month. Such absolute poverty means a diet of rice supplemented with insects (crickets, grubs, and maggots are widely eaten), wild plants, and what fish they can catch themselves. Below this level, which can be sustained only in the countryside, is hunger and the loss of any house or land. For most Thais an income of 2,500 to 4,500 baht per month ($100 to $180) is normal. Since the economic crash in 1997, the poor have only gotten poorer and more numerous as jobs evaporated: in the cities rent will take more than half of the average income, and prices climb constantly. At this income there is deprivation but no hunger since government policies artificially depress the price of rice (to the impoverishment of farmers). Rice sells for 20 baht (75 cents) a kilo, with a family of four eating about a kilo of rice each day. They might eat, but Thais on these poverty wages can do little else. Whether in city, town, or village, to earn it they will work six or seven twelve- to fourteen-hour days each week. Illness or injury can quickly send even this standard of living plummeting downward. There is no system of welfare or health care, and pinched budgets allow no space for saving. In these families the 20,000 to 50,000 baht ($800 to $2,000) brought by selling a daughter represents a year's income. Such a vast sum is a powerful inducement and blinds parents to the realities of sex slavery.

The Always Prospering "Restaurant"

Brothels are just one of the many outlets for commercial sex, but because of their rapid turnover they serve a large proportion of men buying sex. The average brothel keeps between ten and thirty prostitutes, and most average around twenty. In the countryside the brothel may just be someone's house with three or four women working, but it is the brothels in cities and towns that hold girls in debt bondage. Many brothels benefit from economies of agglomeration, bunching together in a red-light district. If they have any sign outside (and most don't), it will be cryptically neutral. One working-class brothel I visited had a small lighted sign hanging by its gate that read "Always Prospering"; below it in smaller type and different paint had been added "restaurant." This addition, I was told, had been made at the suggestion of the police, though no food was for sale inside. The buildings themselves are as a rule dilapidated, dirty, leaky, and cobbled together from scrap. Rats and roaches infest them and sanitation is minimal. The women who must work in them are young, rarely over thirty and often younger than eighteen. There is little difference between them and their customers. Both are from poor backgrounds, though the girls are more likely to be from the northern region. In the far south of Thailand the men may be Malay or Singaporean Muslims, but the girls will still be northern Thai Buddhists. The exception to the regular use of northern Thai girls is the recent increase in women trafficked from Burma and Laos, and enslaved in brothels. Importing women helps meet the rising demand for fresh prostitutes.

Forced prostitution is a great business. The overheads are low, the turnover high, and the profits immense. In this research I have tried for the first time to detail the business side of this form of slavery and to expose the scale of exploitation and its rewards. It is far, far different from the capital-intensive slavery of the past, which required long-term investments and made solid but small profits. The disposability of the women, the special profits to be made from children, all ensure a low-risk, high-return enterprise. For all its dilapidation and filth the brothel is a highly efficient machine that in destroying young girls turns them into gold.

To set up a brothel requires a relatively small outlay. About 80,000 baht ($3,200) will buy all the furniture, equipment, and fixtures that are needed. The building itself will be rented for anywhere from 4,000 to 15,000 baht per month ($160 to $600). In addition to the prostitutes the brothel needs a pimp (who often has a helper) and a cashier/book-keeper; it sometimes employs a cook as well. Pimps will receive from 5,000 to 10,000 baht per month in salary ($200 to $400), cashiers about 7,000 baht ($280), and the cook about 5,000 baht ($200) or less. For electricity and other utilities about 2,000 baht ($80) is needed each month. Beer and whiskey must be bought for resale to clients. This leaves only two other expenses—food and bribes.

Feeding a prostitute costs 50 to 80 baht per day ($2.00 to $3.20). Slaveholders do not skimp on food, since men want healthy-looking girls with full figures. Healthy looks are important in a country suffering an HIV epidemic, and *young* healthy girls are thought to be the safest. Bribes are not exorbitant or unpredictable; in most brothels a policeman stops by once a day to pick up 200 to 400 baht ($8 to $16), a monthly expenditure of about 6,000 baht ($240) that is topped off by giving the policeman a girl for an hour if he seems interested. The police pay close attention to the stability of the brothels: a short side street generates $32,000 to $64,000 each year in relatively effortless income. The higher-priced massage parlors and nightclubs pay much larger bribes and usually a significant start-up payment as well. Bribe income is the key reason that senior police officials are happy to buy their positions and compete for the most lucrative ones.

TABLE I   MONTHLY EXPENDITURE AND INCOME
FOR THE ALWAYS PROSPERING BROTHEL

Expenses		*Income*	
Item	Amount (in baht)	Item	Amount (in baht)
Rent	5,000	Commercial sex*	1,050,000
Utilities and bills	2,000	Rent paid by prostitutes	600,000
Food and drink	45,000	Sale of condoms	70,000
Pimp's salary	7,000	Sale of drinks	504,000
Cashier	7,000	Virgin premium	50,000
Cook	5,000	"Interest" on debt bond	15,000
Bribes	6,000		
Payments to taxis, etc.	12,000		
Beer and whiskey	168,000		
Total	257,000 (U.S.$10,280)	*Total*	2,289,000
		Monthly Profit	2,032,000 (U.S.$81,280)

*Calculated for 20 prostitutes averaging 14 clients per day, at 125 baht per client, for 30 days.

Income far exceeds expenses. Each of the twenty girls makes about 125 baht ($5) for the brothel with each client she has, and each day she has between ten and eighteen clients for 1,250 to 2,250 baht ($50 to $90). A single day's return is 25,000 to 45,000 baht ($1,000 to $1,800) just on sex. And as can be seen from table 1, there are a number of other ways for the brothel to turn a penny.

The profit on drinks, mostly the sale of beer and whiskey, is difficult to measure. The table's sum of 504,000 baht is a conservative estimate based on each client buying a single beer, which has been bought by the brothel for 20 baht and sold for 80 baht. The prostitute's rent averages 30,000 baht per month for her room, and if half the girls are repaying a debt bond the brothel would make at least 15,000 baht each month on the "interest." The sale of condoms is pure profit, as they are provided free of charge to brothels by the Ministry of Health in an attempt to slow the spread of HIV. Clients are charged 10 baht for a condom and most clients are required to use one. Siri explained that she went through three to four boxes of condoms each month; there are 100 condoms in each box.

The income shown as the *virgin premium* requires some explanation. Some customers, especially Chinese and Sino-Thais, are willing to pay very large amounts to have sex with a virgin. This strong preference has two bases. The first is the ancient Chinese belief that sex with a virgin will reawaken sexual virility and prolong life. A girl's virginity is thought to be a strong source of *yang* (or coolness), which quenches and slows the *yin* (or heat) of the aging process. Wealthy Chinese and Sino-Thais (as well as Chinese sex tourists from Taiwan, Singapore, Malaysia, and Hong Kong) will try to have sex with virgins as regularly as possible and will pay well for the opportunity. When a new girl is brought to the brothel she will not be placed out in the selection room with the other prostitutes but kept back in another room, the *hong bud boree sut* (the "room to unveil virgins"). Here she will be displayed, possibly with other children, and her price will be negotiated with the pimp. To deflower a virgin these men pay between 5,000 and 50,000 baht ($200 to $2,000). Deflowering often takes place away from the brothel in a hotel room rented for the occasion. The pimp or his assistant will often attend as well, since it is usually necessary to beat the girl into submission.

The second reason the brothel can demand a virgin premium is the general fear of HIV/AIDS. While Thai men or other non-Chinese customers do not believe in yin and yang, they do fear HIV infection. It is assumed that virgins cannot carry the virus, and even after a girl has lost her virginity, she can be sold at a higher price as "pure" or "fresh." One Burmese girl reported being sold as a virgin to four different clients. The younger the girl, or the younger-looking she is, the higher her price can be, as in Siri's case. The premium might also be paid to a brothel by another, higher-class, commercial sex business. Special "members clubs" or massage parlors might take an order from a customer for a virgin, a pure girl, or a child. If the brothel doesn't have a suitable young girl on hand, it might arrange with a broker for one to be recruited or, if time is pressing, kidnapped. The more expensive establishments don't normally want to get involved in procuring and are willing to pay the brothels to find the young girls. Once used in this way, the girl is put to work with the other prostitutes in the brothel to feed the normal profit stream.

This profit stream makes sex slavery very lucrative. The Always Prospering brothel nets something like 24,384,000 baht a year ($975,360), a return of 790 percent on expenses. Key to this level of profit is the low cost of each girl. A new girl, at 100,000 baht, requires a capital outlay of less than 5 percent of one month's profit. Simply from the sale of her body and the rent she must pay, a brothel recovers the cost of buying a girl within two or three months. Within the sex industry it is the slaveholder that makes the highest profits. "Voluntary" prostitutes in nightclubs and massage parlors charge higher prices, but have only three to five clients a day. Escort girls may have only one client a night. "Voluntary" sex workers, who keep a much larger proportion of the money they make, also exercise some discretion over which clients they will take. By contrast, the slaveholder's total control of the prostitute, over the volume of clients she must take and over the money she makes, means vast profits. There is no good estimate of the importance of the sex industry to the Thai economy, and the total number of sex workers is hotly debated. But if we look just at girls like Siri, the estimated 35,000 girls held in debt bondage, the annual profits they generate are enormous. If their brothels follow the same scheme as the Always Prospering, the annual profit made on these girls is over 42 *billion* baht ($1.70 billion). There is, however, one other cost to be laid against this profit—the price the girls pay with their bodies, minds, and health.

Disposable Bodies

Girls are so cheap that there is little reason to take care of them over the long term. Expenditure on medical care or prevention is rare in the brothels, since the working life of girls in debt bondage is fairly short—two to five years. After that, most of the profit has been drained from the girl and it is more cost-effective to discard her and replace her with someone fresh. No brothel wants to take on the responsibility of a sick or dying girl.

Enslaved prostitutes in brothels face two major threats to their physical health and to their lives: violence and disease. Violence—their enslavement enforced through rape, beatings, or threats—is always present. It is the typical introduction to their new status as sex slaves. Virtually every girl interviewed repeated the same story: after being taken to the brothel or to her first client as a virgin, any resistance or refusal was met with beatings and rape. A few girls report being drugged and then attacked; others report being forced to submit at gunpoint. The immediate and forceful application of terror is the first step in successful enslavement. Within hours of being brought to the brothel, the girls are in pain and shock. Like other victims of torture they often go numb, paralyzed in their minds if not in their bodies. For the youngest girls, with little understanding of what is happening to them, the trauma is overwhelming. Shattered and betrayed, they often have little clear memory of what has occurred.

After the first attack the girl has little resistance left, but the violence never ends. In the brothel, violence and terror are the final arbiters of all questions. There is no argument, there is no appeal. An unhappy customer brings a beating, a sadistic client brings more pain; in order to intimidate and cheat them more easily, the pimp rains down terror randomly on the prostitutes. The girls must do anything the pimp wants if they are to avoid being beaten. Escape is impossible. One girl reported that when she was caught trying to escape, the pimp beat her and then took her into the viewing room; with two helpers he then beat her again in front of all the girls in the brothel. Afterward she was locked into a room for three days and nights with no food or water. When she was released she was immediately put to work. Two other girls who attempted escape told of being stripped naked and whipped with steel coat hangers by pimps. The police serve as slave-catchers whenever a girl escapes; once captured, girls are often beaten or abused in the police station before being sent back to the brothel. For most girls it soon becomes clear that they can never escape, that their only hope for release is to please the pimp and to somehow pay off their debt.

In time, confusion and disbelief fade, leaving dread, resignation, and a separation of the conscious link between mind and body. Now the girl does whatever it takes to reduce the pain, to adjust mentally to a life that means being used by fifteen men a day. The reaction to this abuse takes many forms: lethargy, aggression, self-loathing and suicide attempts, confusion, self-abuse, depression, full-blown psychoses, and hallucinations. Girls who have been freed and taken into shelters are found to have all these. Rehabilitation workers report that the girls suffer emotional instability; they are unable to trust or form relationships, to readjust to the world outside the brothel, or to learn and develop normally. Unfortunately, psychological counseling is virtually unknown in Thailand, as there is a strong cultural pressure to keep any mental problems hidden, and little therapeutic work is done with girls freed from brothels. The long-term impact of this experience is unknown.

A clearer picture can be drawn of the physical diseases that the girls accumulate. There are many sexually transmitted diseases, and prostitutes contract most of them. Multiple infections reduce the immune system and make it easier for infections to take hold. If the illness affects their ability to have sex it may be dealt with, but serious chronic illnesses are often left untreated. Contraception often harms the girls as well. Some slaveholders administer contraceptive pills themselves, continuing them without any break and withholding the monthly placebo pills. Thus the girls stop menstruating altogether and work more nights in the month. Some girls are given three or four contraceptive pills a day; others are given Depo-Provera injections by the pimp or the bookkeeper. The same needle might be used for injecting all of them, passing HIV from girl to girl. Most girls who become pregnant will be sent for an abortion. Abortion is illegal in Thailand so this will be a backstreet operation, with all the obvious risks. A few women are kept working while they are pregnant, as some Thai men want to have sex with pregnant women. When the child is born it can be taken and sold by the brothel owner and the woman put back to work.

Not surprisingly, HIV/AIDS is epidemic in enslaved prostitutes. Thailand has one of the highest HIV infection rates in the world. Officially, the government admits to 800,000 cases, but health workers insist there are at least twice that many. From 1997, a campaign to reduce HIV infection had a significant effect. While the target was 100 percent condom use for commercial sex, the reality was a reduced but steady cross-transmission between men and prostitutes.[12] The epidemic has passed beyond the high-risk groups of sex workers and drug users, who now have infection rates as high as 50 percent in some areas. The group with the greatest increase in HIV infection today is wives exposed through their husbands' visits to prostitutes. In some rural villages where the trafficking of girls has been a regular feature, the infection rate is over 20 percent. Recent research suggests that the younger the girl, the more susceptible she is to HIV due to the lack of development of the protective vaginal mucous membrane. In spite of the distribution of condoms by the government, some brothels do not require their use. Many young girls understand little about HIV and how it is contracted. Some feel that using condoms is too painful when they have to service ten to fifteen men a night. In fact, the abrasion of the vagina brought on by repeated sex with condoms can increase the chances of HIV infection when unprotected sex next occurs. Even in brothels where condoms are sold or required, girls cannot always force men to use them. Most northern villages house young girls and women who have come home from the brothels to die of AIDS. There they are sometimes shunned and sometimes hounded out of the village. There are a few rehabilitation centers run by charities and the government that work with ex-prostitutes and women who are HIV-positive, but they can take only a tiny fraction of those in need. Outside the brothel there is no life left for most of these women, and some will stay in the brothel even when they have the chance to leave.

We're Unfit for Anything Else Now

Occasionally the government will order a raid on a brothel and take all the girls into custody. This is done for show, when newspaper reports or foreign interest makes it necessary. During such raids the prostitutes hide or run away from the police. Since the police normally work for the slaveholders, the girls assume the worst, not that they will be freed. Videos taken during these actions show girls paralyzed by fear and shock sitting numbly in the display room or later in police cells. Sometimes they are taken to emergency shelters, but the rehabilitation workers have learned it is impossible to keep some of them from running back to the brothel. One shelter worker explained, "When the girls are first brought in we say to them—'Don't break any windows in order to leave. Look, we are all going to the doctor now for a checkup, the door is open, just leave if you want'—it is no use to hold them against their will."[13]

The complex relationship between slave and slaveholder helps explain why a young prostitute runs back to the brothel after so much cruel treatment. From the outside it seems simple—one person controls others through violence, taking away their freedom. But slaves have to live on as slaves; they must find ways to adapt to their enslavement. Of course, any adaptation to horror may itself be horrible. Their reactions mirror the words of the psychologist R. D. Laing, who declared that some kinds of mental illness were strategies "invented in order to live in an unlivable situation."[14] Within the brothels perhaps half of the sex slaves escape into a state of shock and withdrawal; the other half find a more active adaptation, which may include close identification with the pimp or slaveholder. This resignation, this giving in, has the important benefit of reducing the violence the prostitutes suffer. Once escape is seen as impossible, any action or obedience that takes away pain, that makes life a little more bearable, becomes viable no matter how degrading or illogical. Whether a girl adapts or withdraws may depend on how much she knew about life in the brothel before her arrival. Some parents admit that they understand exactly what happens to their daughters after they sell them. Some girls realize that they will probably be prostitutes and know something about what that means. For these girls adaptation may be easier. Other girls, especially very young girls, expect to be working in factories or restaurants. They will have heard of prostitution, but have little or no idea what it actually entails. For these girls physical assault and rape can be shattering, and they may react by escaping into shock and numbness.

In the world in which they live, like the world of the concentration camp, there are only those with total power and those with no power. Reward and punishment come from a single source, the pimp. The girls often find building a relationship with the pimp to be a good strategy. While pimps are thugs, they do rely also on means of control other than violence. They are adept at manipulation, at fostering insecurity and dependence. They can be kind, at times, and they can treat a girl with affection in order to increase her pliability and her reliance on them. Cultural norms have also prepared the sex slaves for control and submission. A girl will be told how her parents will suffer if she does not cooperate and work hard, how the debt is on her shoulders and must be repaid. The need to submit and to accept family responsibility will be hammered home again and again. Thai sex roles are clearly defined and women are expected to be retiring, nonassertive, and obedient, as the girls hear repeatedly. Their religion, too, supports this manipulation. Thai Buddhism asserts that everyone must repay the karmic debt accumulated in past lives with suffering in this life. Such beliefs encourage the girls to turn inward, as they realize that they must have committed terrible sins in a past life to deserve their enslavement and abuse. Their religion urges them to accept this suffering, to come to terms with it, and to reconcile themselves to their fate.

As a result the girls become willing slaves, trusted and obedient.

When I met Siri, she had just crossed the invisible line between resistance and submission. Though only fifteen she was reconciled to life as a prostitute. She explained it was her fate, her karma, and each day she prayed to Buddha for acceptance. In the past she had tried to escape; now she dreams of earning enough money to build a house in her village. Her anger and resentment had dissolved, and she willingly accedes to the pimp's wishes, priding herself on her looks and higher price. Her resistance ended, she is now allowed out of the brothel to visit the temple. In his domination of Siri, her pimp has a powerful ally: her mother. Siri's mother had been staying at the Always Prospering brothel for several days when we arrived. She had come down from her village at the pimp's request while Siri had an operation. (Although Siri wouldn't tell us the nature of the operation, she did say that it had cost her 10,000 baht.) The pimp was concerned that while Siri was convalescing she might begin to think of escape. Her mother provided a forceful check on such thoughts, providing basic care but at the same time reminding Siri of her duty and the importance of repaying her debt both to the brothel and to her parents. In time the pimp may allow Siri to go home on holidays as he does some of the other girls. There is little threat that they will run away, for they know the pimp can always find them in their village; they are convinced that wherever they fled they would be found.

This belief in an omniscient pimp is supported by the other, more distant, relationships each girl has with slaveholders and the government. From the policeman who comes each day to the brothel, to the police chief in the city or district, to the political boss that the police chief must answer to, and so on up the ladder of government, the machine of the state is the machine of enslavement. That is not to say that the police or government directly enslaves girls in brothels; instead they provide a system of protection and enforcement for the slaveholders that makes slavery possible. At all levels of government, officials turn a blind eye to the crime of slavery. A complete set of laws on the statute books lies unenforced: they forbid trafficking in women, prostitution, rape, sexual abuse of minors, establishment of brothels, kidnapping, forced labor, debt bondage, and slavery. Some officials profit from bribes; others regularly use the brothels. The result is an unofficial but highly effective system of state enforcement of sex slavery. The power of the pimp is enormously enhanced by the power of the national police. Thailand's Prime Minister Chuan Leekpai admitted in 1992 that "the problem [of sex slavery] would be less if those who have the weapons and enforce the law were not involved," but he added that "if the problem cannot be solved, I won't order the authorities to tackle it."[15] Since 1992 police involvement has, if anything, increased.[16]

On the day that Chuan made these comments, a tragic murder was discovered in Songkhla that exposed the links between police and brothel owners.[17] A young Thai prostitute, Passawara Samrit, from the northern city of Chiangmai was found dead with her throat slashed. After receiving death threats from her pimp and police when she tried to run away from her brothel, Passawara escaped to the local hospital and asked for help. Hospital staff turned her over to the welfare department at the Songkhla provincial hall, and the welfare officials called in the police. At the end of the day, while still at the welfare office, Passawara went to the toilet and disappeared. Her body was found the next morning. Extensive press reports made it impossible for the police to cover up the murder, and in a month's time investigators charged six men: two provincial officers, two police officers, the son-in-law of the brothel owner, and the pimp. A parliamentary investigation found that the local police station received regular payoffs from the brothel owner. Following the investigation, twenty policemen were transferred for idleness and "allowing bad incidents to occur."[18]

Escape and Be Arrested

The same economic boom that has increased the demand for prostitutes may, in time, bring about an end to Thai sex slavery. Industrial growth has also meant an increase in jobs for women. Education and training are expanding rapidly across Thailand, and women and girls are very much taking part. The ignorance and deprivation on which the enslavement of girls depends are on the wane, and better-educated girls are much less likely to fall for the promises made by brokers. The traditional duties to family, including the debt of obligation to parents, are also becoming less compelling. As the front line of industrialization sweeps over northern Thailand, it is bringing fundamental change. Programs on the television bought with the money from selling one daughter may carry the warning messages to her younger sisters. As they learn more about new jobs, about HIV/AIDS, and about the fate of those sent to the brothels, northern Thai girls refuse to follow their sisters south. Slavery functions best when alternatives are few, and education and the media are opening the eyes of Thai girls to a world of choice.

For the slaveholders this presents a serious problem. They are faced with an increase in demand for prostitutes and a diminishing supply—already the price of young Thai girls is spiraling upward. Their only recourse is to look elsewhere, to areas where poverty and ignorance still hold sway. Nothing, in fact, could be easier, for there remain large oppressed and isolated populations desperate enough to believe the promises of the brokers. From Burma to the west and Laos to the east come thousands of economic and political refugees searching for work; they are defenseless in a country where they are illegal aliens. The techniques that have worked so well in bringing Thai girls to the brothels are again deployed, but now across the borders. Investigators from Human Rights Watch, who made a special study of this trafficking in 1993, explain:

> The trafficking of Burmese women and girls into Thailand is appalling in its efficiency and ruthlessness. Driven by the desire to maximize profit and the fear of HIV/AIDS, agents acting on behalf of brothel owners infiltrate ever more remote areas of Burma seeking unsuspecting recruits. Virgin girls are particularly sought after

because they bring a higher price and pose less threat of exposure to sexually transmitted disease. The agents promise the women and girls jobs as waitresses or dishwashers, with good pay and new clothes. Family members or friends typically accompany the women and girls to the Thai border, where they receive a payment ranging from 10,000 to 20,000 baht from someone associated with the brothel. This payment becomes the debt, usually doubled with interest, that the women and girls must work to pay off, not by waitressing or dishwashing, but through sexual servitude.[19]

Once in the brothels they are in the same situation as enslaved Thai girls, except worse: because they do not speak Thai their isolation is increased, and as illegal aliens they are open to even more abuse. The pimps tell them repeatedly that if they set foot outside the brothel they will be arrested. And if they are arrested Burmese and Lao girls and women are afforded no legal rights. They are often held for long periods at the mercy of police, without charge or trial. A strong traditional antipathy between Thais and Burmese increases their chances of discrimination and arbitrary treatment. Burmese women fall below even the denigrated position of Thai women. Explaining why so many Burmese women were kept in brothels in Ranong in southern Thailand, the regional police commander stated: "In my opinion it is disgraceful to let Burmese men [working in the local fishing industry] frequent Thai prostitutes. Therefore I have been flexible in allowing Burmese prostitutes to work here."[20]

The special horror suffered by Burmese and Lao women is the strong possibility of reenslavement once they reach the revolving door at the border. If they escape or are dumped by the brothel owners, they come quickly to the attention of the police, since they have no money for transport and cannot speak the language. Once they are picked up they are placed in detention, where they meet women who have been arrested in the periodic raids on brothels and taken into custody with only the clothes they are wearing. In local jails the foreign women might be held without charge for as long as eight months while they suffer sexual and other abuse by the police. In time, they might be sent to the Immigrant Detention Center in Bangkok or the penal reform institution at Pakkret. In both places abuse and extortion by staff continue, and some girls are sold back to the brothels from there. No trial is necessary for deportation, but many women are tried and convicted of prostitution or illegal entry. The trials take place in Thai without interpreters, and fines are charged against those convicted. If they have no money to pay the fines, and most do not, they are sent to a factory-prison to earn it. There they make light bulbs or plastic flowers for up to twelve hours a day; the prison officials decide when they have earned enough to pay their fine. After the factory-prison the women are sent back to police cells or the Immigrant Detention Center. Most are held until they can cover the cost of transportation (illegal aliens are required by law to pay for their own deportation); others are summarily deported.

The border between Thailand and Burma is especially chaotic and dangerous. Only part of it is controlled by the Burmese military dictatorship, while other areas are in the hands of tribal militias or warlords. After arrival at the border the deportees are held by immigration police in cells for another three to seven days. Over this time the police extort money and physically and sexually abuse the inmates. The police also use this time to make arrangements with brothel owners and brokers and to notify them of the dates and places of deportation. On the day of deportation the prisoners are driven for several hours along the border into the countryside, far from any village, and then pushed out of the cattle trucks in which they are transported. Abandoned in the jungle, miles from any main road, they are given no food or water and have no idea where they are or how to proceed into Burma. As the immigration police drive away, the deportees are approached by agents and brokers who follow the trucks from town under arrangements with the police. The brokers offer work and transportation back into

Thailand. Abandoned in the jungle many women see the offer as their only choice. Some who don't are just attacked and abducted. In either case, the cycle of debt bondage and prostitution begins again.

If they do make it into Burma, the women face imprisonment or worse. If apprehended by Burmese border patrols they are charged with "illegal departure" from Burma. If they cannot pay the fine, and most cannot, they serve six months' hard labor. Imprisonment applies to all those convicted—men, women, and children. If a girl or woman is suspected of having been a prostitute she can face additional charges and long sentences. Women found to be HIV-positive have been imprisoned and executed by the Burmese military dictatorship. According to Human Rights Watch there are consistent reports of "deportees being routinely arrested, detained, subjected to abuse and forced to porter for the military. Torture, rape and execution have been well documented by the United Nations bodies, international human rights organizations, and governments."[21]

The situation on Thailand's eastern border with Laos is much more difficult to assess. The border is more open, and there is a great deal of movement back and forth. Lao police, government officials, and community leaders are involved in the trafficking, acting as agents and making payments to local parents. They act with impunity, as it is very difficult for Lao girls to escape back to their villages; those that do find it dangerous to speak against police or officials. One informant told me that if a returning girl did talk, no one would believe her *and* she would be branded as a prostitute and shunned. There would be no way to expose the broker and no retribution; she would just have to resign herself to her fate. It is difficult to know how many Lao women and girls are brought into Thailand. In the northeast many Thais normally speak Lao, making it difficult to tell whether a prostitute is a local Thai or has actually come from Laos. Since they are illegal aliens, Lao girls will always claim to be local Thais and will often have false identity cards to prove it. In the brothels their lives are indistinguishable from those of Thai women.

"They Didn't Think Those People Were Human Beings"

Women and girls flow in both directions over Thailand's borders.[22] Export of enslaved prostitutes is a robust business, supplying brothels in Japan, Europe, and America. Thailand's Ministry of Foreign Affairs estimated in 1994 that as many as 50,000 Thai women were living illegally in Japan and working in prostitution. Their situation in these countries parallels that of Burmese women held in Thailand. The enticement of Thai women follows a familiar pattern. Promised work as cleaners, domestics, dishwashers, or cooks, Thai girls and women pay large fees to employment agents to secure jobs in the rich developed countries. When they arrive they are brutalized and enslaved. Their debt bonds are significantly larger than those of enslaved prostitutes in Thailand, since they include airfares, bribes to immigration officials, the costs of false passports, and sometimes the fees paid to foreign men to marry them and ease their entry.

Variations on sex slavery occur in different countries. In Switzerland girls are brought in on "artist" visas as exotic dancers. There, in addition to being prostitutes they must work as striptease dancers in order to meet the carefully checked terms of their employment. In Germany they are usually bar girls, and they are sold to men by the bartender or bouncer. Some are simply placed in brothels or apartments controlled by pimps. After Japanese sex tours to Thailand began in the 1980s, Japan rapidly became the largest importer of Thai women. The fear of HIV/AIDS in Japan has also increased the demand for virgins. Because of their large disposable incomes, Japanese men are able to pay considerable sums for young rural girls from Thailand. Japanese organized crime, the Yakuza, is involved throughout the importation process, sometimes transshipping women through Malaysia or the Philippines. In the cities it maintains bars and brothels and trade in Thai women. The women are bought and sold between brothels and controlled with extreme violence. Resistance can bring murder. Because they are illegal aliens and often enter the country under false passports,

Japanese gangs rarely hesitate to kill girls who have angered them or ceased to be profitable. Thai women deported from Japan also report that the gangs will addict girls to drugs in order to manage them more easily.

Criminal gangs, usually Chinese or Vietnamese, also control brothels in the United States that enslave Thai women. Police raids in New York, Seattle, San Diego, and Los Angeles have freed over a hundred girls and women.[23] In New York City thirty Thai women were locked into the upper floors of a building used as a brothel. Iron bars sealed the windows and a series of buzzer-operated armored gates blocked exit to the street. During police raids the women were herded into a secret basement room. At her trial the brothel owner testified that she bought the women outright, paying between $6,000 and $15,000 each. The women were charged $300 per week for room and board; they worked from 11 A.M. till 4 A.M. and were sold by the hour to clients. Chinese and Vietnamese gangsters were also involved in the brothel, collecting protection money and hunting down escaped prostitutes. The gangs owned chains of brothels and massage parlors around which they rotated the Thai women in order to defeat law enforcement efforts. After being freed from the New York brothel, some of the women disappeared—only to turn up weeks later in similar circumstances 3,000 miles away in Seattle. One of the rescued Thai women, who had been promised restaurant work and then enslaved, testified that the brothel owners "bought something and wanted to use it to the full extent, and they didn't think those people were human beings."[24]

Thai women have been imported into North America for factory work as well as commercial sex work. In late 1995 sixty-eight Thais, most of them women, were rescued from a sweatshop garment factory in Los Angeles. Most of these women were in fact garment workers in Thailand and had paid agents for the possibility of good jobs in the United States. When they arrived their passports were taken away and they were placed in debt bondage. Forced to live within a locked factory compound, they worked sixteen-hour days under armed guard.

Told they must repay debts of around $5,000, they were paid just over $10 per day from which the cost of their food was deducted.

Like many developing countries, Thailand exports its people as cheap labor. Thai men regularly find construction and factory work in Middle Eastern and other Asian countries. The vast commercial sex industry in Thailand has led it to be a major exporter of women. The low status of women in Thailand, together with the regular abandonment of mothers with children as men move on to other or minor wives, creates a ready supply of women desperate to find ways to support their families. Hearing about women who have secured legitimate jobs abroad they incur large debts to pay agents' and brokers' fees. For those who are enslaved the result is exploitation followed by destitution on their return to Thailand. Their poverty is compounded by the money, borrowed to pay airfare, that they still owe friends or relatives.

Official Indifference and a Growth Economy

In many ways, Thailand closely resembles another country that went through rapid industrialization and economic boom over one hundred years ago. Rapidly shifting its labor force off the farm, experiencing unprecedented economic growth, flooded with economic migrants, and run by corrupt politicians and a greedy and criminal police force, the United States then faced many of the problems confronting Thailand today. In the 1890s political machines that brought together organized crime with politicians and police ran the prostitution and protection rackets, drug sales, and extortion in American cities. Opposing them were a weak and disorganized reform movement and a muckraking press. I make this comparison because it is important to explore why Thailand's government is so ineffective when faced with the enslavement of its own citizens, and also to remember that conditions *can* change over time. Discussions with Thais about the horrific nature of sex slavery often end with their assertion that "nothing will ever change this . . . the problem is just too big . . . those with power will never allow change." Yet the social and economic underpinnings of slavery in Thailand are always changing, sometimes for the worse and sometimes for the better. No society can remain static, particularly one undergoing such upheavals as Thailand.

Even a cursory look at the record shows that most Thai politicians do not take sex slavery seriously. While it is true that full and complete laws exist forbidding enslavement, trafficking, and exploitation, they are not enforced. Actually, that is not quite true: they are *very occasionally* enforced whenever public scandal requires that politicians need to be seen doing something. When the enforcement crackdowns do occur, they take on a quality of comic opera. After shocking accounts of child prostitution and sex slavery in the press in 1992, the government moved quickly to set up a special anti-prostitution task force.[25] The unit was ordered to raid every brothel in the country that had underage or forced prostitutes. This major law enforcement campaign was undertaken by six men, with one car. And when the tiny task force took its job seriously and pressed ahead with raids in spite of the resistance of local police, its authority to override local police was withdrawn. After further successes working with the support of charitable organizations to free enslaved prostitutes and children, it was disbanded in favor of a group that would work more closely with local police. In 1994 this government special force arrested 64 brothel owners, 472 Thai prostitutes, and 9 foreign prostitutes, and rescued 35 children and sex slaves—in a country with an estimated one million commercial sex workers.[26]

When Burmese or Lao girls are arrested, the Thai police routinely violate their own laws. The Antitrafficking Law of 1928 forbids the imprisonment or fine of women or girls trafficked into Thailand. Nevertheless, the police commonly charge them and imprison them, as we have seen, so that brothel owners can reclaim these women by paying their "fines"—which include a bribe for the police. The conspiracy of gangs, police, and immigration officials allows trafficking to occur on a large and increasing scale. When police or officials are charged in connection with these offenses, they receive the lightest slap on the wrist.

Punishment for the police ordinarily consists of a posting to another job. The same reluctance to apprehend or punish extends to brothel owners as well. Reading through newspaper reports of police raids one is struck by the incredible slipperiness of the brothel keepers. In raid after raid they escape, while the prostitutes are all captured. When they are arrested only a few are brought into court (most skip bail), and even fewer receive sentences. Colonel Surasak Suttharom, the man in charge of the task force, explained that when he did get a case to court, brothel keepers were allowed to plead to lesser violations, after which they paid a fine or settled the case out of court.[27] Obstruction of the investigations and very long delays in the court proceedings, sometimes up to three years, made the conviction rate extremely low. Yet even Colonel Surasak regards the brothel keepers with ambiguity. "These wicked people," he said, "are sometimes good men because they help bring these poor girls away from home for a better living."

Though it represents only a tiny fraction of the problem, Thai cooperation with European law enforcement has improved. In 1992 Thailand passed an Act on International Cooperation in Criminal (Law) Matters. This law allows the attorney general to gather evidence against foreigners who commit crimes in Thailand and send it to their home countries. Under its provisions, evidence was taken from a Thai child to help prosecute a Swedish pedophile. The Swede had been arrested in Thailand, but he skipped bail and fled. Rearrested on the basis of the forwarded evidence he was tried and convicted in Sweden. To bring such a prosecution in Europe required the extraterritorial jurisdiction laws that have existed in the Scandinavian countries for some time. Recently, after campaigns by the End Child Prostitution in Asian Tourism (ECPAT) network, similar laws have been enacted in Australia, Belgium, France, Germany, New Zealand, and the United States. ECPAT and other organizations have also convinced the Thai attorney general not to allow bail in future cases of foreigners accused of child sexual abuse.

At the beginning of 1997 Thailand revised the law on prostitution.

The new statute dramatically increased the fines and prison sentences for anyone who has sex with prostitutes under the age of eighteen (maximum 60,000 baht and three years, respectively) or under the age of fifteen (maximum 400,000 baht and 20 years). This marked a real improvement over the 1960 Prostitution Suppression Act, which made every person involved in prostitution subject to penalties except the customer. Prostitution is still illegal, but now an adult prostitute is liable only for a fine of 1,000 baht and one month in jail. Prostitutes under the age of eighteen are not to be charged, but if arrested they will be forced to go to a rehabilitation center for not more than six months and then sent for vocational training for two years. The law also sets out fines and sentences for parents who sell their children, as well as for the procurers, brokers, agents, and brothel owners who buy them. It is a good start in addressing the issue of sex slavery, but it may have little effect. Leaving aside the question of whether or not the law will actually be enforced, there are a number of loopholes and other problems. For example, there are not enough rehabilitation centers to take anywhere near all the young prostitutes who fall under this law. The key problem, however, is that prostitution remains criminalized in a way that allows pimps and police to continue working together, using the law as a threat to control commercial sex workers.

For girls like Siri the new law will probably have little, if any, impact. In the provincial towns, like the one where she works, the police have a firm grip on the sex industry and few concerns about national political decisions; they worry even less about international concerns. There is no shortage of clear recommendations to help the Thai government reduce sex slavery. In 2003 the United Nations published several distinct steps that the government might take to deal with trafficking in women.[28] But the law has no teeth as long as the police serve the slave-holders first and the public second. And while there are huge profits flowing through the brothels and into the pockets of police, why should they enforce a law that has so little public backing? Most Thais, particularly Thai men, see nothing wrong in using prostitutes and little wrong in using underage girls. That the girls are there to repay a debt makes perfect sense within their cultural context. That it is a wonderful business for those who invest in brothels is another reason not to question the system that supplies girls and women.

In spite of the new law, it is still not clear which side the government is on. Throughout the 1960s, the interior minister publicly championed expansion of the sex industry to promote tourism. Not long after prostitution was made illegal in 1960, a Service Establishments law was passed that legitimated "entertainment" as an industry. The law explained that women in entertainment were expected to provide "special services"—in other words, sex. This law gave power to brothel owners as "entertainment providers" (legal) over the women who had been prostitutes (illegal). It drove independent women sex workers into brothels and set up a legal category for these "service establishments." In the 1960s and early 1970s these service establishments did very well from the 40,000 American soldiers who were stationed in Thailand and the large numbers that were sent there on R&R leave during the Vietnam War. As the U.S. bases closed down in the late 1970s, the Thai government looked to tourism and to sex as important sources of income that might replace those lost earnings. In 1980 the vice premier encouraged the provincial governors to create more sex establishments to bring tourism to the provinces: "Within the next two years we need money. Therefore, I ask all governors to consider the natural scenery in your provinces, together with some forms of entertainment that some of you might think of as disgusting and shameful, because we have to consider the jobs that will be created."[29] Thailand's economic boom included a sharp increase in sex tourism tacitly backed by government. International tourist arrivals jumped from 2 million in 1981 to 4 million in 1988 to over 11 million in 2003.[30] Two-thirds of tourists are unaccompanied men: in other words, nearly 5 million unaccompanied men visited Thailand in 1996. A significant proportion of these were sex tourists. Because they feared it would diminish the large foreign exchange earnings gained from sex tourists, government officials consistently denied the "rumor" of a worsening AIDS crisis throughout the 1980s. As late as 1989 the prime minister declared that AIDS was "no problem" in Thailand.[31] Helped along by sex tourism, HIV/AIDS is now epidemic in Thailand, but sex tourism continues to be a major source of foreign exchange and not one that the government would want to restrict.

But it is important to understand that the direct link between sex tourism and slavery is small. With the exception of children sold to pedophiles, most commercial sex workers serving the tourist boom are not slaves. There is no question that the women and girls working with sex tourists suffer extreme exploitation and degradation, but most are not enslaved through the debt bondage that captures girls into brothels used almost exclusively by poor and working-class Thai men. However, the indirect connection is crucial: sex tourism has created a new business climate conducive to sexual slavery. Thai culture, as we have seen, has always treated women and sex as commodities to be bought, sold, traded, and used. Yet concubines and polygamy are historical patterns; these old cultural forms of sexual exploitation have been transformed into new business opportunities, as Thailand embraces the world of twenty-first-century business and economics. With government support, traditional sexual abuse of women has been modernized and expanded with a vengeance. The brochures of the European companies that have leaped into the sex tour business leave the reader in no doubt of what they are selling:

> Slim, sunburnt, and sweet, they love the white man in an erotic and devoted way. They are masters of the art of making love by nature, an art that we Europeans do not know. (Life Travel, Switzerland)

> [M]any girls from the sex world come from the poor north-eastern region of the country and from the slums of Bangkok. It has become a custom that one of the nice looking daughters goes into the busi-

ness in order to earn money for the poor family . . . you can get the feeling that taking a girl here is as easy as buying a package of cigarettes . . . little slaves who give real Thai warmth. (Kanita Kamha Travel, the Netherlands)[32]

As the country takes on a new Western-style materialist morality, the ubiquitous sale of sex sends a clear message—women can be enslaved and exploited for profit. Sex tourism helped set the stage for the expansion of sexual slavery.

Sex tourism also generates some of the income that Thai men use to fund their visits to brothels. No one knows how much money it pours into the Thai economy, but if we assume that just one-quarter of sex workers serve sex tourists and that their customers pay about the same as they would pay to use Siri, then 656 billion baht ($26.2 billion) a year would be about right. This is thirteen times more than the amount Thailand earns by building and exporting computers, one of their major industries, and it is money that floods into the country without any concomitant need to build factories or improve infrastructure. It is part of the boom raising the standard of living generally and allowing the purchase of commercial sex by an ever greater number of working-class men. Thousands upon thousands of men buy sex on a regular basis, and those who are just now beginning to taste the new prosperity do not want to be left out. Buying women is a mark of success and achievement, a mark that more men expect as Thailand joins the world economy.

Joining the world economy has done wonders for Thailand's income and terrible things to its society. According to Pasuk Phongpaichit and Chris Baker, economists who have analyzed Thailand's economic boom,

> Government has let the businessmen ransack the nation's human
> and natural resources to achieve growth. It has not forced them
> to put much back. In many respects, the last generation of economic
> growth has been a disaster. The forests have been obliterated. The

urban environment has deteriorated. Little has been done to combat the growth in industrial pollution and hazardous wastes. For many people whose labour has created the boom, the conditions of work, health, and safety are grim.

Neither law nor conscience has been very effective in limiting the social costs of growth. Business has revelled in the atmosphere of free-for-all. The machinery for social protection has proved very pliable. The legal framework is defective. The judiciary is suspect. The police are unreliable. The authorities have consistently tried to block popular organisations to defend popular rights.[33]

The machinery for social protection is so ineffectual that slaves are bought and sold. So where does this leave us and those who are enslaved? Many human rights organizations call on the government to enforce its laws. Indeed, if they were enforced to the letter there would be no slavery. But, as we have seen, the law can do little against the combined strength of a sexist culture, rationalizing religion, amoral exploitative economy, and corrupt government.

Thailand is a country sick with an addiction to slavery. From village to city and back, the profits of slavery flow. Once authorities and businesspeople become accustomed to this outpouring of money, once any moral objection has been drowned in it, a justification of slavery is easy to mount, and Thai culture and religion stand ready to do so. The situation is similar to that of the United States in the 1850s—with a significant part of the economy dependent on slavery, religion and culture are ready to explain why this is all for the best. But there is also an important difference: this is the new slavery, and the impermanence of modern slavery and the dedication of human rights workers offer some hope.

Throughout Thailand people and organizations are fighting against slavery. The Center for the Protection of Children's Rights rescues children from brothels, gives them medical and psychological care, and provides sheltered homes for rehabilitation. The Foundation for Women and its sister organization, the Global Alliance against Traffic in Women, ceaselessly press the government to enact and enforce laws.

ECPAT and the Task Force to End Child Sexploitation have had tremendous success in raising awareness in Europe and North America, and particularly in getting laws passed that can punish Westerners who sexually exploit Thai children. But these activists are attempting to shift a mountain of social indifference in Thailand. The surplus of potential slaves—especially in the politically disturbed neighboring countries of Burma, Laos, and Cambodia—their low cost, and the resulting high profits obstruct the reformers' work. At best, these organizations are only able to help a fraction of the slaves in Thailand, and they can do little to attack slavery at its roots; yet, as we will see in the next chapter, such work would be viewed in the context of the old slavery of Mauritania as a great breakthrough.

3

——⟨ 0/0/0 ⟩——

MAURITANIA
Old Times There Are Not Forgotten

MAURITANIA HAS A CERTAIN *Alice in Wonderland* character. The country is a violent military dictatorship, but most people, even the ubiquitous soldiers, are friendly and welcoming. Bribes are expected in most public situations, but everyone is very gracious about it, and often a kind word will suffice. It is a police state where calling for free elections can lead to disappearance and death, but even the police fall all over themselves in apology if they accidentally jostle you in the street. Mauritania has the largest proportion of its population in slavery of all the countries in the world, and it has no slaves at all.

Just south of Morocco in northwest Africa, Mauritania is a geographical buffer: its population and history grow out of the violent relationship between the Black south and the Arab north. Mauritanian society (current population 2.2 million) is made up of three main groups: the Arab Moors, often called the "White Moors" (including the Hassanyi "warrior" caste, the priestly Marabout caste, and the Zenaga vassals); the slaves and ex-slaves, called the Haratines; and the Afro-Mauritanians, who make up around 40 percent of the population and who come from the southern part of the country, where the Arab Sahara ends and Black Africa begins. The exact number of each of these groups can only be guessed. The results of the national census have been kept secret by the ruling Moors, who are well aware of their numerical inferiority. At most the Moors account for 40 percent of the population, but the figure is probably nearer to 30 percent; moreover, their birthrate is lower than that of the Haratines or the Afro-Mauritanians. Under the new Islamic law, supported in Moor newspapers, men are urged to take more than one wife in the hope that polygyny will increase the Moor birthrate. The numbers bring real fear to the warriors and holy men of the dominant Hassanyi castes.

Slavery has been abolished many times in Mauritania, most recently in 1980. On that occasion the government decreed that slavery was ended and no longer existed in Mauritania. A significant part of the population, perhaps as much as one-third, became "ex-slaves." This reclassification came as a shock to the existing population of "ex-slaves," the Haratines. Their name literally means "one who has been freed," and they form a middle layer in Mauritanian society. They are the descendants of slaves, belonging to the White Moors, who had been freed over the centuries. Many families were freed more than two hundred years ago, and they now possess businesses, property, and influence. That a great mass of illiterate and ragged slaves were suddenly lumped in with them was seen as an insult.

For the thousands of slaves who had been legally freed in 1980, life did not change at all. True, the government abolished slavery, but no one bothered to tell the slaves about it. Some have never learned of their legal freedom, some did so years later, and for most legal freedom was never translated into actual freedom. In Mauritania today there is no slavery, and yet everywhere you look, on every street corner and shop, in every field and pasture, you see slaves. Slaves are sweeping and cleaning, they are cooking and caring for children, they are building houses and tending sheep, and they are hauling water and bricks—they are doing every job that is hard, onerous, and dirty. Mauritania's economy rests squarely on their backs, and the pleasant lives of their masters, and even the lives of those who keep no slaves, are supported by their never-ending toil.

"Show Kindness to the Slaves You Own . . ."

Doing research into human rights and slavery in a police state requires subterfuge. To gain entry to Mauritania is not easy, and researchers are often denied visas. I presented myself as a zoologist interested in the behavior of the country's native hyenas and jackals. With my new membership card for the Royal Zoological Society, my collection of articles and books on jackals and hyenas, and my binoculars and scruffy zoologist field study clothes, I managed to get a visa and, with a small bribe, to make it through the airport and into the capital without being searched. Once in Mauritania I was helped by some very brave people who took great risks with their lives and liberty to show me slavery up close. I wish I could tell you more about these remarkable Mauritanians and the work they are doing to bring freedom to slaves, but for their own safety they must remain unnamed and undescribed.

Mauritania was also my first experience at working undercover. It is illegal to take pictures on the street—carrying a video camera means instant detention, and the police are everywhere. A policeman stands on practically every corner in the capital, and to drive anywhere means constant stops at police roadblocks where your papers and passport are checked again and again. The plainclothes police also feel free to stop you regularly. I was prepared for this, but not for the eerie sense of being watched that had clearly infected my co-workers there. To document slavery in Mauritania I took with me very small still and video cameras. The still camera fit into my palm and I was able to take pictures while holding it just outside my trouser pocket, giving me many oddly framed photos of my knee as well. The video camera I carried in a prepared shoulder bag, filming without looking through the lens as best I could, shooting from the hip and getting more oddly framed pictures (though this time of my stomach).

Stepping out of a car onto the pavement might bring a few glances from the people walking or working along the street. But there would always be one person—sometimes in uniform, sometimes not—whose eyes would lock down on us and follow every movement. Unzipping a bag, lifting a camera, or opening a notebook would start this man moving toward us. And unless we quickly dodged indoors or back into the car, the questions would start—"Who are you? What are you doing? Where are your papers?" Mauritania is a police state hiding the dirty secret of its slavery.

What I found was a kind of slavery practiced hundreds of years ago, and now existing nowhere else in the world. Slavery, which has been a significant part of Mauritanian culture for centuries, survives here in a primitive, tribal form. African slaves sold in ancient Rome were captured by Moors in what is now southern Mauritania and transported north. Over the centuries the region has had only a few resources to exploit, and the most durable and profitable of them has always been slaves.

As the overview of the new slavery in chapter 1 made clear, slavery takes many forms. There is the sort of slavery that most people mentally picture as "real" slavery—the bondage of the Atlantic slave trade of 1650 to 1850 and the slavery of the American South. Today we think of the slavery of the nineteenth century as exemplifying "old" slavery. But to understand Mauritanian slavery we must go back even further, to the slavery of Old Testament times. It both treats the slaves more humanely and leaves them more helpless, a slavery that is less a political reality than a permanent part of the culture. It places a greater value on the bodies and lives of slaves, especially female slaves, than do other forms of slavery. It is so deeply ingrained in the minds of both slave and master that little violence is needed to keep it going. The lack of overt violence has also allowed many outside observers, like the French and American governments, to deny that this slavery even exists. The slaves know better.

An escaped slave, Salma mint Saloum, told me, "I was born a slave. I was born in Mauritania in 1956. My mother and father were slaves for one family, and their parents were slaves of the same family. Ever since I was old enough to walk, I was forced to work for this family all day, every day. We never had days off . . . we had to work every day. Even if we were sick, we had to work. When I was still a child, I started taking over my mother's job, taking care of the first wife of the head of the family and her fifteen children. Every day at 5 A.M. I had to make their breakfast. First, I had to get water and wood to make a fire. We were in the desert, and the well was far away, so often I had to walk a long way. I had to cook all their meals, and clean their clothes, and watch all the children. Even if one of my children was hurt or in danger, I didn't dare help my child, because I had to watch the master's wife's children first. If I didn't, they would beat me. I was beaten very often, with a wooden stick or leather belt."

The lives of Salma and her family are typical. The White Moors who control Mauritania, properly known as Hassaniya Arabs, are organized into large extended families, which are further linked together into several tribes. Virtually all extended families of the dominant Hassaniya castes have owned slaves for generations. Any individual slave is the specific property of a male member of the family; as property, the slaves are inherited and, very occasionally, sold. Slave families usually live with their master's household. Some masters are kind, treating their inherited slaves almost as their own children; others are brutal. The Haratines, the ex-slaves freed over the generations, are usually the offspring of slave mothers and White Moor fathers (and thus are sometimes called Black Moors). Slave women prepare food, wash, and clean for the entire extended household. Slave men do whatever work they are ordered to: in the countryside, herding and basic agriculture; in the cities, almost any kind of work imaginable. The slaves are not paid for their work, and generally have no freedom of choice or movement. But the fact that a slave's parents, grandparents, and great-grandparents have worked and lived in the household of the same Moor family often forges a deep emotional link between master and slave.

This is the paradox of Mauritanian slavery. Many slaves think of themselves as members of their master's family. Equally, as devout Muslims, many slaves believe that they are placed by God into their master's household, and that to leave it would be sinful. In one small town I visited, the reporter David Hecht found a black man walking hand in hand with a White Moor, dressed in matching robes.[2] They said they were slave and master as well as best friends. While many slaves would leave their masters but cannot, others are able to leave but will not. Unlike the slaveholders of the new slavery, most of the Moor masters feel a certain responsibility and obligation to their slaves, seeing themselves as good family men and good Muslims. They refer to their slaves as children, needing care and guidance, and they expect their obedience. Willful slaves are punished, but elderly slaves are often cared for after their usefulness is gone. The relationship between master and slave is deep, complex, and long-lasting. Given that a significant portion of the population is either master or slave, individual relationships take every imaginable form, from friendly intimacy to brutal exploitation. To be sure, a master who respects his slaves and treats them with anything like equality is very rare; but extreme brutality, while less rare, is not common. The experience of the great majority of slaves falls between these poles. Their lives are hard, their spirits and potential suppressed, and their freedom taken away. They are slaves, but they are not seen as disposable, as are the enslaved prostitutes in Thailand.

Religion serves both to protect slaves and to keep them in bondage. The Koran declares that only captives taken in a holy war may be enslaved, and that once they convert to Islam they are to be freed. It is possible that the ancestors of today's slaves were captured in just this way, but today all Mauritanians are Muslim and have been for hundreds of years—and no general freeing of slaves has resulted. While the Koran is clear on this point, the Islamic jurists (called *ulemas*) are rather more stingy with the truth. When slavery was abolished in 1980 one ulema responded by proclaiming "the lawfulness of slavery in Islam in general." The opinion of these Islamic judges is important because also in 1980, probably as a condition of financial aid from Saudi Arabia, Mauritania implemented the Sharia, the extreme religious law of Islamic countries. Most people today know of the draconian measures of the Sharia: the stoning to death of adulterers, the amputation of the hands of thieves, and the decapitation of convicted murderers. Less well known are the laws that apply specifically to slaves. For example, one rule states that there will be severe punishment for any man who does not "restrain his carnal desires," but it adds, "except with his wives and slave-girls, for these are lawful to him."[3] The law concerning the freeing of slaves is clear: it is the prerogative of the master alone ("a slave may be allowed to purchase their freedom if you find them to have any promise"). And the power that the Sharia gives any Muslim man over his wives and sisters is extended to his slave women and their children. Though the Koran also orders that a man should "show kindness to the slaves you own," since its institution the Sharia has been used to keep the slaves intimidated and mindful of their place. Ex-slaves have been executed, and one whose hand was amputated for theft died as a result. In contrast, Moors found guilty of murdering slaves have not suffered execution. To make sure that everyone understands the way things are, the judgments and punishments of the Sharia courts are performed in public, leaving little doubt as to the official distinction made between slave and master.

Another important distinction is made between male and female slaves. In Moor society, wealth was traditionally measured in the number of female slaves a man owned. Though they are infrequently sold, a young male slave might go for $500 to $700, a mature female for $700 to $1,000, and a young and healthy female for even more. Children of slave women always became and still become the property of their masters, in spite of the law abolishing slavery. Adult male slaves cannot be required *by law* to remain with their masters, but adult females, especially with children, are rarely protected in the courts. Masters may use force to keep a woman in slavery, or they may simply keep her by taking her children under tight control. To prevent escapes, children are often transferred away from their mothers to a member of the master's family in another part of the country. In several recent cases, ex-slave women have sued for custody of their children withheld by their former masters. A slaveholder usually claims that the slave's children are his own—that their mother is in fact his wife. Judges, and the ulemas of the Islamic courts, can be counted on to accept this argument; after all, they normally have slaves in their households as well. In any event a man is allowed up to four wives, so who is to say that the slave woman is not one of them? The woman herself may deny the marriage, but government magistrates have consistently awarded custody of children to masters rather than mothers—hardly a surprising outcome within a legal system which counts the testimony of one man equal to that of two women and which mandates that any compensation to be paid for the life of a women should be at half the rate paid for a man.

The pervasive nature of slavery also means that slaves have almost no alternatives. A slave who leaves his or her master's household is unlikely to find any other work. White Moor families have no need to hire laborers, as they have their own slaves. Poorer White Moors, the Zenaga caste of herders and cultivators, are also tied to Hassaniya families as obligatory vassals and would not (and could not, because of their poverty) hire escaped slaves. The free non-Moors in Mauritania do not keep slaves, but they normally have plenty of family members whom they would hire before considering any outsider. When slaves do leave a master, they leave with nothing. With nowhere to live, no guarantee of food or clothing, they quickly fall into desperation. Some escaped women slaves become prostitutes and some men find a hardscrabble existence in the city, but for most freedom means starvation. In a country organized into extended families, the escaped slave is an outcast. Immediately identifiable by color, clothing, and speech, an escaped slave would be asked, "Who do you belong to?" by any potential employer. From the perspective of those in control of jobs and resources, escaped slaves have already proved their untrustworthiness by turning their backs on their "families," a view shared by many slaves. On the streets there are already a good number of beggars, many of them disabled, to remind slaves of where they would almost certainly end up. Thus slaves are tempted to flee only if a master is very brutal or violent—but in fact physical abuse is rare. All my informants, even ex-slaves, confirmed this. The beatings that they described were more or less accepted "for the sake of discipline." Generally, they seemed to feel that every once in a while a child or a slave needs the discipline of a spanking to be kept in line. When cases of extreme violence did occur, they were roundly condemned as a violation of Islamic law.

Under these conditions, most masters do not need to force their slaves to stay. It is just as easy for them to say, "Go if you like," for they know the slaves have nowhere else to go and nothing else to do. A slave is free to ask his or her master for payment, but the master is equally free to refuse. The change in the law in 1980 altered the legal obligation of slaves to serve their master, but not the reality of work and exploitation. While legal ownership of slaves was abolished, no change in the working relationship was legislated; masters don't have to pay their slaves or provide any sort of social security. This arrangement allows the legal fiction of slavery's abolition to continue. The Mauritanian government, though admitting that hundreds of thousands of "ex-slaves" do unpaid work in exchange for food and clothing, insists this is not slavery. Violence is rarely needed to keep slaves obedient since the entire social system maintains a culture of order and obedience. Of course, the ruling White Moors and their government hold a monopoly on violence and can and do use it as necessary against perceived threats, such as political opponents or organizations supporting ex-slaves.

To understand this slavery that is not slavery, we must remember the Mauritanian context. This country is not part of the modern world. The culture is isolated: there are very few sources of information, most of which are controlled by the government. International news on television and in the press focuses on the Arab world, concentrating on the international struggle for greater Islamic purity and never touching on human rights. If the illiterate majority of slaves *could* read, there would be virtually nothing they could learn that did not reinforce the status quo.[4] If anything, most slaves are more accepting and more psychologically secure in their slavery than the masters. The ruling Moors know about the international criticism of their practice of slavery. They feel that they must guard against exposure and against the slaves' becoming aware of international pressure on the government, which goes to extraordinary lengths to hide slavery from foreign visitors. One White Moor who worked for the government and has since left the country related the following story:

> In January 1984 four experts arrived in our country, followed by a fifth from London. Their visit had been postponed several times, as we weren't ready. Why did we need to be ready? Because we young people had been requisitioned some weeks before to help the army or the police move the slaves to other regions and to destroy any traces that might disturb or upset our visitors. Sometimes some of us would even take the place of freed slaves and would talk with our visitors, telling them how happy we were to have been freed and to have the opportunity to educate ourselves, to learn to read, write, count, and speak a foreign language. This farce lasted about ten days. We knew exactly the itinerary that had been carefully planned for our guests and we would go ahead of them.[5]

It is a very nervous guard that government officials mount, since the slavery they are trying to conceal is perfectly visible, and they must go through more than linguistic acrobatics of denial and obfuscation to hide it. Their success has much to do with the strange makeup of Mauritanian society: while isolated at the top of the heap, the upper-caste White Moors scramble desperately to hold on to their privileges and their slaves.

Government-Sponsored Lynch Mobs

Feeling pressured and watched, the government has become paranoid and violent. Outnumbered by the non-slavekeeping and often economically independent Afro-Mauritanians, the White Moors will do anything to hold on to power. Beginning in 1989 they turned on the Afro-Mauritanians, who had been pressing for greater recognition and for democratic participation. In 1990 the government whipped up lynch mobs of Haratines to hunt down Afro-Mauritanians and Senegalese. At least two hundred black Senegalese were killed in the capital alone. Under attack by government forces, over 70,000 Afro-Mauritanians were expelled or fled into neighboring Senegal and Mali. The torture, maiming, and murder of over five hundred Afro-Mauritanians, many of them members of the military or holders of public positions, has been documented by the United Nations. With the Afro-Mauritanian opposition shattered and its leadership murdered, the government completed the exercise in 1993 by passing an amnesty law protecting all its employees or soldiers who took part in the massacres and expulsions from pursuit or prosecution.

The massacres, torture, disappearances, arrests and detentions, and extrajudicial executions of 1989 to 1991 made it clear what would happen to anyone who threatened the status quo. As is often the case with dictatorships, the clampdown was a gross overreaction: the Afro-Mauritanians and Haratines are devout Muslims who respect authority and have a scrupulous regard for the preservation of public order. The same level of violence has not been used against slave liberation groups, probably because their smaller numbers represent a much smaller threat. They are hardly free from interference, however. As I prepared to visit Mauritania in early 1997 I arranged secret meetings with the leaders of El Hor, the organization of escaped slaves, and with SOS Slaves, another organization campaigning to help slaves. Ten days before my arrival, the leadership of both organizations and a number of other Mauritanian human rights workers were arrested and imprisoned. Some were let out of prison while I was still in Mauritania, but they remained under house arrest and surveillance. Needless to say, we were not able to meet.

The contradictions within Mauritania are hard to fathom. Here are slaves who are free, but cannot leave; masters who control everything, but fear everyone. Marvelous hospitality is the setting for the most blatant lies: government officials welcomed me into their homes and would then proceed to deny that any form of slavery exists in Mauritania. It is a country so rigidly separated into competing groups that the divisions might have been made with a ruler. One guide describes it as an "austere, almost medieval nation, powered by Islam, riven by racial hatred and flayed by drought."[6] In time I learned how Mauritania was very much a product of its strange environment. And if we are going to understand the lives of individual slaves, we have to look first at Mauritania's cruel land and even crueler history.

All of Our Roads Are Paved, Both of Them

As might be guessed from the radically different groups that make up Mauritanian society, Mauritania is another one of the African nations created artificially by European colonists. The country is vast and empty. It is about the same size as Colombia, or the American states of California and Texas combined, yet it holds only a little more than 2 million people, giving it the lowest population density on earth. Mauritania is practically all desert: it is really just the western end of the great Sahara. Over one-third of the country, the eastern region that borders Mali, is known as the "empty zone." Here, in an area the size of Great Britain, there are no towns, no roads, and virtually no people. The regions of Mauritania are just variations played on the theme of desert. As I traveled across the country I came to understand that there are many kinds of desert. In the center and north are hard pans of rock and broken stony hills where some scrub can grow, and goats and camels can live. In the east, but also stretching fingers into the rest of the country, are the great deserts of live dunes where the constantly moving sand prevents any vegetation from growing. In fact, the Sahara continues to spread, stony deserts slowly being inundated by live dunes and lost to grazing; in the south, the sand oozes over the soil and stops farming. North of the capital whole villages are being reduced to rectangular lumps in the sand drifts. Only on the southwestern border does the unrelenting desert give way. Here the Senegal River irrigates fields and supports the fertile heartland of the Fula, Soninke, and Wolof peoples who make up the Afro-Mauritanians, tribes with a long history of slavery and resistance.

French colonists drove Portuguese traders out of the Senegal River region in the seventeenth century and quickly concentrated on a very profitable business—slaves. Setting up a base, St. Louis, at the mouth of the river, they sent European trade goods up river and into the desert regions. Their influence secured a steady supply of slaves from the feuding and rigidly stratified peoples of the interior. Mauritania's White Moors provided a large portion of these slaves, capturing and trading the non-Arabs of its southern region in exchange for firearms, cloth, and sugar. Sold down the river and shipped from St. Louis, these blacks became the plantation slaves of Haiti and other French colonies, and they were sold throughout the Americas. By the early nineteenth century, as the Hassaniya Arabs tightened their grip on the region, most of Mauritania was divided into competing emirates—highly structured Muslim societies that fought bitterly among themselves. The French fomented civil war within, and animosity between, the Arab emirates to keep them weak and ensure a flow of slaves captured in battle.

By the end of the nineteenth century the French, pushing north from their base in Senegal and south from their possessions in Morocco, had taken over much of Mauritania in a program of so-called protection and pacification. It only required the assassination of a French commander in 1905 to provide the pretext for a full-scale invasion and annexation. By 1920 Mauritania was officially a French colony, though the nomadic guerrilla resistance in the north was not fully "pacified" until 1933. Since the commercial exportation of slaves had ended in the nineteenth century, Mauritania had little to offer economically. And the French gave back next to nothing, using the colony as a place of exile for political agitators from other colonies and pointedly overlooking the endemic slavery of Mauritanian society. By the time the independent Islamic Republic of Mauritania was declared in 1960, the country still could not boast of any paved highways or a railway.

The country's first president was a young White Moor lawyer with substantial political clout with both the Moors and the French (he was Charles de Gaulle's son-in-law). Subverting the new democratic constitution, President Mokhtar ould Daddah absorbed all political parties into his own, eliminated all political rivals, and enshrined one-party rule into law within three short years. To further consolidate White Moor control a new capital was founded at Nouakchott. Though only a dusty village of 300 people, it was well within the Moorish part of the country and thus shifted the country's center of gravity away from the Afro-Mauritanian south. To increase White Moor control, Arabic was made the compulsory language of instruction in schools. When Afro-Mauritanians protesting their rapid exclusion demonstrated in the capital, the army was called out and opposition forcibly suppressed. Merely *discussing* racial conflict was banned. To further reduce dissent, the ruling party took control of all trade unions as well. By the early 1970s government repression had turned a sleepy French colony into a single-party police state relying on racial discrimination. The dictatorship of ould Daddah silenced criticism and forced a program of Arabization on the country, but it could not control two outside threats: the weather and the wreckage left by colonizers—this time, Spanish colonialism in the Western Sahara.

In 1971 even the tiny amount of rain that normally fell on Mauritania dried up. The drought severely punished the Arab north and central part of the country and radically altered the lives of many slaves. As food supplies diminished it was the slaves who went hungry, and without rain there was no hope of their growing more food. The White Moors were traditionally herders, and the drought killed cattle, sheep, goats, and camels. Faced with the starvation of both their families and their slaves, White Moors moved in large numbers to the towns and especially to Nouakchott, as the capital's population exploded. The proportion of Mauritanians living in cities leaped from 14 percent in 1970 to 50 percent by 1990.

While the drought radically altered the face of Mauritanian society, a guerrilla war brought down Mokhtar ould Daddah. Mauritania had long laid claim to the area known as the Western Sahara, a Spanish colony immediately to the north of the country. Unfortunately, Algeria and Morocco also claimed the region, and when Spain abandoned the colony in 1975 all three began to fight each other and the local people (who had formed the Polisario Front, seeking an independent future).

Control of the region is still disputed today, but Mauritania, in many ways the weakest of the four combatants, was knocked out of the fight by 1978, despite support from the French army and air force. The government that sued for peace was a new one, made up of lieutenant colonels who had ousted the president in a bloodless military coup. When this new government abolished slavery in 1980, attempting to divert attention away from the continuing racial discrimination of their policies, it only served to alert the rest of the world to the problem. By 1981 one of the colonels, Maawiya Sid'Ahmed ould Taya, had emerged as the strongman; since that time he has run Mauritania.

It was President ould Taya who directed the attacks on the Afro-Mauritanians in 1989 to 1991, and under his orders leaders of the human rights groups were detained in 1997. His administration has continued the program of ethnic cleansing known as *Arabization*, expanding it into the Afro-Mauritanian heartland in the Senegal River region. Since the late 1980s he has forced through a "sensitization program" that has flooded the fertile southern valleys with White Moor land buyers, supporting development schemes that always hinge on dispossessing Afro-Mauritanian farmers. By inciting hatred against the Afro-Mauritanians the government diverts attention from the plight of the slave population and at the same time encourages the Black Moor ex-slaves to distance themselves from the "traitorous" Afro-Mauritanians. This strategy of divide and conquer requires that the slaves identify with their master's rather than their own interests. For the present, because of the social isolation and powerlessness of the slaves, it is working, but social and economic change is eroding Moor power.

A Slow Train to the Stone Age

Mauritania is an economic basket case. The country carries a staggering foreign debt of over $2.3 billion—more than five times its total annual export earnings. Per capita income has been falling steadily and is now about $340 per year, making its population one of the poorest on earth.[7] Though it is hard to imagine, the economic situation is actually getting worse. Mauritania has only two natural resources: iron ore and fish. Mauritania's only railway connects the port of Nouadhibou with the open mines 350 miles inland. Ore trains slowly haul their loads of rock and rubble to the coast. Mauritania still has a good supply of iron ore, but world demand for the ore, and its price, have been falling for years. The railway itself is shut down at irregular intervals as trains derail and tracks are damaged. Sometimes vast moving dunes of sand cover the tracks and must be ploughed aside. The train might well be the Mauritanian economy: slow, broken down, and hauling products of little value to markets where demand is disappearing.

In the last ten years the government also set out to exploit the fish along the country's coasts. Opening up the waters to foreign companies, the government has managed to deplete fish stocks dramatically without making significant profit. In the north, Russian, Chinese, and Korean factory ships strip out great shoals of fish, and nearer the capital the Mauritanian fleet of small wooden boats feeds its daily harvest to a Japanese processing plant. Japan takes the largest part of the country's exports, while most imports come from France and Thailand. Since most educated Mauritanians speak French, they look to France as the source of culture, fashion, and industrial goods. Most cars on the streets are French; foodstuffs, clothes, and even toys and games come from France along with chemicals, medicines, and other raw materials. Thailand supplies a single import: rice. The government policies attacking the Afro-Mauritanian farmers of the fertile south, together with ongoing desertification, have so reduced output that the country now can supply only 30 percent of its basic food needs. The other 70 percent—in rice, the staple grain—comes from Thailand. Disaster always threatens, for any disruption in the flow of rice would mean large-scale starvation. To ensure the flow Mauritania must give its creditors a relatively free hand in exploiting its resources, marketing their goods, and dictating the terms of business.

Because of the economic collapse of Mauritania, very little has been added to its infrastructure. The country has exactly two roads. These two-lane highways were paved not by the government but by foreign states in an attempt at economic aid. One, the road south to Senegal, is so badly broken up and potholed as to be almost impassable. Bizarrely, the country's second-largest city—Nouadhibou, the center for iron ore export—is not connected by road to anywhere at all. The only way to reach it by car from the capital is to drive (four-wheel drive essential) up the beach on the Atlantic Ocean for about 250 miles, as tides, storms, and drifting sand dunes permit. The lack of modern technology means that this is one of the last places on earth where you can experience what life was like in preindustrial times. Only a fifth of houses have electricity, and these are mostly in the capital and large towns. In the villages night falls with a profound darkness, held back at the tent door by the yellow flame of an oil lamp. Only 3 percent of homes have a telephone: there is one pamphlet-sized telephone directory for the entire country, and each number has no more than five digits. Were it not for the clinics built and staffed by foreign medical charities, there would be no health care except for the rich.

At the personal level Mauritanians suffer poverty almost beyond comprehension. Many people have only the scantiest material possessions: two or three bits of clothing; some plastic jugs, pots, and baskets; a few iron tools; a teapot and some glasses; a blanket or quilt that might serve as carpet, bed, or tent; and nothing more. The hot and dry climate actually helps the poor to live, as most of the year only minimal shelter is needed, and slaves normally sleep on the ground outside their master's house or in crude lean-tos made of brush or scrap wood. For the poor, and for slaves, the diet is little more than rice or couscous (about a pound a day), mixed with the bones and scraps from their master's meal. Slaves are easily identified on the streets by their filthy, ragged clothes, the masters by their flowing and spotless robes. White Moors almost universally wear a large white or sky blue billowing robe called a *boubou*. The precise cut of this robe is uniquely Mauritanian, and its long full sleeves can be pulled up over the head as a covering.

The robes of the Moors are often decorated with gold embroidery, and they are cleaned and starched to perfection. To maintain the distinction of their position, slaves are rarely given a *boubou* to wear. Their clothes tend to be European cast-offs, shipped in great bales from rag pickers in France. In the streets and alleys male slaves live and work in weird mixtures of polyester suit trousers ripped off at the knee and stained T-shirts advertising goods that have never been available in Mauritania. In spite of the heat, and the burning sand and stone underfoot, slaves almost never have shoes or sandals.

Not surprisingly, average life expectancy for a male Mauritanian is only forty-nine years, and somewhat less for slaves. One finds that withered, ancient-looking slave women are in their thirties; and slave children are bony and stunted, often showing cuts and wounds that are slow to heal on their malnourished bodies. Children are everywhere: nearly half of the population is under the age of fourteen. This doesn't lessen productivity, however, since slave children receive no schooling and go to work at the age of five or six. In the town of Boutilimit, behind the large White Moor houses with courtyards, I found lean-tos and shacks that I first took to be crude shelters for goats. From these emerged very dirty slave children dressed in rags. At the same moment White Moor children in bright *boubous* passed up the street carrying books and satchels, on their way to school. The slave children, who aren't allowed schooling, continued to play in the dirt street; their toys were bleached animal bones and old tin cans. Only one person in four can read. In Nouakchott I met an elderly slave woman who, though she made beautiful quilts, could not count above ten. It is this level of enforced ignorance that works to keep people enslaved, even in the less strictly supervised atmosphere of the capital.

The Back End of Nowhere

The easiest place to see slavery in Mauritania, and to see it evolving into new forms, is in the capital, Nouakchott, a city remarkable for its unattractiveness. Only a dictator blinded by racial hatred would have made such an irrational choice. With the exception of an inferior harbor some miles off, there is no good reason to place a capital here, and many, many reasons not to. For nine months of the year, sand storms scour the city. Dunes and drifts of sand fill the streets and press against the buildings. The traffic and the wind whip so much sand into the air that there seems to be little difference between what you walk on and what you breathe. The sky is a uniform sandy brown. Fine sand and grit penetrate everywhere—in your clothes, your food, and your eyes. After a few days the fine blown sand fills your throat and lungs, and you join the locals in their dry, hacking cough.

Nouakchott was a tiny village and French outpost on the unpaved track running along the ocean before being chosen as capital of the new country in 1960. The core of the city was thrown up in a few years, with buildings constructed on fixed dunes; it was designed to hold a population of 15,000. When the first great drought began in 1969 and the city became a center for food aid, refugees from the countryside flooded in. Today it holds between 600,000 and 700,000 people—over a quarter of the country's population. Everywhere one looks in Nouakchott, buildings are being constructed: not offices or stores, but thousands and thousands of small, flat-roofed concrete block houses faced with sand-brown stucco, usually of one or two rooms, scattered across the featureless sand. Slaves do most of the building, mixing the concrete and making the blocks by hand in rough forms, then hauling and stacking the blocks after drying.

Slave labor makes possible a building boom on the cheap. One U.S. government official told me that the embassy could not understand where the money was coming from to pay for all the construction, or how there could be enough economic activity to support the population. If one assumes that workers are paid, and a minimum standard of living exists, he is right: there isn't enough money circulating to sustain everyone. The system works because very large numbers of workers are not paid and receive only poor food and poor shelter. What makes Nouakchott different from the rest of Mauritania is the transfer of slave labor into the urban economy.

When the drought and political unrest drove White Moor masters into the capital, they brought their slaves with them. Working with their relatives in extended families and clans, they began to find ways to make money in their new urban environment. Since Nouakchott was becoming a city virtually from scratch, they had many opportunities. Those who had slaves skilled as blacksmiths opened shops for metal-working. Other slaves could be trained to make bricks and concrete blocks for the new buildings. Some White Moors set up in retail, and thus the market quarter contains garage-like buildings stacked with furniture or tools or car parts. The shopkeepers need never touch the merchandise, for the slaves do all the shifting, carrying, delivering, stacking, hauling, and cleaning. The most able slaves are taught how to serve in small shops, thereby making possible excellent profits based on very low overheads.

In Nouakchott I met a White Moor businessman who owned four shops, like the small neighborhood grocery stores in Europe or America, selling food and household products. Since there are no supermarkets or department stores in the city, any food not bought in the open-air market quarter must be purchased at small, local stores like these. The owner had come to the capital at the time of the drought, and with family help had opened his first shop. From his home village he brought four slaves who could be shown how to run it, while slaves left back in the home village were put to work raising produce to be sold in it. In addition, trusted slaves were sent south to Senegal to buy beans or vegetables wholesale. Profits were good from the beginning, and they financed the construction and outfitting of three more shops over time. Today the businessman "employs" four slaves in each shop and thus can keep his stores open from early morning until past midnight, even when one or two of the slaves are away making deliveries or hauling goods back for retail sale. Meat and vegetables continue to flow into the shops from the master's slave families still living in the countryside, and all of the workers are "paid" in food. The slaves in the city sleep on the shop floor. When I asked about his actual costs and profits the businessman rapidly became vague and disinterested, but since the cost of food is known we can make some estimates. Sixteen people need about five kilos of rice per day, to which perhaps two kilos of scrap meat would be added. This food cost would total $5 to $8, so sixteen workers require an outlay of at most $240 per month—no more than $15 per month each, which has to be one of the lowest expenses for "wages" in the world.

Urbanization has opened up very profitable new areas of business for White Moor masters, who are now engaged in everything from construction to car repair. The slaveholders enjoy the advantages of using slave labor within a modern economy. It's true that the imported goods they buy are costly in the context of the Mauritanian economy, but profits based on slave labor are also high. The benefits pass up the economic chain as well. French exporters supply most consumer goods to Mauritania. A look around any shop shows that the country is a dumping ground for European goods that have passed their "sell by" dates (especially worrying to anyone looking for medicine, for little in the pharmacies is current). To maintain this export market the French government actively supports the ould Taya regime, calling it the "most democratic country in Northern Africa," and funds economic development projects. Many of the projects seem so inappropriate as to be bizarre—in a country where few people have running water, very large sums have been spent on a satellite communications network for the 3 percent who have telephones. Of course, such strange priorities can be assigned when most citizens have no say in how resources are allocated. For the slaves, the new, urban Mauritania is different in how they are expected to work and learn new jobs, but just the same in the fact of their slavery. Perhaps the best way for us to understand this new kind of old slavery is to look at the urban slaves who work to supply something very precious in Mauritania—water.

My Name Is Bilal

Most slaves have only one name, and for many male slaves that name is Bilal. Bilal was the slave owned by the prophet Mohammed, whom he

later freed and made the first *muezzin*, the person who calls Muslims
to prayer from the tower on the mosque. No White Moor would ever
have the name Bilal: it is given only to slaves. The Bilal I met was one
of many slaves who work in the capital distributing water. The task of
distributing water is both simple and enormous. Simple, because it requires only a donkey, a small cart, and one or two barrels; enormous,
because in this parched desert city only 40 to 45 percent of the population have running water. This means that around 300,000 people rely
on human hands and backs for all their water.

As part of this supply system Bilal rises before dawn. He has slept
somewhere around his master's house in the sprawl of Nouakchott,
perhaps on the back porch or under a cardboard shelter in the walled
yard. His breakfast is some rice or leftovers served by the slave women
who got up earlier to begin cooking for the household. By dawn he is
on the street driving his donkey and cart to a public well where he la-
boriously fills his two sixty-liter barrels by hand. The well is just a hole
in the ground with some bricks arranged around its edge. There is no
tap or standpipe or pump, no pulley or crank—just a large metal can
attached to a rope. Working quickly, pulling up bucket after bucket,
Bilal pours the water through a makeshift funnel into his barrels. Once
they are filled, another slave steps in to begin filling his barrels, and
Bilal starts his round.

The slaves hauling water fan out across the city, stopping at most
houses. With a bit of rubber hose they siphon water into bottles, buck-
ets, barrels, and water tanks. Sometimes they are called to building sites
to provide the water for making concrete or mortar, sometimes to garden plots. Bilal will haul at least one load of water back to his master's
house, and perhaps another load or two will go to his master's relatives. The local currency is the ouguiya (200 ouguiya = $1), and Bilal
collects about one ouguiya per liter from those who pay for his water.
When his barrels are exhausted, he returns to one of the public wells
to refill them, sometimes having a moment of rest and conversation as
he waits in line with other slaves hauling water. His day is a constant
round of filling his barrels and hauling the water from house to house.

Bilal's master expects him to sell at least 800 liters a day in addition to the water he hauls for his master's family, making it necessary for Bilal to go to the well between seven and ten times. The rest of the time he is in constant motion, working through the hottest part of the day without rest, keeping up the pace until sundown. At sundown he must return to his master's house, to hand over the money he has collected and to do other work (usually cleaning or hauling) until he can sleep around midnight. The next day is the same; every day is the same, seven days a week. If he returns to his master without the expected amount of money, he is berated or beaten and his food is cut back. If he has a break from the work it will come in the rainy season, a short and chancy thing in Mauritania, when his master will send him back to the country to help with the planting.

Bilal is about twenty years old, and he was brought to the city by his master three years ago. At his master's house in the countryside Bilal did all the jobs young slaves were expected to do—washing, cleaning, tending the goats and camels, gardening, hauling water, digging, and fetching and carrying. For the dominant castes of the Hassaniya, any work involving agriculture is considered degrading. Only the breeding of camels and the nomadic lifestyle are honorable, so virtually all work falls to the slaves. Bilal's father and grandfather were also slaves to his master's family. Before that he doesn't know anything about his own family. His mother continues to work at his master's house in the countryside.

When I first spoke to Bilal, he acknowledged that he had no money but insisted, "I do this, not because I get money, but because I want to help my master." This is a standard response of the slaves when they are unsure of those to whom they are speaking, concerned that what they say might get back to their masters. In time, we convinced him of our interest and he explained that his master had told him never to admit he was a slave now that he was in the city. "But, of course," he said, "I am a slave." Since coming to the capital Bilal has learned a great deal. Now he has a vague understanding about El Hor, the organization of escaped and freed slaves. He doesn't know how to find its members, but he knows that they exist. He has also learned that life has more possibilities than being master or slave. "What I really want," he said, "is a salary—a fixed amount of money for the work I do." He knows now that other people sometimes work for salaries, that they have jobs and at night go to their own homes. "But when I asked my master about a salary, he told me it was better this way, that he gives me food, maybe a little pocket money, and that I should stay in his household—what can I do?" There is very little Bilal can do; he is trapped. He has no money and no other way of making money. He knows how to sell water, but the donkey, cart, and barrels belong to his master. Away from his master he has nowhere to live and no way to pay for a rented room. "If I complain, my master will send me back to the countryside where he has even more control over me," he told me. In addition, Bilal and the others know what can happen to escaped slaves. They have heard the stories of slaves hunted down and killed by their masters, and they know that the courts rarely take any action against the killers.

Where the Money Flows Like Water

It's no surprise that Bilal's master doesn't want to give him a salary: as a slave, Bilal ensures excellent returns for his master. Even though he sells water at the tiny sum of one ouguiya per liter, Bilal's work creates a large profit. In fact, Bilal is just one of four slaves his master has put to work selling water, a small business that brings in a steady stream of cash. Start-up costs are relatively low, and it is unlikely that the master will have to start from scratch since he would normally have some donkeys in the countryside and maybe a cart as well. Even if he does start with nothing, little capital is needed. The most expensive item (leaving aside the slave) is the donkey cart. Made of welded steel, with old car axles and tires, they cost between 30,000 and 55,000 ouguiya ($160 to $290). A good donkey can be bought for 6,000 to 10,000 ouguiya ($32 to $56), and old barrels are about 600 ouguiya ($3) each. Total outlay is, at most, 66,000 ouguiya ($350), and the returns are very good indeed.

On average Bilal brings home 800 ouguiya ($4.25) every day, as do the other three slaves that distribute water. It's not very much, but this is a volume business that provides a regular and reliable income. Bilal collects 24,000 ouguiya ($130) each month—96,000 total from all four slaves—and overhead is very low. In the master's house the female slaves cook for the entire household, making large amounts of rice or couscous. Slaves like Bilal get a portion of rice each day and whatever scraps are left over from the meal prepared for the master. The slave's meal is often rice mixed with the water in which the master's meat has been boiled. If the master has vegetables or potatoes with his meat, Bilal may get the peels and edible scraps. It costs his master about 100 ouguiya (about 50 cents) a day to feed Bilal. Feeding the donkey is even cheaper. The grass, twigs, leaves, thorns, spoiled grain, and scraps given the donkey work out to around 50 ouguiya a day (about 25 cents). The other major expense is Bilal's "pocket money." Because he has to work all day without returning to his master's house, Bilal is given small sums with which to buy cooked rice or couscous from street vendors. Though it would be cheaper to feed Bilal and the other water sellers at home, the extended workday more than makes up for the added expense. For pocket money Bilal receives between 1,000 and 2,000 ouguiya (about $8) each month. The final cost is a fee paid to the municipal worker who oversees the water supply and wells in his neighborhood. The master has to pay a "tax" of 5 ouguiya for every 1,000 liters of water they take from public wells, which works out to about 120 ouguiya (about 65 cents) per month per slave. Table 2 shows how the business breaks down for Bilal's master.

Admittedly a profit of $371 a month doesn't seem like very much, but the profit rate—265 percent—is very impressive. It is also worth remembering that Bilal's master makes every month from his four water-

TABLE 2   WATER SALES: EXPENSES AND INCOME
(IN OUGUIYA)

	Expenses	
Item	Bilal	Four Slaves
Food	3,000	12,000
"Pocket money"	2,000	8,000
Donkey feed	1,500	6,000
Water "tax"	120	480
Total	6,620 (U.S.$35)	26,480 ($140)

	Income	
Item	Bilal	Four Slaves
Sale of water (at 800 liters per day)	24,000	96,000
Total	24,000 (U.S.$128)	96,000 (U.S.$512)
Monthly Profit	17,380 (U.S.$93)	69,520 (U.S.$371)

selling slaves about what the average Mauritanian earns in a year. In local terms it is enough money to buy a good car or purchase several slaves annually. Of course, if a master has to start such a business from scratch, the profit margin falls as he recoups his initial investment; he can expect only 220 percent profit in the first year, with the start-up costs repaid within the first two months.

In many ways the Mauritanian water business is blindingly simple. This is the elegance of slave labor: no pensions, no sick pay, no salaries, no bonuses—just what it takes to keep slave and donkey alive. And the overall sums for the city of Nouakchott are, as the economists say, nontrivial. Something like 300,000 people in the capital don't have running water. According to government figures they use about 25 liters of water per person every day, for a total of 7.5 million liters a day. To be sure, not everyone buys water. The poorest people, who carry their own water from the public wells, account for about 40 percent of consumption. That leaves around 4 million liters to be purchased from Bilal and his fellow slaves every day, after they have brought the water for the master's family and projects. To supply that much water some 5,000 slaves take to the streets with donkey and cart every day, and every year they generate nearly $6 million in profit. For their masters it is an important stable income.

Those who distribute water are just a fraction of the slaves in the capital, who may number as many as 100,000. It is very difficult to estimate the size of their contribution to the economy, or to their masters' pockets, in the way we now understand the water sellers. But if other slaves of Nouakchott are contributing to the economy at the same rate as the water distributors, then they would be generating $160 million in turnover, or about 12 percent of the country's gross domestic product. The profits made on this vast sum flow directly to the masters, supporting the White Moor minority in a rich and comfortable lifestyle.

While making economic estimates is difficult, seeing into Bilal's future is even harder. Unlike many slaves around the world, he faces no serious risks in his work. He is underfed and undernourished, and he must work very hard in unpleasant conditions, but his work is not inherently damaging to his health or well-being. Life might be easier if Bilal were willing to pocket some of the money he collects and spend it on more food. But this he would never do, for Bilal is honest. It is hard to imagine that slaves will not take more for themselves when they have the chance, but it is true. Being enslaved does not necessarily change a person's sense of right and wrong, and for Bilal stealing is wrong. This sense of morality is strongly supported by the White Moors. From the mosques and from the holy men comes a message of honesty and obedience. Slaves are taught that only if they obey their masters will they go to heaven. For the slave, whose life is so appalling, the promise of paradise in the life to come is important. Of course, not all slaves feel bound to obedience, but the culture of slavery is strong enough that many act more like trusted employees than slaves in bondage.

Stadtluft macht frei?

Bilal's future is also hard to see because his work has no cultural precedent. The movement of what was essentially an agricultural form of slavery into the city is transforming both city and slavery. While generations of Bilal's ancestors had been herders and farmers for the White Moors, he is the first to be a water distributor. The same is true for the enslaved retail porters, shopworkers, blacksmiths, and auto repair workers who also labor in Nouakchott. In Germany, in the Middle Ages, people would say *stadtluft macht frei* (city air makes you free), because rural serfs who escaped their lords and stayed in an independent city for a year and a day would be freed from their feudal obligations. Being brought as a slave to Nouakchott clearly isn't enough to ensure freedom, but in the air of the capital one can catch, at least, the scent of liberation. In the countryside and village, everyone can be placed into clear categories—master, slave, vassal, or merchant. On city streets, strangers mingle. They may be slaves and masters, but they may also be Haratines, escaped slaves or ex-slaves, Afro-Mauritanians, Senegalese or other foreigners, or even those strangest of animals, Europeans.

Exposure to this variety of people and customs opens new horizons for slaves. It is not just that many of the people on the streets are neither master nor slave; all sorts of cultural rules begin to erode in the capital. Women are seen driving cars, and some women who are clearly Mauritanian don't even cover their heads. The visible lives of ex-slaves and Afro-Mauritanians may not be revolutionary, but to the slave accustomed to the rigid code of slavery they are a revelation. By their example, escaped slaves show that life in freedom is possible. Yet for many slaves freedom may not be desirable: across the large population of slaves, there are many responses to its possibility.

For many older slaves, freedom is a dismal prospect. Deeply believing that God wants and expects them to be loyal to their masters, they reject freedom as wrong, even traitorous. To struggle for liberty, in their view, is to upset God's natural order and put one's very soul at risk. They push these ideas hard onto the younger slaves, urging them to make the best of their position. In this effort they are supported by the masters, who will reward loyal and hardworking slaves, letting them marry and treating them well. Linked to these objections to freedom are the strong ties that grow up between slave and master. Slave women feed, care for, and raise their master's children. They serve the women of the master's household, and respect and even affection may grow on both sides of the relationship. Male slaves may see their own parents, in their old age, cared for by the master. Generations of exploitation do not necessarily translate into generations of resentment, as slave families and their masters confront drought and hardship together.

But for many slaves a shared history is not enough. The escaped slaves in the capital provide a powerful example and the more visible freedom is, the stronger its appeal. Many slaves know that they want their liberty, but they are unsure what liberty means. Some slaves would happily stay halfway between slavery and freedom. They would continue as part of their master's household, working within their greater "family," and would only ask for a wage and some limited freedoms. The idea of bearing total responsibility for oneself and one's family, which total freedom would require, can be frightening. Freedom of movement does not guarantee food to eat or work to do. Given the choice, perhaps the majority of urban slaves would continue working for their masters, but with greater independence. Slaves in Nouakchott repeated over and over their goal of living independently in their own, as opposed to their master's, household. However humble, this independence is seen as the key to a better life. Yet many slaves remain ambivalent about achieving it—which is not surprising, given their vulnerability and powerlessness. For in spite of the abolition of slavery in

1980, slaves remain in a legal limbo, one that they question at their peril.

The abolition law of 1980 also proposed that compensation be paid to slaveholders when their slaves were freed. Like the other necessary enabling legislation, no law mandating compensation has ever been passed and no such compensation has ever been paid. While human rights workers argue that payment should be made to the slaves rather than the masters, most slaveholders argue that they are not required to free their slaves until they are reimbursed for their loss. At this point the legal arguments again become paradoxical. Slaveholders refuse to give up their slaves until they receive compensation, but at the same time they assert that because slavery was abolished, they are no longer slaveholders. They continue to treat their slaves as slaves while arguing that they are not slaves at all, just a kind of collateral held against the compensation debt owed them by the government. They do so without fear because no legislation has been passed setting punishments for keeping slaves; and following slavery's abolition, the courts refuse to admit that it exists. When a human rights organization, such as SOS Slaves, brings suit against a slaveholder the best the activists can hope for from the courts is a ruling of illegal confinement, a lesser form of kidnapping. Occasionally a court does rule that a kidnapping has taken place, but no "kidnapper" has ever been punished.

This legal farce was acted out in 1996 when an escaped slave woman, Aichana mint Abeid Boilil, asked SOS Slaves to help her recover her five children.[8] She had run away from her master in the Trarza region after severe ill-treatment, leaving her children behind. In the affidavit prepared for the case Aichana was able to list, in addition to her own children, the names and ages of twenty-four other slaves owned by her master. With legal representatives from SOS Slaves, Aichana visited the government prosecutor's office again and again. When the human rights organization threatened to take the case to international aid agencies, the minister for justice asked a court to rule on the case.

In order to avoid international embarrassment the government pressed the court to return her children, and, in time, her master, Mohamed ould Moissa, returned four of her five children. The fifth child (a twelve-year-old girl), he explained, had been given to his daughter, Boika, and was no longer his concern. Ould Moissa argued that he had a right to all the children because Aichana was his wife and he had fathered some (he didn't say which) of the children. Aichana denied she was his wife, insisting that she had never had sex with him. No fine or punishment was levied against the slaveholder, and Aichana is still pressing for the recovery of her fifth child.

The partial victory by Aichana is a rare event. Most claims raised by slaves and ex-slaves are never heard by the courts. Since there are no laws on the books concerning the rights of slaves or setting punishments for enslavement, the Hakem (provincial officials) and the Wali (regional governors) simply refuse to hear complaints from slaves or to register their claims. They argue that since no jurisdiction over such violations has been set by law, they cannot be expected to take responsibility. The courts also claim that they have no jurisdiction and either dismiss any case brought before them or refer the cases to the Islamic courts, which are charged with enforcing the Sharia. As we have seen, the ulemas have already ruled that according to their interpretation of the Koran, slavery is legal, so little help is found in that quarter; indeed, the ulemas often initiate actions against slaves.

In the town of Aleg, for example, in early 1996, an Islamic court took two children away from their parents and awarded them to their original master.[9] The father, S'Haba, and the mother, M'Barka, had run away with their children from their master, Ahmed ould Nacer of the Arouejatt tribe. Since the slaves had escaped into the nearest town, the slaveholder did not feel he could retake them by main force, so he appealed to the ulemas for a ruling. The slave family was brought by the police to the Islamic court; after a short hearing the daughter, Zeid el Mar, and the son, Bilal, were handed over to their master. Though their parents have appealed to the central court in Nouakchott, their case has yet to be heard and the children remain in slavery.

The case of M'Barka and S'Haba illustrates the special powerlessness of women and children. Their lives are so completely controlled that their slavery is sometimes hard to see. In their master's household the women are passed off as domestic workers or family members. As noted earlier, the Koran makes female slaves available to their masters for sex. The sexual use of slave women is a key part of their subjugation, and it is one of the rights that the slaveholders are loath to give up. For the master its importance goes well beyond pleasure. Female slaves produce more slaves, and slaves are valuable. Whether he has fathered them or not, the children of a female slave belong to her master, and the courts will support the master in this. The master decides if and who a slave woman might marry and can annul any marriage he doesn't approve. Temrazgint mint M'Bareck, an escaped slave woman whose master forbade her marriage, felt the injustice keenly: "On top of everything else I didn't have the right to get married. One man wanted to marry me, but my master said he would have to accept at all times these conditions: I would not be freed; my children would remain slaves of my master; and once married I had to remain living in my master's household."[10] Whether the parents are married or not, the master can do what he likes with slave children. By moving the children around other households, lending or selling them to friends or relatives, slaveholders tie down slave women, effectively holding their children hostage.

Slave fathers have no rights over their children and have wives only so long as their masters wish. They are powerless to protect or to hold together any family they make. The result is fatalism and resignation. Denied rights over their dependents, often separated from their families, male slaves find it psychologically easier to run away. Slaveholders are not overly eager to recover escaped male slaves, since they are not wealth producers like slave women. Men who run away may find menial jobs; though free, they often end up living in worse conditions.

For female slaves, freedom is usually harder to support. They have few options: working as prostitutes or as servants, selling couscous in the street, or doing manual work. Their offspring become street children. Without birth certificates they cannot claim what little state aid exists, and without a fixed home or decent clothes they are denied schooling. As children of escaped slaves they have little worth and will be used for the most dangerous and dirty work. The government accepts extensive child labor as the norm, treating it as essential to economic growth. If this is all that freed slaves have to look forward to, what hope is there for positive change in Mauritania?

Forty Acres and a Mule

The Mauritanian constitution guarantees most human rights. Each time a coup occurs the winners proclaim the citizenship of all Mauritanians and promise reform and the distribution of land to the poor. These hollow promises are yet to be kept, as endless commissions "work" on the problems. The issue of slavery is particularly thorny for the government, and the official response is complex. The true abolition of slavery presents a real threat to the government of Mauritania in at least four ways. First, the upper castes of the White Moors control Mauritania and its government, and they are the slaveholders. President ould Taya and his clan rule with the permission and support of the other White Moor families and tribes. Any suggestion of truly abolishing slavery is seen as directly affecting their economic well-being. Whenever abolition has been discussed the reaction has been immediate: masters step up their brutality, ship their slaves into the isolated countryside, and separate children from parents to serve as hostages. If the government were to pass and enforce laws to bring slavery to an end, chances are good that it would be the government, not slavery, that failed to survive.

Second, even the successful abolition of slavery could be sowing the seeds of the government's destruction. Slaves are effectively non-citizens, systematically denied all political rights. If slaves became functioning members of society, White Moor control of the country would be under threat. The worst nightmare of the ruling White Moors is a coalition between freed slaves and the Afro-Mauritanians. The main opposition political parties are run by and for the Afro-Mauritanians from bases in France, Morocco, and Senegal. Many of the Afro-Mauritanians are well educated and experienced in business and administration. In spite of their talents they are normally excluded from government positions, though those loyal to the rulers fill a few figurehead posts. Members of the Afro-Mauritanian opposition are well aware of the political potential in the slaves and make liberation a key plank in their platforms. The Arabization campaign was instituted to counter this threat. Slaves are taught to speak only Arabic and are only rarely allowed to learn to read. Afro-Mauritanians speak their own languages and French, and so are forced to learn Arabic as well if they are to forge any links with the slaves. Meanwhile the government and the White Moors keep up a barrage of anti-African propaganda. Black Mauritanians are referred to as "foreigners," and the Moors circulate terrible rumors among the slaves about their plans to destroy society and attack Islam. Although the slaves themselves are usually more African than Arab, the White Moors also play the race card. They assure the slaves that they are Arabs, despite denials in private; the White Moors would never dream of giving slaves or Haratines the same rights as Arabs.

Third, if slavery were ended and if the freed slaves joined their interests to the Afro-Mauritanians, the White Moors would face another insurmountable problem—land. When the slaves in the southern states of America were emancipated at the end of the American Civil War, most assumed that some payment would be made to help them get on their feet. The common expectation was that each slave family would be given forty acres and a mule, the basic requirements for self-sufficiency in that agricultural region. After all, abolitionists and freed

slaves reasoned, how could 4 million people just be turned loose without a penny to fend for themselves? If they were to be citizens, should
they not have the right to public assistance to make a start in their new
lives? The American government chose to ignore this plea, and equally
chose to ignore the claims amounting to $4 billion in compensation to
the slaveowners for the loss of their slaves. Ex-slaves and ex-masters
were left to fend for themselves, and the result was another century
of sharecropping, prejudice, segregation, and tragedy. The Mauritanian
government is equally intent on avoiding questions of compensation
to slave or master. Taking even the lowest estimate of the number of
slaves, at their current market rates the government would need to pay
compensation to owners of more than $176 million, or about 16 per-
cent of Mauritania's gross domestic product—a sum far beyond the government's means. Yet the abolition law specifically mentions the need
for such compensation. More important, even if the money for the
slaveholders could be found, the land needed by freed slaves could not.
Mauritania might be able to print money, but it cannot make more
land, and in fact its arable land is being lost to desert at a frightening
rate. The only option would be to take land from White Moor families,
land that the slaves are presently tending. But that expropriation would
never be accepted by the White Moors; attempting it could lead to
civil war.

Issues of control of land are now creating tension between slaves
and slaveholders. In the traditional form of Arab slavery, White Moor
families maintained a migratory life as they moved their herds across
large areas. Some of their slaves traveled with them and others were
left to tend crops on land they owned. Today many slave families have
lived as sedentary farmers for generations, and some believe they have
some rights to the land they cultivate—if not ownership, then a certain
amount of security in their tenure. Unfortunately, neither their masters nor the government agrees with them. In case after case brought to
civil or Islamic courts, slaves and ex-slaves have been thrown off the
land they farm. Waste land reclaimed by escaped slaves over fifty years

ago has also been recently "returned" to its Moor owners, who acquired their land deeds only weeks before calling in police and local officials.

There are several reasons why the Moors are expropriating land at an increasing rate. Some fear that slavery may be abolished or controlled and that slaves might be given rights to the land they farm. By throwing them off the land now, the Moors ensure control in the future. Some slaves have learned of the 1980 abolition law and believe themselves to be free. They assume that now they are not required to hand over half or more of their crop to their masters. Confronted with such resistance, the slaveholders simply drive the families from the land. And as the urban economy grows, more slaveholders are finding new uses for the land they control. When they need land for building or development, they take it from the slaves who have been farming it. Whatever the White Moors' motives, the courts regularly support the land claims of slaveholders. If the current government were to try to give Moor land to ex-slaves, another coup would almost certainly result.

Compared to questions of land, White Moor control of the government, and the Afro-Mauritanian opposition, slavery's fourth threat to the government is a minor one. It is only in the realm of foreign opinion that the existence of slavery, rather than its abolition, becomes a problem. International opinion is important to the Mauritanian government because it is so dependent on foreign aid. To ensure the flow of aid, it has chosen the easiest approach: mounting a campaign of disinformation rather than addressing the issue of slavery. We've already seen how the government abolished slavery without telling the slaves, but the smoke screen extends much farther. Since some human rights organizations persist in demonstrating the existence of slavery, the government has set up two "human rights" organizations of its own: the National Committee for the Struggle against the Vestiges of Slavery in Mauritania and the Initiative for the Support of the Activities of the President. While the title of the second rather gives away its role in providing boosters and yes-men, the first works more cleverly. To the United Nations and to other governments, it appears as an "independent" organization with the position that there may be some slavery in Mauritania, but only the *vestiges:* regrettable but tiny pockets of bad labor practice. Members of the truly independent organizations concerned with slavery, SOS Slaves and El Hor, are kept literally under lock and key. When SOS Slaves is finally able to bring a case to court or to win the freedom of an escaped slave against government obstruction, the National Committee responds, "Ah yes, it is good that another *vestige* has been eradicated." It then points to the very low number of slavery cases brought to the courts, failing to mention that judges keep throwing out such cases on the grounds that they lack jurisdiction.

The willingness of UN and foreign countries to accept the word of these government-front organizations can be explained in two words: Islamic fundamentalism. The United States and France, two key supporters of the Mauritanian regime, need the country as a buffer against the Islamic fundamentalists of Algeria and Libya. In the first Gulf War, President Taya supported Saddam Hussein, allowing him to hide part of the Iraqi air force in the Mauritanian desert. This did the country little good with its creditors or with the United States or France, but the concern of foreign powers now is to reclaim Mauritania and prevent it from becoming the next domino to topple to the fundamentalists. The White Moors that rule Mauritania fear the fundamentalists, whose appeal to the poor and dispossessed is a direct threat both to their power and to their relatively Westernized, luxurious lifestyle. The Afro-Mauritanian opposition also fears the rise of the fundamentalists, who reject the opposition's liberal policies. Because of the opposition's frustration and disunity, this threat might push it into an unholy alliance with the ould Taya government. If that happened, then, as one contemporary guide puts it, "the present government's ungodly, undemocratic, corrupt apparatus could trundle on for years."[11]

To prop up the Mauritanian government, the United States and France provide the regime with both large shipments of material aid and great bundles of political excuses. The French, as we have seen, praise the government as democratic and fund large development projects, studiously ignoring questions of slavery. The Americans deflect any suggestions of widespread enslavement in the country. Their 1999 "Human Rights Report for Mauritania" states: "A system of officially sanctioned slavery in which government and society join to force individuals to serve masters does not exist; however, there continued to be unconfirmed reports that slavery in the form of forced and involuntary servitude persists in some isolated areas . . . with some former slaves continuing to work for former masters in exchange for . . . lodging, food, or medical care. Many persons, including some from all ethnic groups, still use the designation of slave in referring to themselves or others."[12]

If these were American children being referred to as "slaves," immediate outrage would follow—but they are not. For the Americans it is politically expedient to stick to the fiction that there are only *vestiges* of slavery in Mauritania. The ould Taya government is a regime that the Americans and the French can do business with, even if it means winking at some of the local customs. This is a disgrace. Slavery in Mauritania is very different from the new slavery that grips the rest of the world and it needs more, not less, attention and intervention. It is more deeply rooted in history and custom than the new slavery and thus more intractable. For this reason it is less likely to give way before economic pressure. Here we find not businessmen who have decided to invest in slavery and who could also choose to disinvest, but rather the entire ruling class of a country united to defend its way of life.

Back to the Future

Mauritanian slavery is old slavery carried into the present. The isolated time warp that is the Western Sahara has kept this particular remnant of the past in a remarkable state of preservation, like some desiccated mummy. And because this is old slavery, it has special problems that are not found in the new slavery. Let's look again at the differences between old and new slavery, this time with Mauritania in mind:

Old Slavery	Mauritania	New Slavery
Legal ownership asserted	Ownership illegal, but upheld by the courts	Legal ownership avoided
High purchase cost	Relatively high purchase cost	Very low purchase cost
Low profits	Relatively high profits	Very high profits
Shortage of potential slaves	Shortage of and competition for slaves	Glut of potential slaves
Long-term relationships	Long-term relationships	Short-term relationships
Slaves maintained	Slaves maintained	Slaves disposable
Ethnic differences important	Ethnic differences accented	Ethnic differences not important

Its closeness to old slavery makes the situation in Mauritania highly resistant to change. Because it never went away or reappeared in a new form, this slavery has a deep cultural acceptance. Many people in Mauritania see it as a natural and normal part of life, not as an aberration or even a problem: instead, it is the right and ancient order of things. And because of the high cost and value of slaves, if slavery is truly abolished the masters have much more to lose than do the holders of new slaves. Having more to lose, they have more to fight for, and they have made it clear they will not relinquish a system in which they have such large investments and which serves them well. Of course, the high cost and value of slaves also means that they are treated and maintained better than are new slaves. This better treatment makes it easier for Mauritanian slavery to be ignored or excused. The arguments can even center on what is good for the slave: "If the masters didn't care for them, they'd go hungry," and "In such a poor country, it's really the best thing all round; it means everyone gets to work and eat." When slavery can be cast as part of a "traditional" culture that serves as a kind of primitive social security, then even countries like the United States and

France can turn a blind eye. If their memories were less self-interested they would recall the same arguments being made in favor of slavery in the American South.

As in the nineteenth-century American South, in Mauritania race matters intensely. Racism is the motor that drives Mauritanian society. Despite extensive intermarriage, White Moors generally disdain their black slaves and regard them as inferior beings. The worldview of the White Moors is clearly hierarchical, casting themselves as superior in all things. That superiority also stirs fear and animosity toward the Afro-Mauritanians who want a fair share in government. This form of racism is sometimes hard for non-Mauritanians to see, since black slaves live in White Moor households and all attend the same mosques and ride the same buses. But it is so strong that no official segregation is needed: the lines of family and tribe are exact and impermeable. The White Moors hold on to what is theirs.

It will certainly be more difficult to dislodge slavery from Mauritania than from countries where the new slavery exists. The ruling White Moors' deep cultural and economic vested interest in slavery makes them as ready to fight for this privilege as the southern states of the United States fought for theirs. And in Mauritania there is no Abraham Lincoln, no Union Army—only a tiny and persecuted abolitionist movement. Moreover, just as the Confederacy had a powerful friend in Great Britain, who needed the South's cotton, so Mauritania is supported by France and the United States, who need help to stop the spread of Islamic fundamentalism. All in all, this portends a long fight. Those who want to stop slavery in Mauritania face a more daunting prospect than did the American abolitionists of the 1850s when they looked south and saw 4 million slaves bound by two hundred years of violence, custom, and law.

Yet there is hope. Despite being deeply embedded in Mauritanian culture, slavery there will eventually end. Some will find freedom sooner than others. Were the Western countries to link the remission of Mauritania's staggering foreign debt to a government program to give land to slaves, thousands more could achieve a sustainable freedom. If food aid and development projects were refocused in order to set freed slaves on the path of self-sufficiency, only the largest of slaveholders would fail to benefit from the general economic growth.

But whatever power and resources the Western governments bring to bear on the problem, they are not going to be the wellspring of freedom for these slaves. Every day, members of the Mauritanian organizations SOS Slaves and El Hor work to help slaves into freedom. The story they bring to slaves, the example they set, shows the way out of bondage. Though their leaders are arrested and imprisoned, though their meetings are broken up and their publications censored, they are not giving up. Many of the leaders and members of both these organizations are ex-slaves, and like Frederick Douglass or Harriet Tubman they are in the fight to the end. But most importantly and most powerfully, the slaves of Mauritania are learning of their rights: the ineluctable urge to become free grows in them, and once it takes root they will not be stopped.

4

~~∽∾⊘∾∼~~

BRAZIL
Life on the Edge

THE NEW SLAVERY FLOURISHES WHERE old rules, old ways of life break down. The much-publicized destruction of the rain forest and the rest of Brazil's dense interior creates chaos as well for the people who live and work in those areas. Much of the slavery in Brazil grows out of this social chaos. Think of the way in which serious flooding or an earthquake can destroy sanitation and spread disease. In even the most modern countries, when natural or human-made disaster demolishes a city's water system and sewers, killer diseases such as dysentery or cholera can erupt and infect the population. Similarly, environmental destruction and economic disaster can cause an existing society to collapse—and the disease of slavery can grow up in the wreckage.

But destruction is never stable; no place or people ever slides into chaos and remains there forever. Economically driven destruction is sweeping like a tidal wave across Brazil. Before it are the scrub forests of the *cerrado* or the rain forests of the Amazon; behind it are the eucalyptus plantations and the new cattle ranches, planted with alien grasses, emptied of native animals, and providing meat for the markets of the cities. At the location of the wave itself is turmoil. The space between the old forests and "civilization" is a battle zone where the old rules are dead and the new rules are yet to come into force. As the native ecosystem and peoples are uprooted, displaced workers, even the urban unemployed, become vulnerable to enslavement. The people caught up and forced to carry out the destruction of the forests live without electricity, running water, or communication with the outside world. They are completely under the control of their masters. The wave is carrying slavery with it. The land ahead is still exploitable, the land behind is stripped, and when all the land is stripped the slaves will be discarded.

We tend to picture environmental destruction as huge bulldozers gouging their way through pristine forests, crushing life under their steel tracks, scraping away nature in order to cover the land with concrete. In fact the process is more insidious. In this case, the people who live in the forest and rely on it are usually the ones forced to destroy it. Tree by tree, the hands of slaves wrench the life out of their own land and prepare it for a new kind of exploitation. The slavery of Brazil is a temporary slavery because environmental destruction is temporary: a forest can only be ruined once, and it doesn't take that long.

Sometimes a forest is destroyed when something of value is taken out; at other times the destruction yields nothing of value. In Mato Grosso do Sul both have happened. Twenty-five years ago when the *cerrado* was cleared to make way for the eucalyptus, the wood was simply dragged into great piles and burned. Today, as the final wave of destruction sweeps across the Mato Grosso, the *cerrado* and now the eucalyptus are again being burned—but this time they are being turned into money. The wood is made into charcoal, just like the kind we use in our barbecues. This is a special kind of charcoal because it is handmade, by slaves. But perhaps it is not so special, after all—slavery has a long history in Brazil.

For the English to See . . .

When Europeans, mostly Portuguese, first came to Brazil, they brought large-scale slavery with them. Eight years after Columbus "discovered"

America, a Portuguese sailor named Pedro Alvares Cabral "found" Brazil, and soon the explorers began to realize the riches they could make from growing sugar there for the European market. The native Indians were quickly conquered and enslaved to serve the new masters, but they proved neither numerous nor durable enough to supply the labor needs of the growing plantations (the Europeans carried diseases that exterminated many tribes). This wasn't a crisis for the settlers, since the Portuguese had already begun capturing slaves on the coast of Africa. Shipping them to Brazil was easy, a shorter trip than sending them to the Caribbean or North America. Soon all the settled parts of Brazil were practicing legal slavery, and a national economy grew up on the backs of slaves.

From the beginning of colonization until late in the nineteenth century slaves were transported from Africa to Brazil in huge numbers. As many as ten times more Africans were shipped to Brazil than to the United States: something on the order of 10 million people. But because the death rate on the sugar plantations was so high, the slave population of Brazil was never more than half that of the United States In the eighteenth century the discovery of gold helped carry slavery deeper into the interior and the Amazon. By the nineteenth century Brazil was locked in a struggle over slavery, but unlike the United States, it did not suffer a civil war. For Brazil the key antislavery forces were the British, on whom the Portuguese had become increasingly dependent for economic support and protection. From 1832 the British navy patrolled the oceans off Brazil, intercepting and freeing African slaves. Inside Brazil the slaveowners worked constantly to whip up the racism and fear necessary to preserve slavery; the government enacted laws *para Inglês ver* (for the English to see), a phrase that is still used to mean doing something by subterfuge. In 1854 the importation of slaves and the international slave trade were abolished, but not slavery within the country. The power of the British had its limits, and in the end it was the Brazilian antislavery movement, led by Joaquim Nabuco, which forged a coalition of nationalists, anticolonialists, and liberals that defeated the landlords and slaveholders after twenty years of political conflict. Full emancipation came in May 1888, when Brazil became the last country in the Americas to abolish legal slavery.

It is hard to know if slavery ever completely disappeared in Brazil. The great plantations of the coastal regions, the areas nearest government inspection, converted from slavery within a few years, but in the remote areas of the Amazon and the far west enforcement was lax. Those distant parts of the country were relatively untouched until the 1950s, when exploration and exploitation began in earnest. Bigger changes began when Brazil experienced an economic boom in the 1960s and 1970s, which affected Brazil much as we saw the boom of the 1980s and 1990s affected Thailand. Lower infant mortality and immigration led to a population explosion, the cities grew and filled, industry expanded, and the pockets of poverty grew deeper and deeper. The military government courted foreign investors with promises of cheap labor and loose environmental and tax laws. But mechanization drove more people from the countryside to the cities than the new industries could absorb, and enormous slums (called *favelas*) ruled by gang lords grew up in Rio and São Paulo. The military rulers also borrowed heavily to support nuclear power and mining projects. A return to elected governments could not forestall the bust of the 1980s, and the uneven development of twenty years crashed. Hyperinflation wiped out savings, and servicing the foreign debt, now $120 billion, crippled the economy.

The economy slowly improved in the 1990s, but the underlying problems of inequality were never fixed. Today, Brazil (along with its neighbor Paraguay) suffers the greatest economic disparities of any place on earth. On one end of the scale are the 50,000 Brazilians (out of a population of 165 million) who own almost everything, especially the land. At the other end of the scale are 4 million peasants who share 3 percent of the land. Most of them, of course, have no land at all. In the cities and the slums are millions more without work. The austerity programs that brought the hyperinflation under control all but shut down the health and education systems. And in the times of instability state corruption, already serious, grew worse.

"A Breast of Iron . . . "

We have already seen how government corruption goes hand in hand with slavery. In Brazil it also fosters environmental destruction. The advent of eucalyptus plantations mentioned at the beginning of this chapter was part of an immense tax-avoidance scheme cooked up in the 1970s by the military government and multinational companies. The exact origins of the scheme are lost, but its gist was clear: the government allowed large companies and multinational corporations to buy up federal land, at a very low price, in blocks of hundreds of thousands of acres. If the companies would then strip away the native forests and plant eucalyptus, the government would allow them to take the cost of the land and the replanting off their corporate taxes. Ultimately, the eucalyptus was to be cut down and fed to a paper mill that the government promised to build. Handed vast tracts of land on a plate, the big companies—including international giants like Nestlé and Volkswagen—then received over $175 million as tax relief.[1] By the 1990s the paper mill remained unbuilt, and many of the owners began to contract local firms to clear the land and make charcoal.

When an exploring geologist combed through the land north of Rio de Janeiro at the beginning of the nineteenth century, he said the country had a "breast of iron and a heart of gold."[2] This area of rich mineral deposits became the state of Minas Gerais (in English, "General Mines"). Today the state is a mining and industrial center producing large quantities of iron and steel. To make steel requires charcoal. And the modern industries of Brazil, whether they are making cars or furniture, are using steel produced with the help of slaves. Many of the plants and smelters are efficient and up-to-date, but the charcoal they use still comes from denuded forests and the hands of slaves.

After the forests of Minas Gerais and the neighboring state of Bahia were cut down, new sources of charcoal had to be found; thus we return to the western state of Mato Grosso do Sul, more than a thousand miles from the steel mills of Minas Gerais. As the frontier moved west, roads penetrated into the *cerrado*, providing a way to haul out the charcoal. And with millions of acres standing in native wood or eucalyptus, charcoal making is a quick way simultaneously to squeeze more money from the land and to clear it for cattle ranching. The only ingredient lacking in this remote area is the workers.

There is an art to making charcoal; it is a skill that must be learned and practiced before charcoal of good quality can be consistently produced. With the forests gone in their home states, charcoal workers congregated in the cities hoping to find work. They found, as have millions of other displaced workers in Brazil, that there was none. Whole families in the eastern cities teeter on the edge of starvation: some live in the public rubbish dumps gleaning scraps of metal to sell, others beg, and some turn to selling drugs. These families are trapped and are willing to do anything to bring in food for their children. When recruiters arrive in the cities of Minas Gerais promising good work at good pay, they leap at the chance.

"They Come with Their Beautiful Words . . . "

From the early 1980s, as the wave of development swept into Mato Grosso do Sul, recruiters began to appear in the slums of Minas Gerais seeking workers with some experience of charcoal making. These recruiters are called *gatos* (cats) and are key players in the process of enslavement. When they drive into the slums with their cattle trucks and announce that they are hiring men or even whole families, the desperate residents immediately respond. The gatos will go from door to door or use loudspeakers to call people into the street. Sometimes the local politicians, even local churches, will let them use public buildings and help them recruit workers. The gatos explain that they need workers in the ranches and forests of Mato Grosso. Like good salesmen, they lay out the many advantages of regular work and good conditions. They offer to provide transport to Mato Grosso, good food on site, a regular salary, tools, and free trips home to see the family. For a hungry family it seems a miraculous offer of a new beginning. In a charcoal camp in Mato Grosso I spoke with a man named Renaldo who described being recruited:

> My parents lived in a very dry rural area and when I got older there was no work, no work at all there. So I decided to go to the city. I went to São Paulo but that was even worse; no work and everything was very expensive, and the place was dangerous—so much crime! So then I went up to Minas Gerais because I heard that there was work there. If there was I didn't find it, but one day a gato came and began to recruit people to work out here in Mato Grosso. The gato said that we would be given good food every day, and we would have good wages besides. He promised that every month his truck would bring people back to Minas Gerais so that they could visit their families and bring them their pay. He even gave money to some men to give to their families before they left and to buy food to bring with them on the trip. He was able to fill up his truck with workers very easily and we started on the trip west. Along the way, when we would stop for fuel, the gato would say, "Go on into the cafe and eat as much as you like, I'll pay for it." We had been hungry for a long time, so you can imagine how we ate! When we got to Mato Grosso we kept driving further and further into the country. This camp is almost fifty miles from anything; it is just raw cerrado for fifty miles before you get to even a ranch, and there is just the one road. When we reached the camp we could see it was terrible: the conditions were not good enough for animals. Standing around the camp were men with guns. And then the gato said, "You each owe me a lot of money: there is the cost of the trip, and all that food you ate, and the money I gave you for your families—so don't even think about leaving."

Renaldo was trapped. Like the other workers, he found he could not leave the camp and had no say in the work he was given to do. After two months, when the workers asked about going home for a visit they were told they were still too deeply in debt to be allowed to go.

The mother of three sons who later escaped from bonded labor explained, "When things are bad here [in the slums], it is as if the gatos can guess things are in such dire straits, and then they come and trick the poor. . . . They come with their beautiful words and promise you the length of their arm, and then when you get there they won't even give you the tip of their finger."[3]

When the workers begin their trip, the gatos ask them for two documents: their state identity card and their "labor" card. These are crucial to life in Brazil. The identity card is essential for any dealings with the police or government and is proof of citizenship; the labor card is the key to legal employment. By signing the back of a person's labor card, an employer creates a binding contract and brings the job under government employment laws such as the minimum wage rules. Without a labor card, workers have difficulty obtaining their rights. The gatos say that they need the documents to update their records, but in fact this may be the last time the workers ever see them. By keeping these cards the gatos gain a powerful hold over the workers. However bad their situation, the workers are loath to leave without their documents. Meanwhile, since the labor cards have not been signed, there is no proof of employment and little legal protection. As one Brazilian researcher put it, "From this moment the worker is dead as a citizen, and born as a slave."[4]

For the gatos, their method of long-distance recruiting has great advantages. Taken far from their homes the workers are ignorant of the surrounding countryside and cut off from friends or family who could help them. Even if they are able to escape, they are penniless and in debt. They have no way to pay for the trip back to their own state. They will often keep working in the most horrific conditions in the hope of getting some cash that they can use to get home. And if they do flee from the charcoal camps, the local people often resent and fear them as outsiders. Without identity cards they can be locked up by the police as vagrants or suspected criminals. Without their labor cards they cannot work; moreover, they remain unregistered in their new workplace and the government labor inspectors and the trade union organizers will have no idea they exist.

In the charcoal camps the workers are isolated, like the young women brutalized and held in the brothels in Thailand: we can see in Brazil another example of the "concentration camp" method of enslavement. The charcoal camp is its own world. The gato and his thugs have complete control and can use violence at will. What they want are workers who have given up, who will do anything that is asked of them. At the same time they want their captives to work hard, so they constantly promise payment and more food and better treatment. Balancing hope against terror, they lock their new slaves into the work. Like the young women forced into prostitution, the charcoal workers are not enslaved for life; in fact, their stay in the camps is usually shorter than the women's in the Thai brothels. The gatos and their bosses don't want to *own* these workers, just to squeeze as much work out of them as possible. The workers I spoke to had been held in debt bondage for anywhere from three months to two years, but rarely longer than that. There were several reasons for the brevity of their employment. A charcoal camp lasts only two or three years in any one location before the forest around it is exhausted, and workers are rarely moved from one camp to another. Also, the workers themselves become ill and exhausted after a few months' work in the ovens. Rather than keep on those who can no longer work at full strength, it is more cost-effective to discard them and recruit fresh workers to take their places. Since they are usually penniless when they are thrown out of the camps, many of the workers never make it back to their homes in Minas Gerais. More often than not they hang around in the towns of Mato Grosso, and many are ultimately drawn back to the charcoal-making camps (called *batterias*).

A charcoal-making camp is called a *batteria* because it has a battery of charcoal ovens (called *fornos*). The batteria may have from twenty to over a hundred ovens, with between eight and forty workers. The heat, smoke, and desolation of the batteria makes it seem like a little bit of hell brought to the forest. The charcoal ovens are round brick-and-mud domes about seven feet high and ten feet wide. They are built in long straight lines, with twenty or thirty ovens standing about four feet apart. A little peaked opening in the oven about four feet high is the only way in. Through this door the workers pack the oven completely full of wood. The wood has to be stacked up from the floor to the rounded roof of the oven very carefully and very tightly so that it will burn down properly into charcoal. After the wood is loaded, the door is sealed up with bricks and mud and the fire is set. Charcoal is made by burning wood with a minimum of oxygen. If too much air gets into the oven, the wood is consumed by the fire and only ash is left. If there is not enough air reaching the oven, useless, half-charred chunks of wood are produced. To control the flow of air, small vent holes in the side of the oven are opened and closed by digging them out or sealing them off with mud. The burn lasts for about two days and the workers have to constantly monitor the oven, day and night, to make sure it is burning at the right temperature. When the burn is finished, the oven is left to cool; then the charcoal is taken out.

All around the camp for a mile or so the land has been stripped and gouged. The exposed earth is red and eroded. The tree stumps, the great patches of burned-over grass and wood, the trenches and holes, and the ever-present pall of smoke turn it into a battleground. The wreckage of the forest is everywhere. Covered with black soot and gray ash and shiny with sweat, the workers move like ghosts in and out of the smoke around the ovens. All the workers I saw were just muscle, bone, and scars; every bit of fat had been burned off by the heat and effort. The overpowering, choking smoke colors and flavors everything. The eucalyptus smoke, full of the sharp oils the tree makes, is acrid and burns the eyes, nose, and throat. All the charcoal workers cough constantly, hacking and spitting and trying to clear lungs that are always full of smoke, ash, heat, and charcoal dust. If they live long enough most will suffer from black lung disease.

Most of the ovens are oozing and belching smoke and the heat is tremendous. As soon as you enter the batteria the heat bears down. This part of Brazil is already hot and humid; take away any protection from the sun that the trees might offer and add the heat of thirty ovens, and the result is a baking inferno. For the workers who have to climb inside the still-burning ovens to empty charcoal the heat is unimaginable. When I got inside an oven with a man shoveling the charcoal, the pressure of the heat had my head swimming in minutes, sweat drenched my clothes, and the floor of hot coals burned my feet through my heavy boots. The pointed roof concentrated the heat and in a few moments I was addled, panicky, and limp. The workers hover on the edge of heatstroke and dehydration. Sometimes in their conversation they were confused as if their brains had been baked. The workers who empty the ovens stay almost naked, but this exposes their skin to burns. Sometimes standing on the piles of charcoal they will stumble or the charcoal will give way and they will fall into red-hot coals. All of the charcoal workers I met had hands, arms, and legs crisscrossed with ugly burn scars, some still swollen and festering.

In front of the ovens are great stacks of wood cut in four-foot lengths ready for loading. Behind the ovens are the piles of charcoal waiting to be shoveled into huge bags for transport to the smelters. The line of ovens is the last step in the destruction of the forests, which disappear in an ever-widening circle around the batteria. At the far edge of the ruined fields surrounding the ovens, workers are burning through the undergrowth and cutting down more trees, pushing the edge of the forest further and further back. Hauled up to the ovens on trailers pulled behind tractors, the cut wood will soon be turned into charcoal.

Two Hundred Years in Two Thousand Miles . . .

It was spring when I visited a number of batterias in one part of Mato Grosso do Sul. I was traveling with Luciano Padrão, a young Brazilian expert on poverty and employment from Rio de Janiero. Our journey seemed to cross not only a large part of the country but also

from this century to the last. Brazil has one foot in the first world
and another squarely in the third world. We began in Rio de Janeiro, a
city that would be at home in the United States. With its McDonald's,
subway system, strings of condos facing the beach, and drug gangs, it
could be an upmarket city in Florida. Though, to be fair, Rio is more
spectacular than any city in Florida: the lushly forested volcanic mountains that range through the city and drop to the ocean make a stun-
ning backdrop. To reach the baterias we flew from Rio to the even
larger city of São Paulo. Everything in Brazil is just so *big*, and flying
over a city of 16 million people was a mind-boggling experience; the
towering buildings stretched to the horizon. In São Paulo we changed
planes and flew a thousand miles west to Campo Grande in Mato
Grosso do Sul.

To go from São Paulo to Campo Grande was to make the first shift
across time and culture. Campo Grande is a cow town full of stock-
yards, cowboy supply stores, battered farm trucks, and dusty, ragged
streets where people seem to move at half speed. In the late afternoon
the beer bars open, and young men in work clothes sit outdoors and
drink and sweat. It was so much like a half-baked, half-broken-down
county seat in Oklahoma, where I grew up, that I felt I had been there
before.

The next morning we pulled out of Campo Grande in a four-wheel-
drive pickup truck. The roads were paved and so straight that I couldn't
understand why Luciano had insisted we needed both a heavy-duty
truck and a driver. For a couple of hundred miles it was as if we were
driving through east Texas. The land was broad and rolling. Clumps of
trees broke up the vast pastures where cattle grazed, and everything
was a deep green under puffy white clouds. Where it had been cut into,
the soil was a harsh red and quick to erode. The watercourses spoke of
heavy rains and flash floods. Miles and miles from anywhere we'd pass
a man or sometimes a boy in ragged clothes walking along the highway,
a bundle on his back. Occasionally a patch of *cerrado* would show what
had been there before.

After a few hours we reached the town of Ribas do Rio Pardo and shifted cultural gears once more. Now we were in the recent past, in the slow molasses of a town that simply marked where a number of farms had coalesced. There were tractors and livestock in the street, and it was clear we were a long way from where world events or national politics mattered to anyone. A few miles out of town we turned onto a dirt track into the countryside. Now I understood why we needed the special truck and driver: we crawled through ravines and up and down washed-out streambeds, bottoming out in great ruts and bogging down in pits of sand. Here the open pastures became more and more patchy as we drove deeper and deeper into the *cerrado* forest. Even with the four-wheel drive it took us almost four hours to travel the fifty miles to the first batteria. During that time we passed only two other vehicles; one was a small old car driven by a man, probably a gato. The other was an equally old and ramshackle truck heaped high with bags of charcoal. It was inching its way along the track at a speed slower than a walk.

When I asked Augusto, our driver, what kind of animals lived in the *cerrado* before the clearances began, he said, "Nothing ever lived here." But as we drove deeper into the forest I saw amazing fauna, especially birds. In the golden afternoon light, we passed a small tree with dark green leaves that was full of bright green parrots. Regularly along the track were snakes—big snakes, sunning themselves in the dust. Once as we came up out of a streambed we startled a flock of about thirty birds from the track. This flock was like nothing I have ever seen: about a third were shiny jet black, another third were also black but with very bright yellow stripes on their wings and bodies. The rest, mixed among these, were a luminous light green with red flashes. At another turning we stirred up a great bird of prey with a wing span of five or six feet. And then, a mile or so down the road, with a double take I realized I was watching a five-foot tall emu watching me.

When we arrived at the batteria we had reached the back of beyond. The camp had been carved out of the dense and tangled forest next to the track. Now I began to understand the control the gatos have over the workers. The batteria is completely isolated; the only link to the outside is the truck that carries away the charcoal and the car that brings the gato. Any worker who tries to leave faces a fifty-mile walk back to the nearest town. Since no police ever come out here, and the workers' families have no idea where they are, it is easy to see how a troublesome worker can just be killed and dumped in the forest. Remarkably, the very isolation that traps the workers opened up their lives for us. In batterias as remote as this one, the gato doesn't bother to stay around all the time. He knows that the workers can't escape and that they are dependent on him to bring food to the camp. Every two or three days, the gato brings supplies to the batteria and checks up on production. We came to this camp because we knew from contacts in Ribas do Rio Pardo that its gato was still in town.

"My Tail Was in His Trap . . . "

At the batteria the workers were surprised and wary when we arrived. Soon, however, Luciano, with years of experience working with poor and bonded laborers, overcame their suspicions and got them talking. As they showed us around the camp, we found it hard to imagine that this was a place where people lived. Poles and branches cut from the forest, but still with their bark, were tied or nailed together to make a crude frame. More scraps of wood were loosely fixed to the frame, making walls that you could see through in a hundred places; over the top was a sheet of black plastic. This was where the workers slept. It was so insubstantial that it couldn't even be called a shack. As shelter, it was markedly inferior to a tent. The floor was just the dirt, and chickens, dogs, and snakes came and went freely. Inside another rough frame of poles had been knocked together so that the men could sleep up off the ground. On this were the small bundles of clothes and a blanket or two that made up the men's possessions. There was only one woman in the camp and no children; they had been driven off, as will be explained below.

Cooking was done over an open wood fire, and the toilet was the forest during the day or a bucket at night. The gato had left behind a tank of water and another tub collected any rainwater. It was a hungry, thirsty, and dirty place for the workers. Although they were working with sharp tools such as axes and with burning charcoal, there were no medical supplies. Several of the men were clearly suffering from infected burns and cuts; others looked weak and sick. I was told that many had internal parasites.

Speaking through Luciano I began to talk with the workers. At first I just asked one man a few questions about where he was from and if he had a family. He asked me why I had come to Brazil and what I thought about it. After a little while I asked him if he had heard about slavery:

Yes, I have, I know a lot about it.

How so, what is this slavery?

Slavery is what is happening right here to us. We're enslaved here, I understand that. Look, I cut the cerrado *and haul it to the ovens for making into charcoal. I was told that I would be paid 2* reais *[pronounced "re-eyes"; about $2] per load. But I get nothing. According to the gato all the work I do just covers the cost of my food and my debt. He charges us much more than the real price for the food he brings out here. We have to pay for everything we get, but we receive nothing. Everything we do counts for pennies and everything we use or eat is very expensive.*

You've been here three months; how much pay have you had in that time?

I haven't had anything, absolutely nothing. See, with this gato my debt is always running ahead of my earnings.

So, if you've been here three months and you've been paid nothing, why do you stay? Why don't you just leave?

I can't just run off and stop working. I have to talk to the gato and see how things are and see if I can get ahead of my debt. A man has to leave in the right way with his debts settled. It is necessary to have your debts paid off, so I have to keep working till then. If I didn't do that then tomorrow or later I would need a job and I would go to other places and the gato would send word: "This man worked for me and didn't settle his debt." Then I would never be able to get work. Today I can't leave, because of my debts; I just have to work hard. If every way I try I don't succeed, then I have to just talk to the gato face to face and say, "Look, what can I do; I've been working and working and still I owe you the same amount. What can we do to make this right?" Sometimes then the gato just says "forget it."

Another worker spoke up:

This kind of thing has already happened to me. At the last batteria where I worked I was a woodcutter. I had my own chain saw and I cut and hauled the wood. When we were going to settle up after three months working there, the gato turns to me and says, "You owe me almost 800 reais." Since I don't want to be in debt to anyone I had to leave my chain saw with him. My tail was in his trap; it was the only way to get free.

A third worker added:

I've been here two months, but I don't know if I'll get anything, we haven't settled up yet. No one says anything about money, the gato only wants to talk about work, about how we have to work harder and make more charcoal.

I asked him if he knew how much he should get when they did settle up.

No, I have no idea, I have no way of knowing this. We don't even know the name of this batteria or where we are. All I know is the name of the gato.

It seemed pretty obvious to us that the gato was tricking these men into working for nothing, and stealing their possessions as well. But these workers, isolated and illiterate, were too honest to perceive how they were being entrapped.

Dishonesty feeds on honesty. The very rules of trust and honesty that guide most of these poor Brazilians in their dealings with each other are key to how the gatos enslave them. All the workers I met had a very strong sense that debts *must* be repaid, that a person who did not pay his or her debts was the lowest of the low. The sly manipulation of this belief achieves the gatos' ends more effectively than violence: the drawbacks are fewer and the workers' productivity greater. Indeed, once a gato does resort to violence, the workers realize that they can never work their way out of debt and their sense of pride can no longer be used against them. For that reason the gato will keep appealing to their sense of "fair play" for as long as possible. They are trapped, believing that trust *might* pay off and knowing that running away is of no avail. A charcoal worker explained the situation to me:

> *The charcoal always goes to the smelter but the money never comes back. So we have to wait and see. Maybe we decide to wait for two more months. From time to time we ask the gato; he always says that he is not paying us because we all owe him so much money, but in fact no one owes him anything. Sometimes we have to borrow money from our friends and everyone is left like this. We are all in this situation and don't know what to do. Sometimes [I think] I'll run away without getting paid. Sometimes I stay because I think the gato will pay me. We never know what to do—go or stay, maybe we get something, maybe not.*

In fact, the gatos will pay some of the workers some of the time. At a few of the batterias I visited the workers were being paid, though usually late, and below the agreed rate. The fact that they *might* get paid (or are paid even a little bit) keeps them working, especially since the alternative is no work, no money, and a walk home of a thousand miles. Alfeo Prandel is a priest who works with families in the charcoal camps.

He told me this story:

> *It is not always the case that there are people with guns holding workers in the camps. They use something that the poor Brazilian people have: the feeling that they must pay their debts. We had a case of one family that were told that they owed the gato 800 reais. They were able to hitch-hike with one of the charcoal trucks back to Minas Gerais to go to a funeral. And then they came back! I asked them, "Why did you come back?" And they said, "Because we owe the gato 800 reais, we had to come back and try to pay him." So I told them, "You know you are being robbed of much more than 800 reais." But they just said, "A debt is a debt and we have to pay."*

Of course, the gatos cannot always rely on the goodness and honesty of the workers. Eventually, it becomes obvious to them they are being cheated, and when that happens the gatos are ready to use violence. Many workers told us of being threatened or beaten and of knowing people who had disappeared. At another charcoal camp I met a man who had been a guard at a batteria, who recalled:

> *The very first job I had when I came here from Minas Gerais was as a guard. I thought I was going to be making charcoal, but the gato thought I looked tough or something. The gato gave me a gun. It was a huge batteria and my job was to stop any workers that tried to leave. I told him I had never had such a job and that I didn't want to be a guard, but he just said I would do it or I would suffer. I had to do it. It wasn't so hard to be guard so I did it for a while. After three months of working at the batteria I still hadn't been paid anything. I didn't like being a guard and pushing people around, so after these three months I told the gato I wanted to quit and to settle up. The gato got really mad and said, "You came here to work. I don't have to settle up with you." So I said, "All right, I'll keep working, but I don't want to be an armed guard, I don't like it." The gato said, "Right, I've got another job for you, get into the truck." Then the gato drove me seventy miles into the deep countryside, to this little shack*

that was completely remote; when we got there he just said, "Get out and stay here," and then he drove off. So there I was, no food, no water, nothing, and seventy miles to the nearest town. But I decided that I just had to run away immediately, so I set off through the forest, not on the road in case I met the gato coming back. After two days I saw someone I knew from another charcoal camp. This person told me that the gatos were looking for me, that they said they were going to kill me when they found me. My gato had left me at the shack and had gone to get the other gatos to help him get rid of me—so it was lucky I ran off when I did. After a few more days I got up close to the road and watched for a car or truck that didn't belong to a gato. Finally I saw one that had a priest driving and I was able to hitchhike into the next town; that was my escape.

Though he had escaped, the man was penniless and more than a thousand miles from home. His only choice was to sign on with another gato and hope that this one would not enslave him.

At the same camp a worker told me this story while we sat with his co-workers:

Six months ago we were all working in this camp, but we had a different gato. This man was very bad. [The other men all murmured their agreement.] He has run away now with all the money. When we got here from Minas Gerais he taught us how to do the work by beating us. We were scared to say anything, as it was clear he would do anything he wanted to us. Very soon we realized that he wasn't going to pay us. When we asked for money he would beat us. Some of my friends from Bahia ran away, but the gato chased after them with dogs and caught them. He brought them back at gunpoint and beat them in front of us. He kept the dogs around us at night so that they would bark if anyone tried to leave. Finally my friends from Bahia managed to slip away at night and escape. Not long after that the gato disappeared, then in a few days the empreitero [the man who had subcontracted the charcoal making to the gato] came and it turned out that this gato had stolen his money as well.

"I Used to Be a Gato . . . "

So far it would seem that the villains of this piece are the gatos. They exploit whole families and children, entice and trick workers into slavery, abuse them, and sometimes kill them. There is no excusing their crimes. Nevertheless, not all gatos are slaveholders. Some pay their workers and treat them well. I would estimate that 10 to 15 percent of baterias are run relatively fairly. Unfortunately, these are not the gatos that last in the charcoal business, because gatos are just subcontractors answerable to the big companies that own the land and the timber. This is easier to understand if we take a quick look at the economics of charcoal.

We can understand how profits are made in charcoal if we look at one small bateria of twenty-five ovens with just four workers. In one month, a bateria this size can make ten truckloads of charcoal, which are sold to the smelter in Minas Gerais for 18,750 reais (around $17,000). Take away the cost of trucking the charcoal to the smelter, and about 12,000 reais are left. If the workers *are* paid, instead of enslaved, it really doesn't eat into the profits. At most a charcoal worker makes between 200 and 300 reais per month. So the whole workforce costs 1,200 reais a month in wages, plus another 400–500 for food. Throw in some tools and fuel and extras, and the monthly profit is still 100 percent. Setting up the bateria in the first place is very cheap: it only costs about 100 reais to build a charcoal oven, and the workers' shacks are mostly made from free wood. About 3,000–4,000 reais gets the bateria into production, and those costs can be made back in the first month with some profit left over. So, this one little bateria can potentially net a profit of 100,000 reais ($90,000) per year. True, a bateria can only produce for two or three years before all the nearby forest is cut down, but it is easy to move the charcoal camp when the time comes.

The very healthy economics of charcoal making raises an obvious question: if the labor costs are so low when compared to everything else, why bother to enslave workers? A wage of 300 reais a month isn't very much, but there are plenty of Brazilians who are ready to work for that. Just as easily workers can be hired for 10 reais a day, or at piece rates of so much per cubic meter of charcoal, or by the number of ovens loaded or emptied. Paying the going rate for workers barely touches the bottom line at all, so why use slaves? The answer to this question has two parts. First, and more important, the people who actually run the batterias, the gatos, don't own them. The owners or their agents, the *empreiteros*, have the whip hand and set the rules. Workers are cheap and easy to trick because there is high unemployment, and the same is true of gatos. The owners can squeeze the gatos hard, offering a small percentage of the total profit and setting minimum quotas for charcoal production. If the gato doesn't like it, there is always someone else ready to try running a batteria. The owners make the deals with the smelters, and payment for the charcoal goes directly to them. Some of the gatos I was able to speak to were on wages linked to production. At one small batteria the gato told me he was paid a salary of 420 reais as long as they produced 500 cubic meters of charcoal a month (this was confirmed by another source). If output dropped below that amount, he got 336 reais—approximately the same pay as any charcoal worker. One charcoal worker told me, "I used to be a gato, but I couldn't make the required quotas, so I lost my truck and chain saw and now I just work like everyone else."

The small shop that sells food at grossly inflated prices near some of the charcoal camps is owned by the *empreitero;* he supplies tools and fuel to the gato, also at a large profit. Often the gato is expected to invest in the batteria as well, or at least put up his truck or chain saw as collateral against the profits. The owners keep the gatos on the edge of going under, pulling every penny they can out of their operations. And why not? There will always be another gato willing to take a chance, willing to be a little more ruthless when it comes to their one source of potential profit: the workers. The only way gatos can win is to cut their labor cost to the bone. The gato is normally expected to pay the workers out of his share of the profits, and while no one is going to give away gasoline or food (the other primary expenses), sometimes the workers can be tricked or forced into giving up their labor for free. To get ahead in the charcoal business, the gato must cheat or enslave workers.

The second reason that charcoal workers are enslaved is simply because they can be. For the gato there is virtually no downside to enslavement; unless he has moral scruples, slavery is a good business strategy and easily accomplished—we've already seen how trust can be abused and used to trick workers. The landowners certainly have no objections; slavery allows them to increase their income without risk. Government inspectors have no clout, and the police are not interested in enforcing the law. Their complete indifference to slavery clearly demonstrates who is paying the bills. Far from the batterias and the slaves, in the office buildings of the state capital, or even in Rio de Janeiro or São Paulo, the businessmen who own or lease the forests chalk up the police as just one more overhead expense.

While a few of the gatos are actually small-time owner-operators of charcoal camps, most of the land is owned by big corporations. Sometimes the multinationals that originally bought into the government forest giveaway scheme still own the land; in other cases, they sold or traded it off after the tax rebates were used up. Other large Brazilian corporations concentrate in this sort of forest "management" and buy up or lease land from the multinational owners. These land and timber companies actually control most of the charcoal production. One medium-size company that I looked at closely in the town of Agua Clara owned a vast tract of forest. The land supported fifty batterias. In addition, the company owned the charcoal trucks, the timber trucks, all the tractors, a garage for repairs and fuel, and an office building for managing it all. The gatos that subcontract from this company are required to use company trucks, have them serviced and repaired at the company's garage, and buy all supplies from the company store (at company prices). The two men that own this company are rich and respected members of the local community. Their hands are never dirty, because they are careful to distance themselves from the operation of the batterias.

Although they own the land and keep most of the profits from making charcoal, these companies insulate themselves from any charge of slavery by arranging the work in a series of subcontracts. The company, for example, subcontracts to a middleman (the *empreitero*) to clear a certain large acreage of forest, large enough to support perhaps twenty or thirty batterias, and to turn the wood into charcoal. The middleman gets a percentage of the income when the charcoal is sold to the smelters. In turn, the middleman will subcontract the running of the batterias to different gatos. The gatos will then be responsible for finding the workers and meeting the quotas for charcoal. Though perfectly aware of what is happening on their land, the owners are able to deny all knowledge of slavery or abuses. If central government inspectors or human rights activists find and publicize the use of slaves, the companies can express horror, dump (temporarily) the guilty gatos, tighten up security to prevent further inspections, and go on as before. Like the Japanese and Thai businessmen who invest in brothels that use slaves, these Brazilian businessmen can focus on their bottom line without ever having to know what really supports their excellent profit margin. It is a perfect example of the new slavery: faceless, temporary, highly profitable, legally concealed, and completely ruthless.

For the Americans to See . . .

The power of these companies and their links with government are clearly shown by events that dramatically altered the use of child labor in the charcoal camps in 1995–96.[5] Beginning in the mid-1980s a number of researchers and human rights campaigners had exposed the horrific conditions and the use of slave labor in the charcoal camps of the Mato Grosso. At that time gatos were recruiting and enslaving whole families, and children were commonly seen loading and unloading the ovens. A number of children died of burns and other accidents. By the end of the 1980s the main human rights organization in Brazil, the Pastoral Land Commission (or CPT), had published a number of reports, picked up by the national press and television, that denounced the situation in the batterias. In spite of this publicity no government action was taken. In 1991 further pressure from human rights lawyers and the churches impelled the government to set up a commission of inquiry. Again, time passed and nothing changed; the government commission never reported. Trying to keep up the pressure, the CPT joined with other nongovernmental organizations and set up an independent commission in 1993 that fed a stream of reports and documentation to the media. Yet two more years passed before any action was taken. By now a decade had passed since unmistakable and ongoing violations of the Brazilian law against slavery had been clearly documented, but national, state, and local governments remained paralyzed.

Suddenly, in August 1995, several things happened at once. First, the governor of the state of Mato Grosso do Sul went to New York to drum up investment. While he was there the BBC showed a film about charcoal making in his state, and the *New York Times* ran a front-page story on the use of slave labor in Mato Grosso.[6] The American investors balked at such clear evidence of slave labor, and the governor was told there would be no investment until the problem was resolved.

Back in Brazil the governor blasted the CPT and the activists for bringing shame on the state, threatening them with investigations and injunctions. But at the same time, and undoubtedly as the result of another series of unpublicized meetings among the governor, landowners, and businessmen, all the gatos in Mato Grosso do Sul abruptly came out against child labor. This universal change of heart surely came at the orders of the *empreiteros* and owners, but however it occurred the results were dramatic. Women and children were expelled from over 200 batterias, and hastily printed signs were nailed to trees at the entrances to charcoal camps: "No women or children are allowed to work here." As the threat to foreign investment percolated up to the large corporations, the federal government—with admirable coordination with the *empreiteros* of Mato Grosso—introduced a system of education grants that paid 50 reais a month to every child of a charcoal laborer not working in the batterias.

For the families the outcome was both good and bad. On one hand, some families were able to flee enslavement in the batterias altogether and return to Minas Gerais. On the other hand, about 3,000 women and children were trucked into the town of Ribas do Rio Pardo and dumped there. Destitute and with nowhere to go, they now live in a shantytown built on wasteland at the edge of Ribas. Without help from the church and the "education grants," they would starve. Nevertheless, about 1,000 children are attending school for the first time. I found children still living at several of the batterias I visited (and so not attending school), but there was no evidence at all that any of these children were working. One CPT worker told me that child labor can now be found at only the most remote of batterias.

Nor did the Brazilian government's public relations campaign end with the education grants. There had always been some government workers who had agitated for reform and now a small group of these were given a special assignment: to set up a special demonstration camp for charcoal workers (and foreign investors). I visited this project, and it is very impressive. Located between *cerrado* and eucalyptus forests, it has the largest batteria I saw, with over 400 ovens. Near the ovens is a mill that extracts the oil from the leaves stripped from the eucalyptus trees. For the workers it is close to a paradise: electricity, plumbing, flush toilets, a school with teachers, vegetable gardens, large communal kitchen and dining hall for the workers, and playing fields and toys for the children. Here the families live in neat brick-and-stucco houses with tight tile roofs. It is the only place in all the charcoal camps I visited where the workers were animated and told jokes, the only place I heard anyone singing, the only place where everyone had shoes. The families who lived there couldn't believe their luck—and they were indeed very lucky, for they were the only families, out of thousands in the state, to live like this.

The demonstration project is window dressing. Using money from foreign charities, the government has set up an island of good treatment in an ocean of exploitation. It wasn't easy to separate the charcoal workers from the ever-watchful government officials, but when we did we learned a great deal. Though they were extremely happy with their living conditions, the workers explained that their relations with the landowner and *empreitero* were unchanged. While not enslaved, they continue to work for a pittance, in the same dangerous conditions, and without any say in the work they do. From what they understood, the landowner was laughing all the way to the bank: he had his workers making charcoal at the usual high profit; the government was paying him rent and building roads, houses, and barns on his land; and the foreign charities were providing food and medical care for his workers. All he had to do was meet with groups of foreign visitors occasionally and talk about how this new system was *so* much better. There are no plans to extend this demonstration project to other batterias; it is just another case of *para Inglês ver*, this time aimed primarily at American investors. All it really demonstrates is that a government subsidy to a token group of workers can significantly protect the profits of the landowners and large corporations.

On the subject of the economic development of this rural state, the last word has to go to the state secretary of agriculture. When asked about job creation in the region, he replied with stark honesty: "There's nothing left there, just the charcoal and the slaves."[7]

A New Antislavery Movement?

For all the hypocrisy evident in the swift end to child labor in the charcoal camps and the setting up of the demonstration project, there are important lessons to be noted in what happened. The sudden reversals and changes in government policy after years of inaction suggest tactics and strategies that can be brought to bear on slavery. The first key point is the very real power of the media. The combination of a BBC documentary and a *New York Times* front-page article alerted those who had the power to influence Brazilian officials. The second key point is more important: it was *economic* pressure that brought about the rapid and demonstrable improvements in the charcoal camps. If we are looking for ways to bring people out of bondage, we have to recognize that money shouts where pleas for human rights go unheard.

But the connection between media exposure and economic pressure is by no means firm. The outrage generated by today's big story fades quickly as tomorrow's takes its place. The discovery of slavery and abuse is sensational; the deep analysis of the long-term social and economic development needed to end slavery is a yawn. The media, especially the Western media, are enormously powerful in confronting slavery, but their impact tends to be short-lived. In much the same way, business interests can have profound effects on the practice of slavery but rarely sustain them for long—and we should not fault them for that. The development companies that refused to invest in Mato Grosso until the labor situation improved acted admirably, but long-term human rights monitoring is not their job. They want to see the improvements that make business possible and then get back to work. The link that must be forged is between government and business. Purely political or economic attempts to end slavery in the developing world rarely work. When human rights compete with profit, profit wins. If North American and European governments are going to make a dent in slavery, they must work through tight controls on the businesses that are involved, even indirectly, in the use of slave labor.

In Brazil these questions of economics and government action are extremely complex. The slavery in the charcoal camps of Mato Grosso do Sul is just one example of many, many kinds of bondage in the country. Slaves cut down the Amazon rain forests and harvest the sugarcane. They mine gold and precious stones or work as prostitutes. The rubber industry relies on slavery, as does cattle and timber. Indians are especially likely to be enslaved, but all poor Brazilians run the risk of bondage. Yet unlike Thailand or Mauritania, Brazil is a reasonably modern and democratic country. There is a large and educated middle class, the press is free and vociferous, and there are well-organized action groups such as the CPT freely lobbying and working against slavery. Admittedly, these activists run risks. Human rights workers, trade union leaders, lawyers, priests, and nuns have all been murdered while working against slavery and abuses. Eight antislavery campaigners in the small town of Rio Maria in the state of Para had their names circulated on a "death list," and six are now dead. Rio Maria is now known as "the town of death foretold."[8] This is ominous but it doesn't stop the reformers; all of the activists I met in Mato Grosso faced these dangers with a calm resolution.

The activists, however, can only react to the problems they confront. Proactive enforcement of human rights law and economic controls must come from the government. Now that democracy is reestablished in Brazil, the citizens have to ask themselves how long they will tolerate slavery in their country. Foreign newspapers and investment banks can have an influence, just as British policies did in the nineteenth century, but putting a real end to slavery—now, as in 1888—is a job that only the Brazilians can do.

5

PAKISTAN
When Is a Slave Not a Slave?

IN THE SOFT MORNING LIGHT, IN AN AIR still thick with the night's dew, children are mixing water and soil and kneading it into lumps that look like loaves of bread. They chat and laugh as they work. For the moment the work is easy; the sun is low and the day is still cool. It's just after six in the morning and the Masih family has been at work for almost two hours making bricks. The work of the children—two boys, age eleven and nine, and a girl, age six—is crucial to their family's survival. They mix and prepare the mud that will be shaped into bricks by their parents. Using a hoe to hack at an earth bank in the pit where they work, the children then break up the soil by hand. Fortunately this Punjabi soil is not too rocky or hard. The little girl has hauled a two-gallon water can from the well, and the children work the water into the dirt, making the smooth mud needed for bricks. When the mud is mixed they toss a loaf-sized lump across to their mother. She is squatting next to a long line of bricks formed by her husband. She kneads the lump again and dusts it with dry earth. Now it is ready for the mold and she pushes it over to her husband, who picks it up and slams it down into a wooden frame. Beaten into the frame the lump makes a solid block of clay; the excess is trimmed off, and a new raw brick is flipped out onto the ground to dry.

Every ten seconds a lump flies from child to mother to father and into the wooden frame. The line of bricks on the ground stretches out as the sun rises over the pit. From time to time the work slows as a new row of bricks is started or the children have to wait for more water to come from the well. By the eight hundredth brick the soft morning has turned into an oppressively hot and humid day. The temperature is in the 90s and the air in the pit is thick. The children stop chatting or laughing; their movements grow sluggish. They begin to pant and sweat, and addled by the heat they work like automatons, digging and mixing, digging and mixing. Now they drink more of the water brought from the well, and wrap pieces of cloth around their heads and shoulders against the sun. By the time twelve hundred bricks are lined up in the pit, the sun and humidity are pressing them down, and they are faint from heat and hunger. Still they work, digging and mixing, keeping up the flow of mud to their father as he molds brick after brick. Finally, after about fourteen hundred bricks, between one and two in the afternoon, they stop. Now, in the greatest heat of the day, work becomes impossible, and they drag themselves back to the single dirt-floored room where they live, to eat a quick meal and then fall asleep. Sleep is the only way of coping with the great heat of the day.

After a few hours the day cools slightly. Now there's time to put in another two or three hours digging from the pit wall, building up a pile of loose earth and wetting it so that it will be ready in the morning. Of course there's other work to do as well. Mother is preparing the main evening meal, and if not digging in the pit, father and children may be fetching, hauling, or stacking bricks around the massive brick kiln. The Masih family is just one of fifteen families making bricks at the kiln, and sometimes, in the late afternoon, the children of the different families may get time to play together.

Children are an important part of the workforce at a brick kiln in Pakistan. Laboring with their parents they mix the mud for the raw bricks. Other children may work with the haulers who carry the raw bricks from the pits to the kiln, or they may help stack the bricks in the kiln, a more specialized job. If the bricks are not stacked just right, the kiln can collapse with disastrous consequences. Later, the hot, fired bricks have to be taken from the kiln and stacked outside; when sold, they must be loaded onto carts or trucks and hauled away. Before that happens, the coal for the kiln has to be carried to the top of the kiln and shoveled into the fire holes. The temperature here is well over 130 degrees and the workers, including the children, wear sandals with thick wooden soles against the heat of the kiln. For all their heavy footgear, the workers tread lightly, and the children have an advantage, for as the fires rage in the kiln below them sometimes the top level of bricks gives way. When this happens a person can fall through. If workers fall completely into the kiln there is no hope for them; the temperature inside is over 1,500 degrees, and they are instantly incinerated. If only a leg or the feet push through, there may be hope, depending on how quickly they are pulled up and out. But the burns will be serious and disabling.

In spite of the risk, the children work on: their families need their help to get by. And many families, even with the efforts of the children, still cannot make ends meet. The value of their work means that as I visited many brick kilns across the state of Punjab, I found only a handful of children who attended the local school. Often no children were receiving any schooling. At others, perhaps three or four boys were able to go (when children are sent to school, girls are rarely included). At a few kilns a man would come once a week to tutor the children in the Koran, but this was only for the Muslim children and excluded the many Christian children also working there. For the children of the brick kilns the work is long and hard, but hard work and diligence don't guarantee success.

If the *conditions* of work were not bad enough, the *system* of working in the brick kilns presents other dangers and hardships. Virtually all of the families making bricks are working against a debt owed to the owner of the kiln. These debts pose a special danger for the children. Sometimes, when a kiln owner suspects that a family will try to run away and not pay off their debt, a child might be taken hostage to force the family to stay. Such children are tricked away from the kiln and held by force, locked up in the owner's house or in the house of a relative. Here they will be put to any work the owner chooses and fed as little as the owner can get away with.

Holding children as collateral is bad enough, but not the worst aspect of the system. The debt owed to the owner of the kiln does not end if the father of the family dies. Instead it passes to his wife and sons. A boy of thirteen or fourteen can be saddled with a debt that he will carry for many years, perhaps his entire life. The inherited debt binds him to the kiln and to the incessant mixing and molding of raw bricks. In addition, the cost of his father's funeral will be added to the debt. Inheritance of debt is a key factor in the type of enslavement I have been calling *debt bondage*, a system that holds many Pakistani families in a life of grinding toil.

. . . Another Day Older and Deeper in Debt

It doesn't take much capital to start a brick kiln in Pakistan. While beyond the reach of most small farmers, the business is open to people with some savings. This is one of the reasons that there are approximately 7,000 brick kilns in the country, not counting the tiny backyard kilns for homemade bricks. The remarkable thing about the kilns is that they are made of what they make—bricks. Since the bricks are made directly from the soil, the kiln just grows, emerging from a field and converting the earth and mud into a vast structure topped with a tall brick chimney. The building of a large kiln is a great feat of primitive engineering, for it is virtually all done by hand.

When a site has been chosen for a kiln, two groups of workers are immediately brought in—the families of Muslim Sheikh or Christian brick molders and the specialist kiln builders. Almost like seed corn, the first major delivery to the site will be a load of bricks from another kiln to be used to build the small houses for the workers. As the kiln builders, helped by carpenters, put up the housing, the molders begin the process of digging and mixing the mud and forming it into raw bricks. They may begin digging and molding on the site of the kiln itself, excavating and leveling a great oval field. Unlike the small ovens used for charcoal making in Brazil, the Punjabi brick kiln is an enormous affair, nearly the size of a football field. The kiln grows like a low, flat-topped hill out of the fields and its chimney is visible from a great distance. The whole structure is put together from raw, unfired bricks and the outside walls are packed over with mud to seal them. When the fires are started the bricks of the kiln itself will also be baked, and after one or two months of operation the kiln will be hardened and sound.

Once the kiln is constructed more workers are called in. Some crews work with donkey carts to take raw bricks from the field to the kiln, and inside the kiln specialist stackers begin to fill the space where the bricks will be fired. This stacking is a delicate and skilled job. The raw bricks must be placed so that the heat can circulate around them while they bake. At the same time the bricks must hold up the roof without any mortar being used to hold them together. The result is a huge honeycomb, stacked up like children's building blocks. At the top the stackers fit the bricks into a pattern that forms a roof, and the whole is covered over with sand and gravel.

Loading in coal and wood through holes in the top of the stacked bricks, they light the fire. Once started it will burn continuously for four to five months. As it travels incessantly around the oval kiln, the fire demands a constant supply of raw bricks. Day in and day out the stackers work ahead of the fire, unloaders behind it, and fireworkers on top of the kiln. Depending on the size of the kiln, the entire oval will hold from 500,000 to 2 million bricks. To fire this number of bricks, and to carry the fire one time around the oval of the kiln, takes four to six weeks.

One trip of the fire around the kiln is called a *gher*, and the kiln will accomplish five or six *gher*s in each of the two brickmaking seasons.

Given the 7,000 kilns in Pakistan, this means an annual production of some 65 *billion* bricks. Each one of those bricks is shaped and formed by hand by the families that take on the piece-rate work of molding raw bricks. With fifteen to thirty-five families at each kiln, there must be between 150,000 and 200,000 families at this work. Knowing that the average family size is 5.3 people and that children often work along with their parents, we can estimate the total workforce of molders at around 750,000 people.

The workforce available to go to the kilns grew just as the demand for bricks expanded after World War II. Before the independence of Pakistan, most of these kiln workers would have been agricultural laborers tied to the land or working on daily rates. In the forced migrations after partition, property abandoned by Hindu and Sikh landlords was broken into smaller plots and redistributed to Muslim refugees. These new Muslim farmers were owner-cultivators who had no use for the day laborers or peasants of the old feudal system who were bound to the land. Massive rural unemployment resulted, which was made worse during the 1960s. At that time the government began two major projects: the modernization of agriculture and land reform. The threat of land redistribution frightened many large landowners, who believed that their property would be expropriated and given to the resident peasant farmers. To forestall that outcome many landlords simply evicted the families who had lived on and worked their land for centuries. To replace their labor, the landlords ordered tractors and other machinery, thus achieving the government's other goal of modernization. But when land reform did arrive, the landless peasants were excluded; redistributed land went instead to existing small landlords. With more land the small landlords were in a better position to mechanize, and the landless peasants at the bottom of the economic ladder were pushed down another rung. Recent estimates suggest that one-third of all farmland in Pakistan is owned by 0.5 percent of landlords. There are about 15 million landless peasants.

Left with few options and often homeless, many peasant families sold

Every day, all day, this young boy in Pakistan digs mud for making bricks. (Courtesy International Labour Office; photograph by Jean-Pierre Laffont/Sygma)

This child in Pakistan has been molding bricks since before sunrise; her family is enslaved by the manager of the brick kiln. (Courtesy Anti-Slavery International; photograph by L. Roberts)

Working in furnace-like heat, these bonded laborers unload bricks just fired in a kiln in Pakistan. (Courtesy Anti-Slavery International; photograph by Ben Buxton)

During the brickworkers "revolution" of 1988 in Pakistan, a trade unionist puts up posters calling on bonded workers to leave the kilns. (Courtesy Anti-Slavery International; photograph © Ben Buxton)

Enslaved workers have been found on government-sponsored construction projects in India. (Courtesy Anti-Slavery International; photograph by Ben Buxton)

Much of India's agricultural production is done by bonded laborers, such as these women gathering fodder. (Courtesy International Labour Office; photograph by J. Maillard)

Father Ricardo Rezende with seventeen-year-old José Pereira Ferreira, who was captured by gunmen, shot in the neck, and left for dead after he tried to escape from an estate in Brazil. A fellow worker who also tried to flee was killed. Father Ricardo persuaded Ferreira to testify to the police in order to free the sixty other workers on the estate. (Courtesy Anti-Slavery International; photocopied from CPT archives)

The first demonstration against bonded labor in India, in 1982. (Courtesy Anti-Slavery International; photograph by Krishna Murari Kishan)

Sixteen-year-old Sita Ram, who had been held in debt bondage since age eight, plays the drum at a sit-in organized to highlight the plight of bonded laborers in Raipur, India. (Courtesy Anti-Slavery International)

In the Dominican Republic enslaved Haitians harvest the sugar that flows into the food we eat. (Courtesy Anti-Slavery International; photograph by Jenny Matthews)

In many parts of the developing world, manufacturing is still human-powered, often by children in debt bondage, as in this can-producing workshop in Bangladesh. (Courtesy Anti-Slavery International; photograph © Mark Edwards Picture Library for Publishers)

In a workplace that is more like a prison camp, these Brazilians held in debt bondage wait for the rations that are the only payment for their work. (Courtesy Anti-Slavery International; photograph by Joao R. Ripper/Imagens de Terre)

While his master's children attend school, this child slave in Mauritania spends the day watching his master's camels. (Courtesy Anti-Slavery International and United Nations; photograph by Jean-Pierre Laffont [PK])

themselves into debt bondage to owners of brick kilns, whose numbers were increasing. Bricks were needed for the rapidly expanding infrastructure—roads, buildings, and bridges were using bricks at a phenomenal rate, and the number of kilns increased. The first generation of brickworkers was drawn almost entirely from the ranks of the displaced farmworkers. Today their children and grandchildren inherit both the job and, often, the debt that holds them in it.

Except for the degree of enslavement, life in the kilns is fairly uniform. A long, low, and narrow building is put up next to the kiln and divided into single rooms, each with a door to the outside. Each family is allocated one room measuring about eight feet by eight feet. The floor is dirt or brick, usually with a small, glassless window in the wall opposite the door. In one corner is a small earthen stove for cooking and warmth in the winter. Into this room will go all the family and their few possessions—a string cot or two, some pots, pans, and jugs, and their clothes. In some kilns electricity may run to the houses; then there will be a light and, possibly, those few luxuries a family might afford, like a radio or an electric fan. There is no running water or refrigeration for food, though at one kiln I visited, families had banded together to buy a small black-and-white television. The toilet is a communal brick outhouse, and water for bathing, cooking, washing, and drinking must be carried from either a hand-pumped well or a watercourse. Many kilns dig their own wells since water is needed for mixing up the mud for bricks. There is no guarantee that the well is clean and free of disease, and one researcher stated that half of the wells at brick kilns are not potable. Cassandra Balchin, a journalist living in Pakistan who investigated the kilns, found that "Unable to afford the small fees at government clinics, the kiln workers who live in crowded communal huts are affected by tuberculosis, typhoid, malaria, cholera and diarrhea—some of their children simply dying of cold in the winters."[1]

Like the work of the Masih family described at the beginning of this chapter, the toil of all the brickmakers is hard and monotonous. The families must work hard because the piece rate pays just enough to get by on, and a lost day means greater debt or going hungry. As already noted, the rate is so low that families can rarely work their way out of debt. On average, families are paid 100 rupees ($2) for every thousand bricks they produce. Working full tilt a family makes 1,200 to 1,500 bricks a day, but perhaps 10 percent of these will not dry properly and thus will be spoiled. If not thwarted by rain, the family might earn 700 to 800 rupees ($14 to $16) in a good week. But the costs of the minimum essentials needed to keep a family alive are exactly this amount. On weekly earnings of 700 rupees, a family of four or five can have a bare diet of wheat roti (flat, unleavened bread), vegetable oil, lentils, onions, and sometimes a few other vegetables. If they are lucky enough to own a goat or some chickens they might add a little milk or eggs to their diet, but they very rarely eat meat. One woman explained that her family ate meat only twice a year, on the Muslim holidays of Eid and Shab-e-Barat. "Rarely," she said, "will we have any vegetables; we survive on roti and lentils, and occasionally some green chilies or tomato chutney." This exact balance of income and living costs sinks the family deeper and deeper into debt. If the work goes well the family breaks even; but any accident, illness, or natural loss due to rain makes the family lose ground.

Illness can be a catastrophe. If a family goes hungry in an attempt to pay for medicine, it can't work well and its income falls. Other life events have the same dire impact: a wedding, a funeral, the arrest of a relative (bribes will be needed), an accident, heavy rains, drought, *any-thing* that brings extra expense will increase the family's debt. The brick-making families are in a no-win situation. A few families *do* manage to get ahead of the game and reduce their debt. This is most likely in a year when a family's children are old enough, perhaps eleven or twelve, to work as hard as adults; the weather is good; and no accidents or illnesses occur. Of course, even these families will not be able to get ahead should their kiln manager be dishonest. If everything goes right some families might work ahead of their debt, but they can *never* win against a manager's false accounting.

There are two types of managers at a brick kiln. One, the overall manager, is called the *munshi*, and he reports directly to the kiln owner. Under the munshi are the foremen of different work gangs, who are called the *jamadar*s. Some large extended families of brick molders will have their oldest male as their jamadar, and he will deal with the munshi in the calculation of piece rates and debts. But at many kilns the jamadar is an independent contractor who recruits families to work in the kiln and receives a fee according to the volume of the bricks they produce. These independent jamadars often work at the most oppressive kilns, enticing families into the work with promises of good pay, and then working with the munshi to trap them in debt bondage. The ever-deepening debt and exploitation lead to increasing tension at the kiln. The manager and foreman intimidate the workers and prevent them from leaving. Armed guards are hired to patrol some kilns, and "disobedient" workers will be severely punished in order to frighten and coerce the workers. Human Rights Watch related the case of "Salman,"

> a Muslim Punjabi man in his thirties, [who] did not get along with the jamadar at a brick kiln near Kasur as the jamadar beat him on any excuse. He had a number of scars from this treatment. Once, in June 1993, after a disagreement with the jamadar, he was beaten unconscious and then locked in a small shed with no food for three days. After the third day he was brought out in front of the other brick kiln workers where he was hung upside down by a rope and beaten with a long stick. The jamadar laughingly told the other workers that this would be their punishment if they disobeyed him. "Salman," who was told by the jamadar that his outstanding debts were in excess of 5,000 rupees, tried to seek redress by complaining to the brick kiln owner. The owner laughed at him and told him he should work harder.[2]

As the debt builds up, the families lose more and more of their freedom. A remarkable insight into the lives of these workers comes from a former kiln owner named Zafar Iqbal. Iqbal inherited a brick kiln, but soon sold it when he discovered the horrific treatment of the workers. "The idea," he explained, "was that the worker should never have a single spare rupee in his hand so he can run away."[3] In the worst kilns, Iqbal said, "the brickworkers are completely dependent on the owner's will. Wives and daughters will be repeatedly assaulted by the kiln owner and his thugs, and no marriage can take place without his consent." A reign of terror can be instituted: "To intimidate them, the owner just comes along and smashes all the freshly made raw bricks, a whole day's work—for no reason." No bricks means no pay, and the worker can live in fear of even worse treatment. Zafar Iqbal confirmed reports of torture in some kilns—"If a young worker lifts his head or causes trouble, they will put his leg in the kiln oven for a second to burn it. This is common. They make the other workers come to the kiln and they make them watch."

That marriages require the owner's consent takes on special meaning when a man dies or runs away, abandoning his family and his debt. The wife inherits the debt, but the owner knows that she will never be able to repay it working alone or with her children. When this happens the munshi will put pressure on some single man to marry the widow or the abandoned woman and thus take over her debt. If the man gives in, the debt is transferred to his account. Muslim Sheikhs will accept this because it is their custom that a man pay "bride-price" to his wife's family before marriage, and taking on her debt is reckoned to be the equivalent. In one case that was publicized, a kiln owner tried to force a brickmaker named Yaqoob Masih to buy his cousin's wife when his cousin ran away from the kiln. No one will marry a woman who is too old or unwell, and the kiln owner will do almost anything to avoid writing off a debt. Some widows will be forced to prostitute themselves to the kiln owner or manager. As Zafar Iqbal explained: "It may be the only way to reduce the debt they owe."[4]

If an owner feels that a family is not working hard enough he may sell the family, by selling their debt, to another kiln owner. This can be the main way that kiln owners in remote areas get new workers. In the Punjab the kilns of neighboring Rawalpindi district are notorious for bad working conditions and bad treatment. For that reason kiln owners and munshis in the Punjab can control worker families by threatening to sell their debt to the kilns in Rawalpindi. When a family's debt is sold, the munshi from the new kiln will arrive in a truck with an armed guard and remove the family. This method of selling families is one aspect of their slavery. When people lose control of where they live and work, and are not able to protect themselves or their families, they have lost fundamental human rights. An essential part of the experience of old slavery in the American South was that even slaves on "good" plantations lived in terror of being sold "down the river," into the hands of a violent master. In the late 1980s a large extended family of forty-four people, mostly women and children, was sold from a kiln in Rawalpindi to the remote region of Azad Kashmir. At the kiln in Kashmir they were locked up and worked from dawn to dusk. They were given two meals a day, but no payment. After just over a year they were thrown out—a clear example of the new slavery: cheap and disposable slaves kept just long enough to get the maximum return.

Debt bondage is bad enough, but one more factor complicates the picture. It is a problem that affects the whole country as well as many individual kilns: the sexist and abusive treatment of women. It seems odd at first that sexism would have a disruptive impact on brickmaking, but it does. I discovered this as I spoke at length to brickworkers in Pakistan. Conflict arose time and time again when families fled a kiln, abandoning their debt and sometimes their possessions. After the families ran away, kiln owners would pursue them, take hostages, or bribe the police. When I asked brickworkers why they had run away they usually said it was because of dishonest accounting, a charge denied by the kiln owners. When we probed more deeply, a different story emerged. Repeatedly the brickworkers explained how the manager or the kiln owner had begun to molest "their" women, especially the young women of the family. Managers and kiln owners abused the power they had over the brickworkers, taking advantage of the confined space of the kiln and the constant presence of the women to approach and even assault the women. In the worst kilns women would be abducted and raped. It is a sad comment on Pakistani society that its almost complete segregation of men and women tends to place women in one of two categories. There are the women a man respects and protects, normally his family members; and there are all other women, whom many men are willing to violate if given the chance. For women from a minority ethnic or religious group, as are those in most brickmaking families, assault is even more likely.

In such a society men feel intensely protective of "their" women. They will go to great lengths to prevent their women from being seen in public and to stop any unrelated man from speaking to, touching, or sitting near a woman of their family. An important social division exists between families rich enough that the women may remain secluded in the home and those so poor that the women must work outside. Brickworker families are obviously in the second group, and for that reason they have to be constantly vigilant. Their concern is often justified. In Pakistan to be economically or socially deprived is to be vulnerable to sexual attack. And such attacks have larger consequences: in this macho world, with its codes of male honor, the insult of sexual assault can lead to bloody feuds that decimate families. A proud man is one who can protect his women. When the women of a family are molested everyone is shamed, especially the men. Seen in this light the flight of poor families from the kilns makes more sense. These families are trapped between the need for work and the need to preserve their pride. But in Pakistan shame is worse than hunger, and the brickworkers will not hesitate to flee a kiln where the manager molests their women. They feel that an assault on their women voids any work agreement they might have. But they do not want to admit the reason they have run away, for it is an admission of shame.

Our Policies Are Liberal!

As I traveled around the Punjab and Rawalpindi, I met a number of brick kiln owners. I am sure that I spoke at length with some of the better kiln owners, ones who were (reasonably) honest. At kilns that seemed to have more coercion, where the workers seemed frightened to talk, the owner or his munshi was more likely to dissemble, to refuse to talk, or to show me and my Pakistani colleague the way off the property. We were never threatened or roughed up at the kilns, but then we never said we were interested in debt bondage. By telling the kiln owners that we were economists interested in overhead rates, fuel costs, transportation charges, and taxation we learned a great deal about the nature of the brick business. Sooner or later the subject of the workers and the system (called *peshgi*) of advance payment and debt bondage would come up, since labor costs made up part of the kiln's budget.

Some of the owners were remarkably forthcoming about kidnapping or holding children against a worker's debt, actions they said were regrettable but necessary to prevent being cheated. In their view, many workers could not be trusted. One kiln owner told me this story, which he explained was "typical":

> I had a family of workers here, two young men and their mother. They owed me 3,200 rupees [$64] and wanted more. I wouldn't advance them more so they found another kiln owner who would take over their debt and advance them another 20,000 rupees [$400], which they claimed they needed for a wedding. There was no wedding, and one of the sons spent the lot on gambling and drugs (you have to understand that all the molders here are using hashish). After he had spent all their money, his mother came to me and begged me to take them back. She was a good woman, so I agreed and paid their debt to the other kiln owner. After they had been here a short time, the mother became ill. What with medical treatment and then the funeral after she died, they ran up another 20,000 rupees in debt. Then last week these two young men ran off. I

traced them back to their village and found their father, who agreed that his sons had cheated me. Their father led me to another kiln where they were working. When they saw me they asked if I would take them back, because their treatment at this new kiln was very harsh, with armed guards watching them. I had a talk with the owner there and decided to leave them for a while to teach them a lesson.

When he finished telling this story, speaking Urdu and with many gestures, he turned to me and said in English, "Our policies are liberal!" Yet within minutes the same owner was telling another story of unreliable workers that was resolved when he held two people (and three cows!) hostage against their debt. Perhaps by comparison his policies are liberal, for his workers did not seemed frightened and spoke freely of their situation. But it was difficult to become too enthusiastic when of the ten or fifteen little children who gathered around, many with skin diseases or hacking coughs, only one boy could be produced who actually went to school.

The owners often lay the problems of the kilns at the feet of the workers, particularly the minority Muslim Sheikhs and Christians. The president of a regional brick kiln owners association told me that the Muslim Sheikhs were wily manipulators of the peshgi system:

They just keep the debt as high as they can; they never intend to pay it off. If they get some money in their pockets, they just go off and spend it having a good time. When they know you've got a big order for bricks and the kiln is under pressure to produce as many as possible, they slow down and then ask for an even larger advance. Or they'll even stop working for a few days and say they've got to go off to a wedding or something— anything to get you over the barrel and get more money out of you.

The chairman of the All-Pakistan Brick Kiln Owners' Association also felt that outsiders didn't really understand the peshgi system:

You see, if we don't give the advances, the workers won't come. At the end of the brickmaking season, the workers go off to do casual labor.

They want the loan to tide them over this period, and if you don't give it to them, they'll go to another kiln. But the kiln owners want to reduce the amount they are loaning out. This is a lot of money to pay out before you even get any work from them. The money would be better spent buying coal in bulk. In fact, we'd like to end the whole peshgi system. It would be much more economical for us to pay the workers like they do in a factory.

Where is the truth in all this? How many kiln owners really feel this way? How many deal honestly with the workers? How many are using the peshgi system to enslave workers through debt bondage? The best answers to these questions have to be educated guesses. The national chairman of the kiln owners' association admitted that some owners were abusing workers and that some terrible problems had occurred, bringing shame on the whole industry. He suggested that 2 or 3 percent of kiln owners were exploiting and cheating their workers. Even the leader of the Brick Kiln Workers Union admitted that only a portion of kiln owners were dishonest, but he thought that 30 to 40 percent of all owners were cheating and enslaving workers. I found kilns whose workings seemed to be completely transparent, where they allowed us to photocopy all of their financial records and show them to the workers for confirmation. Analyzing the earnings and debts from the kiln that had the most complete records, I found that some families were increasing their debts and others were reducing or even completely paying off their debts in a season. And while some owners recognized that the piece rates were at the subsistence level, they argued that if they paid a higher rate they would cease being competitive and go out of business.

From my own study, I suspect that up to 30 percent of kilns regularly cheat their workers, if only in small ways. And from other reports and the testimony of many workers, I also think that up to 10 percent of kilns regularly practice serious abuse of workers. This is not as widespread as some human rights organizations have argued, but it still represents approximately 75,000 people being held through violence in debt slavery. Of course, we will never know the exact truth until a complete census is made of all kilns, ideally by some international organization. As Zafar Iqbal, the man who inherited a kiln, explained: "the Pakistani government labor inspectors come to the kilns once a year, take their bribe money, and go."[5]

There is another reason to be cautious in estimating debt bondage and abuse: the kilns are constantly changing. The records of one district kiln owners' association showed that half of all kilns started in the previous two years were owned by people who had never previously owned a kiln and who sometimes had markedly different attitudes than longtime owners. We should not be surprised at this fluctuation, for kilns are used to lower and level agricultural land. When the land is ready for irrigation, after two or three years, the kiln is shut down. The owner might start hauling soil to the kiln, but the added transportation costs would price the bricks out of the market. For a family that has some land and some capital (it takes about $24,000 to start up a kiln), brickmaking can be a reasonably attractive option. Lack of experience is not considered a serious obstacle, since an experienced munshi can be hired to get things organized and run the kiln. Some of the young and educated kiln owners I spoke with clearly thought that debt bondage was more trouble than it was worth. They wanted to keep their advances to a minimum in order to hold on to their money, and to concentrate on selling bricks.

The situation in the kilns is certainly altering, but it is difficult to say how much and in what ways. Another new variable is the arrival of migrant workers from Afghanistan. These families refuse to take any advance and equally refuse to commit themselves to working for the entire season. The kiln owners were unanimous in their description of these Afghan workers, who were said to work very hard and very quickly, sometimes producing twice the number of bricks per day of the Muslim Sheikh or Christian families. At the same time, all the owners and managers agreed that their work was sloppy and slipshod, complaining that they could not be trusted to make the high-quality bricks that many buyers wanted. By taking no advance the Afghans saved the owners money, but the managers never knew if they would still be working from one week to the next. "At least with the families on the peshgi system you know they'll be here when you need them," said one manager.

Bound by Eternal Debt

The peshgi system of debt bondage is hundreds, if not thousands, of years old in Pakistan. Rooted in the feudal relationship of landlords and peasants, over time it evolved into a system in which money advanced to a worker has the potential to enslave him. But this system, if operated honestly and without coercion, is not necessarily a bad thing for the workers. Working properly, it goes like this: A brick kiln owner will be approached by a family that is looking for work. Perhaps they have lost the right to land where they were traditionally peasant farmers or were turned off the land when their landlord mechanized, replacing peasant cultivators with tractors. They might even be refugees, driven from their home by the fighting in Afghanistan or the Kashmir. Whatever the reason, the family will be desperate, willing to accept even the hard and hot work in a brick kiln.

If the kiln owner agrees to take them on as workers, he will advance them a sum of money. This will be enough to settle them into the housing provided at the kiln, to get any tools they need, and to buy some food. Housing at the kiln can be attractive to the family, especially if they are homeless refugees. It is crude and basic, but it is a roof over their heads with water and fuel nearby. Having taken the advance payment, the family is now committed to working for the owner until it is repaid. There is no salary for the family: the job is paid by piece rate. The more bricks the family can make, the more they will earn. The more days they can work, the better; but if it rains, work stops and they earn nothing. A kiln owner or his munshi keeps a record of their advances and the number of bricks they make. Some families keep their own record of the number of bricks counted at the end of each day. But many families are illiterate and innumerate, and must rely on the manager's records.

The bricks made are credited against the debt, but since the debt is usually a large one, equal to several weeks' worth of brickmaking, the family soon will have to borrow more money from the munshi to buy food and other necessities. Depending on how many bricks they make and how much more they borrow, the debt may slowly diminish over a few months or it may slowly increase. If the family works hard and doesn't cause any trouble, the munshi and owner don't care if the debt is not being paid off, for it keeps the workers at the kiln. The owner needs to bind the workers because the kiln requires a constant supply of raw bricks. Firing up a kiln is expensive; if workers leave in the middle of a "season" the kiln will have to be shut down, with serious financial losses.

There are two brickmaking seasons a year, one ending in late December and another in late June. At the end of each season families can choose to carry their debt over to the next season, which begins about six weeks later, or they can try to get another kiln owner to "buy" their debt from their current manager and move them to a new kiln. Work stops in July and August because there are rains that make the work impossible, and in January and February because it is too cold and dark to dry the raw bricks before firing.

Under this basic system, the workers get enough money when they need it to maintain a subsistence lifestyle and a certain security of employment. The owners also know that they will have the workers they need when they need them. The work is hard but it is regular, and the housing it provides can be a first step up for a family that has been evicted or made refugees. With good luck and hard work, a family can work off its debt and perhaps move on to better things. If the family has a setback such as an illness or a death, the debt can be increased to pay for medical treatment or a funeral, and the process of paying back the debt begins again. An advance payment against promised work may be beneficial to both worker and kiln owner. To be sure, it is a benefit to the families of workers only when compared to destitution. If there were security of employment in Pakistan, or some provision for a living wage, no family would choose to work in the peshgi system. Although peshgi pays slightly more than working as a casual laborer, it still means living in very stark poverty. Binding a family in debt to the brick kiln is a sign of desperation, not the free choice of a free worker. Even when run honestly, the peshgi system is an onerous and oppressive way of life.

If run as I've described it so far, peshgi is not a form of slavery through debt bondage. It is a terrible way to make a living, it is hard on the children and the adults, but it is only as bad as many other kinds of work in the developing world—and it is better than having no work at all and going hungry. Unfortunately, the peshgi system doesn't always work honestly. It can easily be converted from a system of advance payments and piecework into a system of enslavement, turning a brickworker into a slave. Two methods are key. First, managers can dishonestly manipulate the debt and the piece rate in order to keep the family permanently in debt. There are several ways to do this, all made easier by a largely uneducated workforce. Most commonly the manager will simply record more debt than the family has. If the family asks to draw a small amount for food, the manager will give it the money but mark its account at twice that amount. Other charges can be entered into its debt as well—for spoilage, breakage, fuel costs, transportation, or taxes. At some kilns the workers are expected to buy all their food from the manager. The cost of this food is very high and is entered, sometimes inflated even further, directly into the debt. When it comes time to count the bricks the manager will undercount and deduct a fixed percentage as "spoiled." Later the records may be altered again, reducing the amount of money due to the family from the bricks it has produced. The result is a debt that can never be paid off, no matter how hard the family works. This is what the United Nations focused on in defining debt bondage in the Supplemental Convention on the Abolition of Slavery (1956). According to this document, debt bondage occurs when someone is working or providing services against a debt but "the value of those services as reasonably assessed is not applied towards the liquidation of the debt or the length and nature of those services are not respectively limited and defined." In other words, the family is trapped by dishonest accounting.

Thus families are tricked and held until they begin to realize that no amount of work is bringing their debt down. Families who know that they are being cheated by managers often start planning an escape. At this point the second factor comes into play—violence to enforce the bondage. As we've seen, children may be taken hostage as a security against the "debt." At some kilns, gates around the housing are locked at night and armed guards are posted. Hiring armed guards does add to the costs of running the kiln, but it is cheaper to hire three armed guards than to pay wages to fifteen families. If a family, or even one person, does escape, the manager and the guards set off in pursuit. In Pakistan the police are for hire, and they are sent after the escaped laborers. The manager's record of the family's debt legitimates family members' arrest, and the police return them to the kiln. Once there, the workers may be beaten up to "teach them a lesson," and the cost of paying off the police will be added to their debt.

When the basic contract of the peshgi system is broken, family members are working only for the food they receive and their lodging. They have lost their freedom and live under the threat of violence. As is the case with most types of new slavery, a legitimating device conceals their enslavement. If questioned, the kiln owner points to a record of debt and low productivity that justifies his control over the working family. And, like other victims of the new slavery around the world, members of the working family are disposable. The actual debt the family might owe is small compared to the profits the kiln owner is making from its labor. For that reason if the owner decides to shut down the kiln, or if the main workers in the family become ill or injured, the easiest thing to do is simply run them out of the kiln and make them homeless again. Of course, if the owner can "sell" the family and its debt on to another kiln, so much the better. Because the debt can be inherited, a clever kiln manager can keep a family trapped for generations, paying out just enough to keep members reasonably healthy but keeping their debt large enough to bind them permanently to the kiln. When this happens, the workers begin to adapt psychologically to their situation. The debt becomes a fixture in their lives as constant as the sun in summer and the rain in winter. Isolated at the kiln, they have only fading ideas of other opportunities. And for their children, there is little knowledge of any other way of life.

One other force works to bind them as well: their honesty. Like the Brazilian charcoal makers, even when cheated the kiln workers feel bound to pay their debts. Perhaps they are unsure of being cheated, but they know that they have drawn money from the manager for food. If they have had to face a family crisis of illness or death, they will have added a much larger sum to their debt. The poorest workers may have almost no possessions or prospects, but they do have their pride and their reputation—and they cling to them. It is important to remember that a good name is worth a great deal to these people. A casual laborer known for fecklessness and dishonesty will never be employed; a kiln worker with a reputation for bad debts will never be able to secure the advance payment to cope with a family emergency. They are squeezed between the rock of honor and the hard place of economic need.

It would be helpful to those of us trying to understand the new slavery if the brick kiln owners would divide themselves neatly into two groups: the honest operators within the peshgi system and those that subvert the system into debt bondage. Unfortunately, being human they won't do it and instead exist along a continuum from the perfectly honest businessman to the brutal slaveholder. This makes debt bondage all the harder to see and increases the difficulty of even estimating the scale of the problem. In some kilns a little dishonesty and miscounting stretch the debt and increase the profits of the owner, but do not threaten the lives or ultimate freedom of the workers. And there are two further complications that we must consider. First, no interest is normally charged on the family's debt. In many countries where debt bondage enslaves people, the levying of very high interest rates is the mechanism of entrapment. Indeed, interest rates of 50 percent a month leave little need for dishonest accounting, since the debt will grow inexorably beyond the control of the debtor. But Pakistan, like Mauritania, is an Islamic republic; and though Islamic law does little to prevent debt bondage, it does prohibit usury, the lending of money at exorbitant rates of interest. It is a baffling nicety that while brick kiln owners may violate the most basic of human rights, they do not charge interest on their workers' debts.

The second wrinkle in the system of peshgi and its related debt bondage concerns the movement of workers at the end of each season. At the end of June and the end of December when the kilns are allowed to cool and production stops, a transfer market in workers begins. At this time, most heads of families can get a slip of paper from the manager that lists their name, their job (raw brick maker, fire tender, oven unloader, etc.), and the total amount of their debt. Then they visit other kilns and negotiate with the managers to buy their debt and move them. Only the man is allowed to leave—the rest of the family remains behind as security. In those kilns where peshgi has turned into debt bondage, no workers may be allowed to leave. But in that case, the owner must feed them until the next brickmaking season begins. For the workers, the transfer market is a gamble. Kiln managers who intend to enslave workers will actively recruit families with promises of high piece rates and good conditions. A family may exchange the small dishonesty of one kiln for the violent oppression of debt bondage in another. Other workers may better their rates or conditions by making a good choice. Dishonest kiln owners can't lose on the deal: they either retain their workers for another season of bonded labor or they receive hard cash against a falsely inflated debt. The movement of workers at the end of each season also serves the owners by concealing the power they have; when families and debts move between kilns, owners can point to the "free movement" of labor.

Client, Servant, Vassal, and Slave

"Freedom" is a malleable concept in Pakistan today. In the recent past it had little meaning at all. In the seventeenth and eighteenth centuries, the free movement of workers was part of Europe's passage from feudalism into early capitalism. Another important change was the breakup of the rigid hierarchies that had structured and controlled lives. Landlord and peasant, aristocrat and artisan—in the feudal world all were linked together by strong personal obligations reaching up and down a strict system of social class. In Pakistan these hierarchies never disappeared. It is a feudal land overlaid with the thinnest veneer of twenty-first century capitalism. Many historians feel that modern society emerged when impersonal, but ostensibly rational, bureaucratic organizations supplanted the personal power of strongmen or clans. It is easy to forget when living in Europe or North America that not very long ago, in the feudal world, justice was dispensed by a local chief or strongman, not by a structure of law—and it was a "justice" that could be arbitrary, unjust, cruel, and more likely to serve the interests of the strongman than some abstract sense of fairness. This historical point is important to help us understand the context of debt bondage: in Pakistan feudalism is alive and well.

Imagine that some fundamental change rocks the town you live in and the power of the police and local government, of the public health authorities, and even of the national government disappears overnight. Who's in charge? If you are a shopkeeper, how do you stop people from just walking off with your goods? How do you stop people from taking your home? Who makes sure that the basic rules of commerce are upheld? You will find yourself relying on power and your personal relationship to the powerful. In Pakistan if you are a shopkeeper you are likely to have an armed guard at the door of your shop, and even street vendors club together to hire men with machine guns to patrol the sidewalks where they set up their stands. But the armed guard offers little protection. Real power belongs to the chief who controls many armed men, who can mobilize overwhelming strength when he must. And when all the power in a society is divided among such chiefs, the only safety is to be found in ties of mutual obligation with a strong chief.

Personal relationships become crucial in such a world. They are your protection and your livelihood, providing your prospects and your security. In Pakistan, especially in the rural areas, such relationships are of overarching importance. If you are cheated or brutalized, going to the police is generally no use. They are just another armed gang serving their own interests, and usually for sale to the highest bidder. If you are wronged you must go to your chief, the man who can bring his reputation and power to bear to right the wrong you have suffered. But how do you get a chief? How do you become the client or vassal of a strongman who will protect you?

Most people are born with a chief already looking after them. When power is personal, family becomes crucial. Blood ties are the immediate and critical first division between *us* and *them*. In Pakistan you *know* your family, all the way out to the third cousins and great-granduncles. You know who has power in your family and who doesn't, and you look to those that do have power for preferential treatment, jobs, and protection. Furthermore, arching over these power relations of families are distinctions of caste and religion. Caste position carries social power independent of financial status, and every Pakistani knows his or her own caste position well. The Sayids, lineal descendants of the prophet Mohammed, are at the top of society and often share the surname *Shah*. The ranking of castes descends through farmers and cultivators, businessmen and artisans, to the lowest castes connected with distasteful jobs such as working with the dead or cleaning the streets. Those jobs are often assigned to groups who were late converts to Islam or who are not Muslim at all.

The people at the bottom of the caste system, not surprisingly, are the poorest and least educated. In the brick kilns, the workers come almost entirely from two of the lowest castes in Pakistan: the Muslim Sheikhs and the Christians. The Muslim Sheikhs, often referred to by the denigrating term *Musselis*, pay the price of late conversion to Islam. Several times in Pakistan I asked people why the Muslim Sheikhs suffered such disdain and discrimination. Each time I was told it hinged on their being "converts." But, I would ask, weren't all Muslims at one time "converts"? Yes, I was told, but these Muslim Sheikhs were raw and untutored, having converted only two or three *hundred* years ago. Caste prejudice, like racism, is never logical. But if the Muslim Sheikhs are poor relations, Christians are beyond the pale. Some families are historically Christian; others converted from the lowest castes when Pakistan was part of the British Empire. All are considered both untrustworthy and simple. In describing their Christian workers, Pakistani brick kiln owners used exactly the same words I heard from racists in Alabama twenty years ago. "You have to understand," one told me, "they're not capable of planning or saving; they only live for the moment—if they get a little money they just drink it up or throw it away." The only thing missing was an insistence on their natural sense of rhythm. I was assured that the peshgi system worked in favor of these simple Christians, saving them from the responsibility of having to manage their own finances and keeping their wild impulses under control.

The Muslim Sheikhs and the Christians often lack the all-important link to a chief. Since they can never be related to men of power, their only way into a protective sphere is to attach themselves to a powerful person as a client. *Client* has a nice modern ring to it, like the relationship between an attorney and her or his client—but I mean something quite different. The old feudal word for a feudal client was *vassal*, and this is much closer to the reality in Pakistan. My dictionary defines *vassal* as "humble servant or subordinate, slave." Vassals, being on the lowest rung of the power ladder, are the most easily forgotten or thrown away. Some of the brickworkers wandered into the kilns when their landlords, the nearest thing they had to a chief, tossed them away as an obstruction to the modernization of their landholdings. Many, never aligned with a powerful family, just fended for themselves the best they could and suffered regular exploitation. To be a vassal is to have obligations to one's chief and to expect, at minimum, physical protection. In the brick kilns, the peshgi system is a means of creating the relationship of vassal and chief in a concentrated, if temporary, form. The kiln owner's obligation is immediate and quantifiable in the money advanced. In addition he offers protection against hunger and the elements. In return the family gives up its freedom and all of its productive labor for at least a season. Peshgi is feudalism translated into short-term capitalist production.

Throughout Pakistan there is an uneasy tension as feudal relationships and modern capitalism mix. Foreign media saturate the country, especially in the form of television programs beamed down from satellites, creating anger and frustration in the conservative Muslim population. While some politicians and intellectuals try to drag Pakistan into the modern world, fundamentalists blame all of the country's problems on the corrupting influence of the materialist, godless Western powers. To the traditionalists, the gyrating dancers on MTV spread a message of rebellion and consumerism that pollutes the minds of Pakistan's youth. The conflicts that erupt from this tension are not historically unique. As Europe left behind feudalism it embarked on hundreds of years of war, violence, intolerance, and terror. Predictably, the tension between feudalism and modernism in Pakistan also expresses itself in conflict and violence. In fact, it is difficult to find an issue of contention in Pakistan that is not soaked in blood. As more and more of the society involves itself in the religious or political violence playing out this basic tension, issues like slavery and debt bondage become obscured. The problems of brickworkers are ignored in the heat of holy war.

Putting the Feud into Feudalism

Conflicts in Pakistan can be intensely personal or impersonally political. For most people, most of the time, the shadow of violence is linked to family feuds. Reading a Pakistani newspaper is a sobering and puzzling experience. Every day there are reports of killings, of armed gangs blasting whole families, of kidnappings and rapes, and the same motive is given in every case: an "old enmity." The downside of the personal protection that a chief must guarantee is that he can never rest. Any slight, any insult, must be avenged, or the social power of the chief, and so his whole clan, declines. Every act of revenge calls forth another act of violence, and the cycle of death and destruction rolls on and on. The violent feuds between families and clans can last for generations. One man told me in all seriousness, "A man needs many sons, for some will always be killed in feuds." If the combatants had to hack at each other with swords and knives as they did in the past, perhaps the death toll would be lower. But the war in Afghanistan flooded the country with weapons: a Kalishnikov assault rifle costs about $100 in any gun shop. Automatic weapons and Toyota pickups make for lightning strikes with deadly force. As I was leaving Pakistan, the parliament was bringing in a law to require all motorcycle passengers to ride "sidesaddle" in an attempt to slow the number of assassinations committed from speeding motorbikes. One of the more horrific outcomes of this feuding is the high incidence of rape and torture of women. A sure way to repay an insult and to cause your enemy to lose face is to capture and rape a woman of his family. Next to the reports of murder in every day's newspapers are the reports of girls and women kidnapped and raped by groups of men. Though the press does not usually attribute these to an "old enmity," I was assured that these assaults were continuations of feuds.

Where are the social institutions that should work to stop this cycle of violence? Sadly, they are also engaged in their own little wars. In this

Islamic republic, where a state religion has tremendous power, religious leaders have little interest in working together to bring harmony. Running parallel to and interpenetrating with family blood feuds are the ongoing wars between Islamic factions and sects. In some neighborhoods, mosques with divergent interpretations of the Koran duel with the loudspeakers attached to their towers. All day and night the supercharged sound systems boom out prayers and sermons vilifying their religious opponents and calling on the "faithful" to shun or even attack them. The 1996 report on human rights in Pakistan reported a significant breakthrough: "No instance was reported in 1996 of a frenzied mob burning or stoning to death a heretic."[6] But it admitted that by other markers, religious intolerance and violence remained high. In the fighting between the Shia and Sunni sects of Islam the annual death toll is around 400. In one rural area in 1996, a series of insults chalked onto a wall led to a battle lasting ten days. Communication with the rest of the country was cut off as the two sides hammered each other with mortars and rocket launchers. The official government tally was 97 killed and 89 wounded; human rights researchers put the death toll at over 200.[7]

Such pitched battles are the tip of a sectarian iceberg. A constant stream of assassinations takes place as the groups target each other's leaders. In 1996 the Shias alone lost twenty-two leaders and officials to murder. In retaliation for such assassinations, armed gangs carry out indiscriminate attacks, spraying machine-gun fire into worshiping congregations or religious rallies. In 2003 grenades thrown into a crowd of worshippers in a mosque killed fifty-three. Six or seven mosques are bombed each year. One Sunni death squad arrested in Lahore was reported to have confessed to twenty-one murders over two years. With such high casualties, the sects have had to find ways to increase the number of new recruits. Because Pakistan lacks an effective state education system, militant sectarian groups have established their own schools. In the single state of Punjab there are over 2,500 of these *deeni madressahs,* or religious seminaries. By government accounts there are 219,000 children, mostly male, in these schools. In a country in which half the population is under the age of eighteen there is no shortage of young boys to instill with suicidal religious fervor.

At a level below the full-scale war between the Shia and Sunni are the violent actions by both these sects of "mainstream" Muslims against smaller, nonconformist religious groups such as Ahmadi Muslims, who are seen as heretics. Together with Christians and Hindus, they suffer both violence and regular discrimination. Laws against blasphemy and divergent religious practice, though in conflict with Pakistan's constitution, are effective weapons in the hands of zealots. In 1996, 2,467 Ahmadis and Christians were arrested under these laws and charged with such crimes as "preaching" or "posing as Muslims." Across the country Ahmadis and Christians also suffer systematic discrimination; they are refused jobs, loans, housing, and even mail delivery. Crowds of mainstream Muslims attack Christian churches and Ahmadi mosques, physically abusing worshipers, tearing down buildings, and desecrating cemeteries. One Muslim family refused to accept their son's conversion to the Ahmadi sect and went ahead and betrothed him to his cousin, a Muslim girl. When he had not relented two months later, the bride's parents charged him with deception and fraud in addition to the crime of adultery,[8] which in Pakistan is punishable by death.

Death also stalks government officials and the political parties, some of which are fronts for the religious sects. Virtually all political parties have armed wings and regularly attack each other as well as the government. Each year over 300 people die in attacks on political workers. In the largest city, Karachi, the summer of 1997 saw violence spiral out of control, as armed assaults and gangland-style executions were reported every day. The day before I left Pakistan, a bomb in Karachi destroyed the headquarters of one political party, killing more than twenty people. The level of violence forces government officials to tread very carefully around contentious issues. Constitutional guarantees of religious freedom or workers' rights are conveniently ignored by bureaucrats who fear retaliation from fundamentalists. The killing of lawyers and judges has paralyzed the judicial system: when a case might lead to a ruling that will anger the fundamentalists, the judges simply "take the matter under consideration" for years at a time. One lawyer, a human rights specialist who had taken cases on behalf of brick kiln workers, was singled out for "inducing young people to rebel against religion." Religious leaders decreed that she "merited stoning," giving zealots permission to assault her. Perhaps because of the armed guards in her office, none has done so yet

Confusion in and around the law has helped thwart any resolution to the pervasive violence. Like Mauritania, Pakistan has a schizophrenic legal system, divided between state (meaning civil and criminal) law on one hand and the Koranic law of the Sharia courts on the other. This twin-track system leads to constant fights over jurisdiction and precedence. Since both sets of law are considered legally valid and yet are sometimes in conflict, the pressure of fundamentalist or political groups will often decide the judicial outcome. Take, for example, two cases in 1996 that involved the right of women to choose their own husbands. Two adult Muslim women who themselves chose and married their husbands, and claimed to be acting as free individuals under the Pakistani constitution, were charged with adultery by their own parents. The courts, following Koranic law and under extreme pressure from fundamentalist groups, ruled that marriages undertaken without parental permission, even by adult women, were invalid. Moreover they ruled that the "police should investigate the cases and take them to their logical conclusion"—which meant charging the husbands with adultery, a capital offense.[9]

This legal confusion and the breakdown of law are important for our investigation because they create a context in which slavery can grow. If the only laws enforced are those pushed by pressure groups, if the law only works for those with power, then for the powerless there is no law. Brick kiln workers and other bonded laborers are without influence, political power, or economic clout. They are on the wrong side of divisions by religion and caste. Laws controlling debt bondage go un-enforced, and the law is even twisted to support slavery. When armed gangs can run roughshod over the legal system, the law loses any meaning. Pakistan is teetering on the edge of collapse into rule by force. The United Nations special reporter, Nigel Rodley, stated that "torture of persons in the custody of the police and paramilitary is endemic, widespread, and systematic in Pakistan. Torture is inflicted to obtain information, to punish, humiliate, or intimidate, to take revenge or to extract money from detainees or their families."[10] He then went on to number a horrific list of specific tortures, which included rape, electric shocks to genitalia, and use of an electric drill to bore holes into parts of the body. When the police become criminals, slavery can take root.

The violent enforcement of debt bondage by the police is a key element of the new slavery. In old slavery the written law supported the ownership of one person by another, but in the new slavery, where slavery normally occurs in defiance of written law, law enforcement turns criminal and aids not outright ownership but control. The government is supposed to have a monopoly on force and violence, to be used legally and only as a last resort. When the control of force is decentralized, spread to whatever group can control the most firepower (usually the police), slavery flourishes. This important theme is repeated as the new slavery spreads. In Thailand, Brazil, and now Pakistan, we find governments that prohibit slavery even as the police encourage and profit from it. A story told to me by a brick kiln worker named Ataullah makes clear how the police take part in the control of bonded laborers:

> *About five years ago part of my family went to work in a brick kiln in Rawalpindi [about 200 miles from their home in the Punjab]. They went there because we understood that the piece rate for making bricks was 100 rupees [$2] per thousand bricks. In the Punjab we were only getting 80 rupees [$1.60] per thousand, and so they thought they could do better. Altogether there were about twenty who went, counting the children: my father and mother, my brother and his family, and my sister and her*

husband and their four children. The total debt they owed the Punjab kiln owner was 70,000 rupees [$1,400] covering the ten or eleven of them who were working. I stayed at the kiln in the Punjab with my family.

They were happy that the kiln owner in Rawalpindi was willing to take over this debt and they moved there and set to work. Immediately they began to realize that they had got themselves into something that wasn't right. True, the piece rate was higher, but the soil was very different, much harder to work and make into bricks, and there were real problems with getting the water they needed to make up the bricks. They were making even less than they had been in the Punjab! Even worse, the kiln was like a prison. An armed guard kept anyone from leaving and the manager was very rough with them. Some of the people in my family can read and write, and soon they began to suspect, and then they were certain, that they were being cheated on their accounts.

The situation came to a head when two of my sister's children got ill. My brother-in-law asked the manager for some money [to be added to their debt] so that he could buy medicine for them. The manager refused, and just told him to get back to work. My brother-in-law was very upset about this and worried about his children, so he began to plan their escape from the kiln.

A few days later, after the morning's work, he told the guard he was going to get some medicine and took two of the children and headed for the nearby village. After a little while my sister took the other two children and a bundle of clothes and walked off toward the watercourse saying they were going to wash clothes. As she left the kiln she asked the armed guard to keep an eye on their hut, and leaving it open and all their other possessions in it, she and the two children went to meet her husband near the village. They then made a quick walk to a highway where they could get a bus back to the Punjab.

When they made it back to the Punjab they came and stayed with me and my family at the kiln, hoping to go back to work for the owner there. About a week later the kiln owner from Rawalpindi showed up with five or six men, and ordered my brother-in-law to come back with him. My brother-in-law refused to go, and when the Rawalpindi kiln owner tried to force him, all the other workers living here stood up to him and wouldn't let him take my brother-in-law.

Ten days later, at eleven o'clock at night while we were all asleep, a detachment of police burst into our house. They arrested me, my brother, and my brother-in-law, saying that we were thieves and that we were hiding illegal weapons (of course, we didn't have any weapons; we could never afford weapons and have no use for them). We were all handcuffed and beaten and then thrown in the back of a truck for the four-hour drive back to Rawalpindi. These police were from a station about twenty miles from the kiln in Rawalpindi and had no jurisdiction in the Punjab, but they were in the pay of the kiln owner, and they had paid some of the local Punjab police to come with them when they raided my house.

My brother-in-law was arrested, but my brother and I were never legally arrested, just handcuffed, beaten, and then put into cells. After a few days in the jail, the police took my brother-in-law to the magistrate and arranged to have him in custody for fifteen days while they "investigated." My brother and I were still locked up and we weren't allowed to speak to anyone. In the jail we were starved and roughed up. When the fifteen days were up we were all taken to the magistrate and my brother-in-law was released when a relative of ours came from the Punjab and spoke to the judge. My brother and I were now sent back to the jail while the police continued to "investigate." After another eight days we were taken back to the magistrate who released us since the police weren't bringing a case. We'd been locked up for a month.

From the court we were turned out onto the street without a penny, just the clothes on our backs. One of the court police asked us if we had any money to get home, and when we told him we didn't, he offered to drive us to the bus stop and loan us enough for the ticket. We couldn't believe our luck, and we shouldn't have, because when we got into his car he showed us his gun and then drove us straight to another police station. Here the kiln owner from Rawalpindi was waiting, drinking tea with the police chief. They locked us up again, and several hours later, after the kiln owner had settled his business with the police chief, they took us to the kiln in Rawalpindi.

This was crazy! I had never been to this kiln before in my life and I had never worked there; I didn't owe this man any money, and I told him this all had nothing to do with me. The kiln owner just said that was tough, he was holding my brother and me as ransom against my brother-in-law's debt. At the kiln they made me work and told me that if I tried to escape they would beat me or shoot me. At night my brother and I were locked up in a windowless room where the heat was terrible. Finally we convinced them to let us sleep outside, but they shackled us with chains to the beds where we slept. The other workers lived in a compound that was locked at night, and all day a gunman kept an eye on everything and threatened anyone who stepped out of line.

After three weeks like this, someone came from the Punjab. My family had managed to convince a landlord from there to pay off my brother-in-law's debt, and he then went to work for the landlord. My brother and I were released and managed to get back to our kiln in the Punjab. We'd been held prisoner for almost a month, starved, chained up, and beaten. My family was more in debt than ever since I hadn't been able to make any money the whole time, and they had had to spend money going back and forth trying to get us released. The police and the Rawalpindi kiln owner had done all this to us, but we knew that it was no use trying to get any justice. The kiln owner in Rawalpindi had got all of the work out of us and never paid a penny, and then had got back his original advance as well. I suppose he did have to pay out to the police.

Ataullah's story is long and involved, but it is typical. The links that stretch across family groups and involve people in the coercive and manipulative actions of the kiln owners match the entanglements that lead families into feuds and conflict. If Ataullah's family were not landless and powerless Muslim Sheikhs, who have already given up any hope of recompense, they would be plotting how to revenge themselves against the kiln owner. And it is just as well that they don't try for revenge, since retaliation would come from the police, who are happy to do any dirty work the kiln owner needs. With other armed groups around, the police don't have a monopoly on the use of violence, but they are the only group to use it with complete impunity.

Perhaps it is easier to understand the oppression of the brickworkers where the physical environment is harsh and the struggle to get by desperate. But in the Punjab, where I looked closely at life in the kilns, there is a natural richness that should provide enough for everyone.

The Soil of the Punjab

In many ways the Punjab seems an unlikely place to find such coercion and bondage. It is a land of tremendous fertility and a lush beauty. The hot summers and monsoon rains make possible two good crops a year, and the region has long been the breadbasket of the subcontinent. Rice, wheat, soy beans, lentils, maize, sugarcane, cotton, and mustard seed are the main crops. Lemons, limes, and oranges also grow in the fields. In the farm gardens are almost every type of vegetable you can think of, including watermelons, squash, okra, tomatoes, potatoes, onions, garlic, and tobacco. With alfalfa for fodder and room to graze the animals, the Punjab can provide a healthy living for its farmers.

Because it is so rich and accessible, the Punjab has been struggled over for thousands of years. Today most of the land is held by landlords, but the combination of the ongoing division of land between sons each generation and the effects of land reform has reduced the size of individual holdings. Until recently, most of the people in the Punjab were attached, like feudal serfs, to the land. The British in their long period of imperial control saw no reason to change this arrangement. When the country became independent in 1947 the region of the Punjab was split between Pakistan and India, and the partition brought great human suffering. A large population of Sikhs fled east into the Indian Punjab while Muslims moved west to the Pakistani side. This two-way exodus was marked by massacres, violence, and expropriations of land and property.

The time since partition has brought many changes to the Punjab. Fifty years ago the caste lines were still rigid. Muslim Sheikh peasant farmers lived lives of unrelenting poverty—never owning the land they worked and always serving the same landlord, generation after generation. The lower castes suffered extreme discrimination. Lower-caste people, including the peasant farmers, were not allowed to touch foodstuffs or to even sit on the same bench as someone of a higher caste (hence one term for these castes: "untouchables"). Today they are unlikely to be actively excluded from any type of work. There has also been an easing of discrimination in social interactions; Muslim Sheikhs now sit on the same benches, shake hands, and share tea with people from "higher" castes. In part, this change is due to the breakdown of the old labor market. The feudal system has changed as agriculture has mechanized and outside money is invested in farming. At the same time, the lower castes have become more aware of their rights. Some political groups have worked to educate and include the lower castes in the political system. Most of the brick kiln workers I spoke to had begun voting in the 1970s or 1980s, though many have now given up as they believe politicians have nothing to offer them.

Rapid population growth has also had a great impact. Improvements in health care and the increased amount of food produced by modern farming created a boom in the rural population. The results are dramatic: Pakistan has a higher birthrate and larger family size than India, and most telling is the fact that one-half of the country's population is under the age of seventeen. As one might expect, this means children everywhere, and the Punjab is no exception. Children are working or playing wherever one looks, though they are rarely in school, the education system of Pakistan having pretty well broken down in the countryside. It is a scandal that as Pakistan's population grows younger, less and less provision is made for their education. The extremely large number of children means that the per capita income of Pakistan is very low, around $450 per year. This is near that of Mauritania, but the lifestyles of the poor in those two countries could not be more different. The pervasive Mauritanian desert means that every scrap of food must be struggled for, and the birthrate is suppressed by poor nutrition and exhaustion. In the Punjab, as long as there are no droughts or serious flooding, food is sufficient, if not plentiful. The diet has variety and there is even some time for leisure.

In spite of the turmoil of partition and the upheaval of social change, the Punjab has continued to be fertile and productive. The great canal projects of the late nineteenth and early twentieth centuries have only increased that fertility. It is a region that can supply almost every need a person has—including shelter. The rich soil of the Punjab has another remarkable characteristic: most of it is good for making bricks that are heavy, dense, and durable. Almost every house, barn, or shed in the Punjab is made of brick, as well as the walls of animal pens, the paving of sidewalks, the floors of many houses, and the curbs around streets and gardens. Brick is everywhere, used to construct ovens, troughs, platforms and shelves, and benches and stairs. Wood is used very sparingly—for the doors and windows, for ceiling joists and lintels. A special thin and flat brick is used for roofing shingles on most buildings. It is highly appropriate for the climate: thick brick walls are cool in the oppressive heat, and I heard several Pakistanis complain of the baking heat they suffer in "modern" concrete buildings with metal roofs. As the universal building material, bricks are big business, yet they are still made in a traditional way that relies on thousands of Muslim Sheikh and Christian families.

In the late 1980s these families were caught up in a sequence of events that threw the entire brickmaking industry into turmoil and led some kiln owners to give up their business entirely. Not just in the Punjab but all across Pakistan, the peshgi system fell into disarray and it looked as if brickworkers' lives might change for the better. The tale, like so many stories in Pakistan, is a twisted one, full of characters who change from good guys to bad guys depending on who is telling it. We might call it the story of the Brickworkers' Revolution of 1988.

The Revolution of 1988

At the end of 1988, Rehmat Masih faced a terrible problem. Rehmat, a Christian brick kiln worker, was part of a desperate family of brickworkers who had been freed from a kiln where they had suffered terrible abuse. Three of their group had been recaptured by the kiln owners, and all of them felt hunted and threatened. They fled to the city of Lahore, but they had no lodging or food. Finally finding refuge with local labor activists and trade union workers, Rehmat contacted the human rights lawyer Asma Jehangir, and took the bold step of sending the following telegram:

To: The Chief Justice of the Supreme Court of Pakistan

We plead for protection and bread for our family. We are brick kiln bonded laborers. We have been set at liberty through the Court. And now three amongst us have been abducted by our owners. Our children and women are living in danger. We have filed complaint. No action taken. We are hiding like animals without protection or food. We are afraid and hungry. Please help us. We can be contacted through Counsel Asma Jehangir. Our state can be inspected. We want to live like human beings. The law gives no protection to us.

Darshan Masih and 20 companions with women and children

The chief justice, Muhammad Afzal Zullah, was moved by the plight of the workers and sent a messenger to the head of police in the Punjab ordering him to investigate the case personally and report back immediately. It is a mark of the relationship between the courts and the police in Pakistan that the head of police ignored the order. Instead he passed it to a deputy head who passed it to a district chief who passed it to a local police chief who gave it to a policeman. The policeman, now armed with an order from the chief justice of the Supreme Court, went straight to the kiln owner involved and handed the order over to him. Thus warned, the police and the kiln owner immediately brought a case against all the escaped brickworkers, charging them with taking 400,000 rupees ($8,000) in advance and then running away with the money. The police then found and arrested fourteen of the workers accused.

When the chief justice opened an inquiry on the case two weeks later, things became even more complicated. The three workers supposed to have been held hostage by the brick kiln owner were no longer detained, but had disappeared. Some of the brickworkers who came to the court seemed terrified of the police and barely answered the questions asked by the judge. Many were deeply concerned about relatives who were still being held in police custody. Two of the workers who seemed most frightened by the police were examined by the chief justice and were found to have scars and bruises from being beaten while in police custody. In spite of this, they refused to make a complaint. One of them, according to the court record, was "still terrified and virtually speechless when he was asked to disclose the circumstances in which he was allegedly detained and physically harmed."[11]

Under questioning by the chief justice, the policeman who had taken the court order to the kiln owner broke down and admitted that workers had been locked up and beaten by the police, who were paid by the kiln owner. The next day, more of the hostages showed up, and under questioning admitted that they were frightened and had been in hiding. By the end of the day all the hostages, whose seizure had originally occasioned the inquiry, were accounted for. The chief justice, however, continued the hearing in order to get workers, owners, local religious leaders, social welfare officials, and others together to work out some long-term measures for the "prevention of bonded labor in the brick kilns." Some of the welfare officials and brickworkers brought forward evidence that the police were working for the kiln owners and using "illegal detention, torture, and the registration of false cases." Then the groups fell into attacking each other. The laborers complained about forced labor and abuse while the kiln owners accused the laborers and the union of "cheating, malpractice and intimidation."

After a week of this the chief justice called a halt and issued a court order. It declared, among other things, that (1) the peshgi system should be stopped, except for an advance limited to one week's wages; (2) all outstanding peshgi loans were still valid, but all repayment should be put on hold for six months while the court investigated the industry; (3) no women or children could be forced to work in the kilns; and (4) all piece-rate earnings should be paid in full. All sides accepted this order and the court settled down to consider if any new law should be drawn up. But what seemed a victory for calm jurisprudence was shattered within a week.

A few days after the Supreme Court order, brickworkers all over Pakistan began leaving the kilns en masse. To the confusion of managers and owners, the workers produced an apparently official mandate freeing them of all debts by order of the Supreme Court. Some of the owners reacted violently, trying to force the laborers back to the kilns, but it was little use: virtually all the workers had walked off, and too few were left to run the kilns. Suddenly, the brick industry was shut down. Stocks dried up and some kilns went bankrupt and had to close. All kiln owners, whether they had abused workers or not, lost the money they had advanced as peshgi. The current president of the Brickworkers Union, Inayat Masih, explained to me that after reports of the Supreme Court's ruling had been published in the newspapers many workers in the kilns came to believe that the government had cancelled all debts. Some workers joined together and approached the kiln owners brandishing copies of the press reports of the ruling. Since the workers vastly outnumbered the kiln owners, and for once were acting in concert, there was little that could be done to stop them. About 500,000 families are thought to have left the kilns at this time.

Capitalizing on the publicity surrounding the case, the Brickworkers Union was making the most of the court order by transforming it into direct action. Four weeks after his court order the chief justice called everyone back to the inquiry. Confused by the walk-out from the kilns, the chief justice began to understand when, as is reported in the Supreme Court records:

The cause of the new development was discovered by chance in a complaint received from the labourers of a brick-kiln who made the grievance that despite the Court having absolved the labourers of all responsibilities with regard to their part of the contract and their liability to return the money having been waived by the Court, they could stay away from the work while the brick-kiln owner was insisting upon his rights under the contract. And they appended the copies of the information—rather wrong information supplied to them. (All Pakistan Legal Decisions, 1990, XLII, pages 534–535)

By this time, early spring 1989, the new brickmaking season was starting and workers began to return to the kilns. Since no one had been earning through the winter months, both owners and brickworkers were anxious to get back to work. The chief justice issued a new order, reiterating the earlier requirements and adding two important ones: (1) past loans made by the owners for such expenses as weddings or medical treatment were now void and should be considered a "donation"; and (2) all owners were ordered to give the returning workers a written assurance that they would not use any coercion or illegal police action against them. The "donation" plus the loans that the brickworkers still refused to repay represented a transfer of funds from owners to workers of millions of rupees, with the families with the largest debts benefiting most.

The mass walkout and the effective scrapping of all outstanding loans was a tremendous breakthrough for the workers. The chief justice called it a "revolution," stating that while it was unjust to the kiln owners, there was no other clear way to resolve the issue without demanding the impossible: repayment from hundreds of thousands of poor workers who had neither the means nor the will to do so. From the beginning of the 1989 brickmaking season the relationship of workers and kiln owners was, temporarily, on a new footing. Coercive owners had to restrain themselves, other owners started keeping better and more public records, and all over the country the piece rate paid to molders almost doubled as owners bid for workers (many families had used their sudden freedom from debt to walk away from brickmaking). If the Brickworkers Union had then concentrated on making sure that the provisions of the court orders were followed, debt bondage might have faded away. Sadly, it was not to be. The current president of the Brickworkers Union recalled:

> *After the brickworkers walked away from their debts, people started coming to the union from all the other jobs that use the peshgi system, like farming and carpet making. They wanted to be released from their debts as well.*

The sudden increase in demands from other sectors of the economy put a real strain on the Brickworkers Union. Just as they were trying to establish other programs for workers, such as schools for their children, they became the focus of international campaigns. Just when the brickworkers needed leadership to consolidate what they had won, their leadership was both overwhelmed by the work involved and by government hostility. One of the original supporters of the Brickworkers Union was the President of the Public Health Association of Pakistan, Professor M. Aslamkhan, a medical geneticist. When I interviewed him, Professor Aslamkhan explained how he had inspected kilns and treated injured and ill brickworkers and their families as a volunteer. But sometime after the "revolution of 1988," he explained that many of the original protagonists fell out with each other. Outrageous claims are bandied about as one side or the other is accused of failing the brickworkers or using them to further political ambitions. As I interviewed the various personalities involved in the "revolution," I felt more and more worried that I was being used to advance personal grievances, especially when the records and the accounts I was given failed to match up.

The rapid growth of the Brickworkers Union attracted a harsh response from the government. The feud that grew up between some organizers meant that public attention was diverted from questions of bonded labour and directed toward the in-fighting. Other organizations grew up to help workers exploited by the peshgi system, but over this period the Brickworkers Union lost ground. The current union has just 5,000 members and their president explained that after the experiences of 1988, they refuse to have anything to do with "intellectuals" or foreign human rights organisations. "It is best" he told me "if we just keep to ourselves."

The reverberations of the 1988 revolution continued, however, and in early 1992 a new law was passed abolishing bonded labor. *Bonded labor* was defined as the giving up by any laborer of his or her freedom of employment, or freedom of movement, or right to a minimum wage in exchange for a peshgi loan. The law specifically outlawed the use of coercion and the forcing of labor. The law also voided any debts owed by bonded laborers and forbade the seizure of any property against the debt. In addition, anyone found to be holding a bonded laborer ninety days after the law came into force could be punished by up to five years in prison. This extraordinary law came about through a coincidence of national and international interests. From the mid-1980s on, human rights organizations had been publicizing the plight of bonded labor in Pakistan, especially in the brick and carpet industries. The Pakistani government was feeling increasing international pressure to do something. Still, it is unlikely that the government would have responded were it not for dramatic events at home. In 1989 the country's military dictator, General Zia, was killed in a plane crash, and elections were held. The new prime minister, Nawaz Sharif, who reopened parliament and guaranteed a free press remained in office until April 1992. Just before his administration was replaced by an "interim government" the Bonded Labor Abolition Act was passed. A few months later Benazir Bhutto, a British-educated lawyer, became prime minister. More sensitive to international opinion, it was hoped that her government would devote more energy to human rights issues and enforce the new law. But to date no one has ever been prosecuted under this law.

All in all, it was an excellent law and it should have had an immediate impact. But because the police can't be relied on to enforce the laws impartially, relatively powerless groups need advocates. Kiln owners, wanting to prevent any loss of peshgi, cracked down on workers, increasing security at the kilns. In 1994 the Human Rights Commission of Pakistan found that "forced labour continued to be practised on a wide scale . . . estimated in the region of 20 million people."[12] Today, as I've described, families are again building up huge loans and being forcibly held against the debt. The 1989 increase in piece rates has disappeared with inflation. The workers' rights of free movement and fair wages are regularly denied. The peshgi system is alive and well, despite being illegal. At kiln after kiln I was told by owners and brickworkers that after the disturbances of 1988 and in spite of the passage of the new law, things were going back to the old ways.

Dirt, Money, and Brickmaking

What is going to happen to the brickmaking families of Pakistan? In many ways it is too soon to tell. Given the country's descent into civil conflict and worsening corruption, there is little hope of government action for change. Yet brickmaking in Pakistan is in one way fundamentally different from most types of the new slavery: it does not generate high profits. The raw material for bricks is dirt cheap, because it *is* dirt. It is the other inputs that cost. On average, bricks in Pakistan today sell for 1,000 rupees ($20) per 1,000 bricks. We've already seen that brickmaking families receive around 100 rupees ($2) for turning mud into 1,000 raw bricks. Then the haulers, the stackers, the fireworkers, the unstackers, and the transport workers all have to be paid as well. This adds another 200 rupees ($4) to the cost of making 1,000 bricks. By far the largest expense in brickmaking, however, is not labor but fuel. To keep a kiln running at 1,500 degrees twenty-four hours a day takes a lot of coal—hundreds of tons each month. The fuel costs for coal, wood, and oil add another 500 rupees ($10) per 1,000 bricks. Add to that the salary of the manager and the expenses for repairs, water, rent, vehicle maintenance, and so forth, and the kiln owner is spending 900 rupees ($18) to make bricks he will sell for 1,000 rupees ($20).

A profit of 10 percent to 15 percent is about as good as it gets in the brick kilns. Even if the workers are enslaved and paid nothing, the profit rises to 25 percent at best. Some kiln owners improve their situation by going into the construction business, using their kiln to cut out the middleman (the brick merchant). But for most owners a modest return is all they can hope for. With some 7,000 kilns in the country there is always enough competition to keep prices down, and overall demand is now slack. This low rate of profit, combined with the unstable and temporary nature of the business, puts Pakistani brickmaking into a special category of new slavery. Although the peshgi system arises from an economic reality that is grossly unjust and unequal, it is almost the only functioning source of credit available to the poor. It blends some of the owner-worker relations of feudalism with the transient economics of modern capitalism to create a kind of bondage halfway between the old and the new. For that reason it is hard to see what will become of the industry.

At first glance brickmaking appears to be very vulnerable to mechanization. After all, we are talking about *handmade* bricks. Modern brick-forming machines work ten times faster than the hardest-working family, and even the smallest automatic kilns can turn out 40,000 bricks a day, double the rate at which handmade bricks can be produced. But to date mechanization had not threatened to drive out the small producers. The cost of the new equipment is high, and only over the long run would an investor be able to undercut the rock-bottom price of handmade bricks. So the brickmaking industry is stuck: bricks are so cheap that even machines can't compete, but profits stay permanently low. Thus the brickmaking family, even at the best of kilns, is locked into a subsistence lifestyle. And in Pakistan's current economic distress, brickmakers who lose this work could quickly slip from subsistence to destitution. Here we are presented with one of the fundamental moral dilemmas of slavery: which is preferable, freedom with starvation or bondage with food?

Sexual abuse in the workplace, subsistence wages, increasing debt, the low profitability of the kilns, religious and ethnic discrimination, police corruption, and unenforced laws all combine to create a trap of poverty and, in the worst cases, debt bondage. Since all of these factors are getting worse, the prognosis for the brickworkers is not good. Were the fundamentalists who hold such sway in Pakistan to pay more attention to fostering respect for women, honesty in business, and protection of the poor—as the Koran requires—the situation might be different. If the government enforced its own laws, rooted out corruption, and brought the police under the rule of law, there might be hope. Even if the brickworkers could find the strength of their numbers and organize effectively and recover from the events of 1988–89, there could be dramatic change. But as conflicts increase there is no sign of change. The dismal prospect is all the more discouraging when we see that a short distance over the border with India, the situation is very different. In a country beset with many of the same problems as those faced in Pakistan, families are leaving debt bondage behind. The key seems to be our old friend the mule, and those forty acres.

6

—⁓⟨⦿/⦿/⦿⟩⁓—

INDIA
The Ploughman's Lunch

WHAT'S IT LIKE BEING AN INDIAN FARM laborer in debt bondage? You can get a sense of their daily life by trying the following experiment at home.

In the kitchen find a bag of rice, or even better some plain, unground wheat. Fill up a coffee mug four times with the rice or wheat. Now feed a family of five for one day with the grain you have measured out. For every meal you'll need to give each person only one-third of a coffee mug of grain so that it will last all day. If you are having wheat, you'll need to grind it into flour and mix it with water to make soft unleavened bread. If it's rice you can just boil it as usual. Repeat this recipe every day for the rest of your life.

There *are* some possible variations. Once every two weeks replace half the grain or rice with beans or lentils. From your backyard find some dandelions or clover and add the greens to the rice when you boil it (believe me, after a week or so, even weeds will begin to taste very good). And while you've still got some strength, grow some peppers or onions or some more beans. Then work even harder so that you'll have enough onions to trade for some cooking oil and salt. This work will continue for twenty or thirty years.

If you were really going to make the experiment realistic, you'd carry it out in the right conditions as well: you'd need to live in a one-room

195

mud hut with a dirt floor and carry the water for cooking at least half a mile before using it. In addition, cook your food and keep yourself warm by burning cow dung in one corner of your room. When one of your children develops a lung infection from the smoke, sell your grain instead of eating it and use the money to buy some medicine. For those days eat nothing.

This is slow starvation, a cruelly balanced way to get the most work from the bonded laborers for the least input. The different systems of bondage in India have been refined over centuries; these may be the most ancient and long-lasting of all the world's enslavements. Thus India can help us see how bondage began in human history. But much more important, it also gives us a glimpse of the end of slavery. India, which may have more slaves than all the other countries of the world put together, is making more progress than any other country toward ending bondage.

Abolishing slavery is an enormous task. In addition to the antiquated forms of bondage in the countryside, many examples of the new slavery are growing up in the cities. In India, bondage comes in a baffling variety. Given the country's poverty and the magnitude of these systems, it is astonishing that it is now making headway against slavery. What has it done that has eluded Thailand, Brazil, or Pakistan? The difference is certainly not resources: India is poorer than any of those three countries. And like them it is riddled with corruption and discord. For clearer answers, we must get away from the global measures of economic growth or gross domestic product and talk to the farmers who have been freed from bondage. But to find our way to their rice paddies, we have to look first at the country as a whole and its many slaves.

Their Daily (Unleavened) Bread

We can be so exact in our experiment above because one kind of Indian debt bondage has very precise rules. Each worker trapped by debt receives no money for his or her daily labor, instead getting just over one kilogram of wheat (usually), rice, or beans (rarely). In return for this daily supply of grain the laborers will work all day, every day, for their landlord. If they can find any time or strength they can try to grow some other food on the acre or so of land the landlord lets them use. Debt bondage in India is a long way from the peshgi system of Pakistan. Back at the brick kilns there was a piece rate paid for brickmaking and it was possible, though not likely, that a family could keep track of their earnings and their debt payments. In agricultural bonded labor in India, a family loses all freedom and receives no wage or piece rate. After taking on a debt or sometimes after just placing itself under his "protection," the family is provided with two things by the landlord: the daily bag of grain and access to a small plot where the family can raise other food.

This bondage is a survival of the oldest enslavement on the planet. Slavery as we know it began when human beings started to settle and farm instead of wandering as hunters and gatherers. What we often call the beginnings of human history are also the beginnings of bondage. About 11,000 years ago this settling began in three places: Mesopotamia, Egypt, and the plains of India. The beginning of agriculture led to the invention of new kinds of societies. These new societies were made up of people instantly recognizable to us: farmers and city folk, rulers and followers, soldiers and civilians, masters and slaves. The bureaucracies needed to manage these big concentrations of people were something like ours today. Some people sat in rooms and pushed paper (well, clay tablets anyway), while most people had to sweat. Food for the rulers, soldiers, bureaucrats, and masters had to come from the work of the people in the fields, and it was much easier to appropriate this food when these farmers were rigidly controlled. This was where the soldiers came in, "conquering" (enslaving) people and keeping them under control; so things went for millennia. Over the last three hundred years conditions in Mesopotamia and Egypt changed dramatically, but in spite of invasions and climate change, India's farmers worked on under the thumb of their landlords. It is a frightening and awesome thought that one of the bonded farm laborers we will meet later in this chapter might be the direct descendant of a bonded laborer from that time, an ancestor so distant that naming him would take three hundred "greats" before "grandfather."

Bonded labor in India is not just long-lasting, it is vast. The plough-man and his family are among millions of agricultural laborers who live in bondage, and hundreds of other jobs are filled by those living similarly. The tea you drink may have been picked by bonded workers in Assam. Jewelry, precious stones, bricks, timber, stone, sugar, fireworks, cloth, rugs—almost any handmade good in India might be produced by a bonded laborer. Making and selling food, carrying and hauling, caring for animals, prostitution, and even begging and thievery may also be done by those in debt bondage. No one knows how many bonded workers there are in India: estimates suggest millions, but whether the number is 2, 10, or 20 million is not clear. The government reports are notoriously low: many Indian states insist that no debt bondage exists within their jurisdiction despite repeated documentation to the contrary.

Of course, trying to describe anything in India as a whole is a problem because of the country's size. With a population of one billion (up from 350 million fifty years ago), it holds one-sixth of all the world's people. These people speak more than one thousand languages and dialects. There are about six hundred recognized "tribes" of indigenous people, with several hundred more subdivisions. These tribes together speak over three hundred languages. Some of the twenty-two states that make up India are as different from each other as distant countries, and traveling a hundred miles can mean confronting new customs, language, social and family organization, and lifestyle. There are very few things that are common to all of India, but bondage might be one of them.

With so many different cultures in one country it is not surprising that there are many variations on the theme of bondage. Some debt bonds are passed from parent to child. In other cases, a family gives a child over into bondage to a landlord or merchant, usually for jobs like cattle tending or domestic service. Some forms are just feudalism: laborers work for their master and get daily food in return. They are available for work at any time and don't have the right to work for anyone else or to leave without the master's permission. Widows often fall into bondage; in return for giving up any independent life or control over their work, they receive two meals a day and normally move to the master's household, often living in a cattle shed or some other farm building. The type of debt bondage that opened this chapter is called the *koliya* (or land) system. Here the worker gives up freedom of movement in exchange for the use of a small plot of land and a food allowance. We'll look closely at the lives of several families who are held in this kind of bondage in the state of Uttar Pradesh.

These varieties of bondage share certain characteristics. All the bonded workers live under the threat of violence. They have all lost the right to free movement and to sell their labor as they choose. They all have extremely long working hours and receive either no wages or wages far below the subsistence minimum. And it goes without saying that they are often treated as subhuman and have lost their dignity. Because these are often traditional forms of enslavement, there may or may not be high profits generated from the bonded labor. The sheer volume of bonded labor in India means that many variations of both old and new slavery exist side by side. Some types use custom and superstition to control the enslaved person.

Consider the case of the *devadasi*, a young woman who is married to a god, which is not as pleasant as it might sound. Poor families, in an attempt to appease local gods and guarantee a happy future, will sacrifice a daughter by "marrying" her to one. Once married the girl is declared a "saint" and must move into the local temple and care for it. She must not do any other work, cannot leave the village, cannot "divorce" and marry anyone else, and is in the control of the men who run the temple. For centuries these men have turned the girls to prostitution, so that the temple doubles as a brothel. Any female children born to the "saints" are raised to be *devadasi* as well, and the women live out their lives as enslaved prostitutes, while the men who run the temple pocket the profits.

Children also form a large part of the bonded workforce in India. A particularly well-known group are the children that produce fireworks and matches around the city of Sivakasi in the state of Tamil Nadu. Some 45,000 children work in these factories, making this perhaps the largest concentration of child laborers in the world. Between 3 A.M. and 5 A.M. every morning, buses from the factories visit the villages in the surrounding countryside. Local agents have enlisted the children, whose ages range from three and a half to fifteen, paying an advance to their parents and creating the debt bond. The agents make sure the children are up and get on the bus for the trip to the factory, where they will work for the next twelve hours. A study by UNICEF, surveying thirty-three buses, found 150 to 200 children jammed into a single bus each day. They will not be back in their villages until after 7 P.M. In the run-up to the big Diwali (festival of lights) holiday, the factories extend their hours and are in production seven days a week.

The children roll and pack the fireworks in dark and dingy sheds. The gunpowder mixture is corrosive, and over time it eats away the skin on a child's fingers. When this happens blisters form and the child can't work, as the chemicals burn quickly into the exposed flesh. To wait for the blisters to heal takes five or six days, but to stay off work for that long would mean being fired. Instead, a hot coal or a lit cigarette normally is applied to the blister, bursting it and cauterizing the wound. In time the children's fingertips become a mass of scar tissue. The powdered potassium chlorate, phosphorus, and zinc oxides also fill their lungs and lead to breathing problems and blood poisoning.

The *devadasi* and the children making fireworks are just two examples of the many types of bonded labor in India. Describing the hundreds of variations of bondage across the country would fill many books, and the lives of those enslaved spell out millions of tragedies. To challenge the rise of the new slavery we have to understand India, but it is so big and there are so many kinds of bondage—where should we look? I chose to focus on Uttar Pradesh.

Where Death Transports the Soul

If one state can be said to best represent India, that state is Uttar Pradesh. It is one of the most populous and varied areas in the country, dominating much of the culture and politics of India. It is the heartland of the Hindi language, the main indigenous tongue and the official language of government. Its northern end touches China through the Himalayas, where the sacred river Ganges has its source. At the other end of the state is the sacred crossing of the Ganges at Varanasi, the place where Hindus believe death carries the soul over to its final liberation. The area was one of the cradles of prehistoric agriculture. Holy places of Hindus, Buddhists, and Muslims are all located there. And it is a part of India most foreign visitors will have seen. In the city of Agra, the capital of all India under the Moghuls, is the famous Taj Mahal. Further to the east is the city of Allahabad, home of the Nehru family, which has provided India with three prime ministers in the last fifty years. For the tourists riding to the Taj Mahal the scenery of Uttar Pradesh, flat and rolling fields tilled by workers ploughing behind oxen or irrigating rice paddies, is the typical view of the Indian countryside. What the visitors rarely realize is that the picturesque farmers they are photographing are likely to be in bondage.

Bondage is endemic to Uttar Pradesh. It goes by a number of names and can be any of the many types noted earlier. Men, women, and children work in bondage in agriculture, stone quarries, brick kilns, mines, and matchbox and firework factories; they make cigarettes, brassware, glass bangles, pottery, and carpets. Especially in the north of Uttar Pradesh, where the rural landlords have great power, families can be broken up when the women or children are auctioned off against a man's debt. No one knows how many bonded workers are in the state. One study looked at 235 villages and estimated the total at 500,000 bonded laborers. However many there are, most are caught up in farmwork and are from the lower castes (officially called "scheduled" or "backward" castes in India). Their debts tend to arise from one of two problems: either an urgent crisis—illness, injury, or famine—or the need to pay for death rites or marriage celebrations. Of course the debt may have first been contracted some generations ago. In fact, the families of the bonded laborers and the landlords may have been locked in this parasitic relationship for centuries.

Almost all of the landlords come from the upper castes and own significant parcels of land. Almost all of the bonded laborers are illiterate and own no land, and those that do often have to mortgage it (and ultimately lose it) against their debts. With such a large proportion of the rural workforce in bondage, there are many possible outcomes. Just as there were "good" and "bad" plantation masters in the American South, there are "good" and "bad" landlords in Uttar Pradesh. Most do not allow their laborers to leave their land or to work for anyone else in their free time. Some are careful to maintain the families of their workers, while keeping them in long-term dependence. Others brutalize and abuse their laborers, and sexual assaults on women are not uncommon.

In the isolated northern part of the state, near the mountains, the landlords have virtually complete power over the landless workers. The upper-caste Brahmins and Rajputs hold all the official positions, own the land, and are the moneylenders. Farmworkers in debt to them endure the system described above—giving all of their labor and receiving two meals a day and the use of a plot of land. Since the local magistrate is a landlord, the law is routinely used to control the workers. False charges will be laid against free laborers and the fines levied against them can only be met by borrowing and becoming bonded. The fines are heavy on the bonded laborers as well, who might be punished for "leaving the farm" or "stealing a potato," and their payment keeps the workers' debt high. To compound the problem, paying bride-price is traditional in this region. Men must go to the moneylenders for the cash they need to marry. In this way young men whose parents are bonded, but who have not been bonded themselves, are drawn into the game. These mountain regions also supply a large number of the prostitutes to the lowland cities. In a horrific irony, men sometimes sell their wives into prostitution in order to get the money to pay off the debt they took out to marry them. This practice has burgeoned in the last fifty years as the victims of old-style bondage try to improve their lot by selling women and girls into the new slavery of city brothels.[1]

Throughout Uttar Pradesh, if a man runs away, his belongings, sometimes even his children, will be seized and auctioned. The debt owed is then inherited by the oldest son, whose labor is counted against the debt interest. Unlike Pakistan, where there are religious rules against charging interest, in India interest rates can be as high as 60 percent; but the basic arrangement is that *all* the worker's labor equals the interest and the principal must be paid in cash. As debts increase, more and more of the family members are taken into bondage by the landlord, with the women and children doing housework, gardening, and caring for animals. The laborers are required to put their thumbprints (the standard method in India for the illiterate to "sign" a document) on "contracts" and account books that the landlords hold in case of any outside inspection. Being illiterate, the laborers have no idea what they have "signed."

Occasionally large projects in Uttar Pradesh require special efforts on the part of the landlords and officials. Construction projects need more workers than can be spared from the fields, and local officials will import families from other states in much the same way as the Brazilians are recruited from great distances to service the charcoal industry. In a recent case nearly one hundred bonded laborers were found locked in a tin shed measuring 60 by 15 feet.[2] They received little food and water, and many were ill and receiving no medical care. Family leaders who had been advanced 600 rupees when they left the state of Orissa were then charged for their transport to the construction site.

The nominal daily rate of 16 rupees did not come anywhere near reducing the debts, which increased as the officials charged the families for food. The workers were under armed guard during the day and imprisoned at night. Even the Indian government's own National Project Construction Corporation in Uttar Pradesh has been indicted for enslaving workers in this way.

By the Banks of the Magic River

On the southern end of Uttar Pradesh, in the Ganges River valley, is the city of Allahabad. The city was built at a site sacred to all Hindus, where three great rivers come together. Here the Ganges and the Yamuna join the magical, though invisible, "river of enlightenment"—the Sarawasti, which wells up from mystical regions. Their confluence is a holy place, one of the great pilgrimage destinations in India. The religious festival held here is the largest in the world, attracting more than 3 million visitors who set up vast tent cities on the floodplains and riverbanks.

About thirty miles from the city, a mile off a state highway, is the village of Bandi. The thirty miles to Allahabad, with its university, office buildings, and factories, might as well be three thousand for the difference between the two places. Here, the modern improvement is the three hand-pumped wells that the government recently installed in the village. *Village* is in fact almost too grand a word to describe Bandi; *settlement* might be closer to the mark. Its thirty-five scattered households bring the population to around 225. There is one small shop, which is attached to a little mill that grinds wheat, husks rice, and extracts oil from mustard seed. "Civilization" is not too far away, since along the state highway are a number of stores and the chance of a bus to the city if you have money. The focus of the place is a small government-built lake, where people bathe, wash clothes, fish, water and wash their animals, and draw water. There are usually a few water buffalo lying about in the water as well. On one edge of the lake the villagers have built a small brick Hindu shrine.

Bandi is a fortunate village. It is not too far from the river, and the irrigation canals serve part of the land nearby. The lake also waters the fields that make up most of the village itself. The land is divided irregularly into small plots of just a few hundred square yards, which are bordered by raised banks just wide enough to walk along in single file. Over 70 percent of the land is held by two landlords, one of whom also owns the shop and mill. Farming is the only game in town and almost everyone works for the landlords.

In Bandi I met a number of bonded laborers, and over a period of several weeks one summer I learned about their lives. A young Indian researcher, Pramod Singh, had spent time in the village and prepared the workers for my visit. Since they were expecting me and had come to trust Pramod, many of the laborers spoke frankly to me about their situation. Some of the children remained frightened of me, as I was the first (tall and sun-burned red) white person they had ever seen. Other children just had to laugh at this ungainly thing in funny clothes who was constantly drinking from a water bottle in the ferocious heat. Most of the villagers were welcoming and gracious in that way of the very poor which shames the miserliness of the well-off. The diet I described at the beginning of this chapter is the one they eat, yet they still offered to share it. Many of the workers I met were on the koliya system, receiving their kilogram of grain every day and the use of a plot of land in exchange for all their labor while they remained in debt. Some of them had been born in debt and fully expected to die in debt. Others had freed themselves, and their stories are especially important because they show a way out of bondage.

Village Tales

BALDEV When I first met Baldev he was ploughing. Behind a small single ox he guided a primitive plough up and down a small plot. Its wooden blade dug a shallow groove in the soil, barely turning it. The soil would have to be ploughed many times to make it ready for planting. Much of his life is spent like this, for Baldev is a bonded *halvaha*, a ploughman. His landlord calls him "my *halvaha*." The morning I met him Baldev was working hard, but was having a good day. To demonstrate that the day was going well, the first thing he told me was that he had eaten breakfast. Breakfast is a rare meal for Baldev, but since he needed strength for ploughing, he had eaten some soaked chickpeas boiled with a little salt and a green chili pepper. When we spoke it was about 11 A.M. and he had been ploughing since 7 A.M. In another two hours he would stop work and lie down through the hottest part of the day. From 3 to 7 P.M. he would be working again.

As we shared our water and sat on the bank at the edge of the field, Baldev squatted in front of us. As a member of the Kohl caste he was "untouchable" for upper-caste people and out of politeness he wouldn't sit next to me—he assumed I must be upper caste, in spite of my assertions otherwise. I asked him how long his family had lived in Bandi, and he replied:

We have always lived here. I do not know about before my grandfather,
but he said we have always lived here. My grandfather was halvaha
to the landlord, and later my father was also his halvaha. *They were*
both bonded by debt—my father by his father's debt, I don't know about
my grandfather's debt. It's a regular thing. Kohl people like us have
always been bonded to Brahmins like my master. That's the way it
has always been around here.

Does everyone know that you're a bonded laborer?

Oh sure, everyone around here anyway. Like I said, my family's worked
for the same master for a long time. It's a small place after all, and every-
body knows everybody else's business. I don't know if anybody in the city
knows, or the government inspectors. I thought maybe you two were gov-
ernment inspectors at first, when I saw your clothes. But I doubt they care
much about what goes on here. Anyway I inherited my father's debt so I
always knew I'd be a halvaha. *I guess everyone did.*

How big is your debt?

Well, when I first become halvaha *to my master, that was about fifteen years ago, I don't remember what it was then. Now it is about 900 rupees [$25]. Once we went to my relative's wedding and to get there and to buy new clothes I borrowed 500 rupees; that was a few years ago. A couple of times I had to borrow some money to buy medicine when one of the children was sick. Mostly, though, it just adds up from little amounts that I borrow to buy things like fertilizer. My master gives me two* bighas *[about three acres] of land to use and that's where I grow our beans and lentils. To get a good crop I have to use fertilizer. I could borrow fertilizer from the master instead of the money, but then I'd have to repay one and a half times the amount when I harvested. Any kind of thing like that, seed or pesticide, you have to repay one and a half times at harvest. I also have to pay for the irrigation for the field; that's a charge to the local government that runs the canal. If I don't have the money when it is time to pay I have to borrow from the master, because if you don't pay for the irrigation they won't let you have any more water for your crop and then you lose it.*

Can you make anything from this crop?

Well, that's what keeps us from starving. I have to put every spare minute into caring for that crop because I sell part of it to get the other things we need. See, I can grow about 400 kilograms of beans and lentils on my plot. They sell for about 10 rupees a kilogram. If I was able to sell it all that would bring in 4,000 rupees [$110], but I don't make anything like that amount. It takes about 60 kilograms of seed for planting and that costs about 15 rupees per kilogram. Anything I borrow from the master I have to pay back 50 percent more. If I've borrowed the 60 kilos of seed from the master I have to pay back 90 kilograms. The same for the fertilizer and anything else. Some of the crop we keep back to eat through the year, and the rest I sell.

What do you do with the money?

That's what pays for everything else. There are four things that we have to buy: oil for cooking, that's about 10 rupees a week. Then there's salt—

it's pretty cheap, we spend maybe 4 rupees a month on that; vegetables cost more, about 20 or 30 rupees a week. We burn kerosene for light, but that's only 6 rupees a month because when it's dark we go to sleep and don't use the lantern very often. When we start to run out of money we don't buy vegetables and just eat the grain we get from the master and any lentils we've saved.

At harvest time, when I've sold my crop, there is the one big expense of the year. That is when we buy new clothes. We only have one or two changes of clothes, and after a year the old clothes are completely worn out; anyway, the kids outgrow their things as well. There are five of us, so that is a lot of money, more than 1,000 rupees [$28]. The only time I have that much is when I've just sold my crop. Most years the money runs out before the next harvest; sometimes we can make it without borrowing, but sometimes we have to borrow.

Later that evening we stopped by the house Baldev shares with his wife, Markhi, and their three sons. Their house is just one room, about 7 by 15 feet. The walls are made of mud packed onto a frame of branches. The roof is thatch resting on poles. Hanging from the roof poles where animals can't get at them are a few bags of beans or lentils and any herbs they have found and brought back to dry. There is a low entrance, but no door to shut, and two small openings high in the walls serve as windows. In one corner of the dirt floor is a small stove also made of mud; it has no chimney pipe and the smoke pours into the room, rising to blacken the thatch. Markhi cooks all their meals on this little fire of cow dung and brush. All of their possessions would probably fit onto their one bed, a rope-bottomed frame five feet long with no mattress. There are a few pots, some hand tools, a couple of shirts, a jug, a lamp, and a pair of sandals. Around the front of the house they have grown a fence of thorn bushes enclosing a space of about 100 square feet with a shade tree. Much of their home life is spent under the tree, their bed serving as a bench for sitting. Often in the hot weather they sleep there as well, where they might get a little breeze.

About fifty yards away is an open well where Markhi hauls up water with a rope and bucket. I asked Markhi if she had grown up in the village:

No, I'm from Chandpur in Madya Pradesh [a neighboring state about sixty miles from Bandi]. My father died when I was a little girl. He was bonded to a master there. We lived there just the way we do here. About ten years ago I came here and married Baldev. Some relatives arranged it. I've been here all the time since then.

What kind of work do you do most days?

Besides the cooking and washing, I work in the fields like Baldev. I do a lot of weeding, pulling up weeds from the master's fields. I'll do planting and sowing, or harvesting when it's time. Almost anything except ploughing; only Baldev does ploughing. I have to keep the boys busy as well. There are green leaves and things that can be gathered from some of the plants and weeds that grow in the fields that we can cook up. I get them to gather these things.

Do they go to school?

No, not any more. We sent the older two to school a couple of years ago, but it didn't do any good. It didn't seem like they were learning anything. Sometimes they would just leave and go play in the fields. To buy paper and things for school was really expensive, so now we keep them home. They help me here.

Baldev started pointing around the house, and added:

Anyway there's plenty to do here. See these mud walls—I have to repack them twice a year. In about two weeks I'll have to start. They have to be repaired before the rainy season starts, or when the rain comes the walls just melt and fall off the frame. You have to be ready for the rains: you have to have your field ploughed, and your walls ready. And then every two or three years you have to put new thatch on the roof. The thatch only lasts that long. This is a problem, because the only person who grows thatch around here is the landlord, so you have to get it from him or borrow the money from him to buy it somewhere else. When the thatch is no good you can't wait, or when the rains come everything is ruined. This is what happens, even if I get a really good crop there's always more going out than coming in and I have to borrow.

I asked Baldev if he had ever paid off any of his debt.

No. It has just built up little by little over the years. With the children there is always something, and if anyone gets sick we have to buy the medicine. Sometimes I don't have enough money in the spring to buy the fertilizer I need, so it just goes up and up. Maybe when the boys get older they can work and we can get ahead. I'll just keep at it till the debt is paid, and when I'm too old to work my sons will take care of me.

What about your landlord? How does he treat you?

Well, I've known him all my life; my father worked for him too. He is a pretty old man now. He's always given us the grain we should have and treated us all right, but in the last few years he has become very strict. Now if someone comes to the village, maybe from the government or something, he won't let me meet them. When he knows someone is coming he sends me off to do some work. He tries to keep us here and he's started ordering me around a lot more—just "do this, and do that." Of course I have to do anything he tells me.

Later that day I had a bizarre interview with Baldev's master. Up on the highway to Allahabad he kept a small bicycle repair shop where we stopped to chat with him. An old man, Baldev's master became more and more flustered and agitated as we spoke. First he told us that he farmed sixty acres by himself except for the two acres that he lets Baldev use. Then he said that Baldev's father worked for someone else and that Baldev had only been in the village for three years. When we asked about the amount of grain grown on his land and on Baldev's plot, he said that he had never let Baldev use any land and then stated that Baldev doesn't work for him at all. A moment later he said he paid Baldev 100 kilos of grain every season. The contradictions piled up as he became increasingly nervous, and finally we just gave up and left.

We had earlier spoken with other landlords and found them smooth rationalizers of the koliya system, full of official doublespeak and acting out their warm feelings toward their "attached" workers. Baldev's master seemed to be one of the last of the very old school, a man unable to comprehend that the ancient system had to change at least its surface appearance.

It may seem as if Baldev and Markhi are just very poor sharecroppers, like other very poor farmers in the developing world. But we should not be fooled by the lack of overt violence: these are slaves. Baldev's master sees him as property, a docile beast of burden. The koliya system has even greater stability than the old slavery of the American South. Obviously, this is not the vicious and brutal short-term bondage of the new slavery, but what it lacks in violence it makes up for in hopelessness. Baldev and Markhi are completely resigned to their fate. Violence is rarely needed to keep them enslaved. Those who suffer the new slavery, like the women in the brothels of Thailand, sometimes abandon any hope of freedom, but Baldev was born without hope. Living constantly on the edge of hunger, he and his neighbors work themselves to an early grave. They rarely complain. They told me their stories with complete passivity. After generations of being *halvaha*, they see little alternative. Baldev believes that as long as he can plough, his family will at least eat. But the situation around Baldev is changing and his master has good reason to keep him hidden away. Other families in the village have come out of bondage through government assistance. Baldev is the last ploughman this landlord has, and without him the landlord would have to pay the going rate for farm labor to get his fields ploughed and harvested.[3] The story of Baldev's neighbor Munsi, however, suggests that his master might make a profit by "rehabilitating" him.

SHIVRAJ AND MUNSI Shivraj's wife ran inside their house when we came into the yard. She pulled a thin cotton cloth over her face and then peered at us from around the doorway. For our entire stay she would duck inside if we glanced toward the house; meanwhile her friends stood just outside the thorn fence and silently watched us with their faces covered. A little girl perhaps three or four years old, Shivraj's grand-daughter, stumbled and giggled around us while we talked. She did all those things that toddlers can do to embarrass adults when company comes: drooling on our shoes, poking at our clothes, then standing in our midst as we spoke and urinating on the ground. One of Shivraj's white Brahma yearling cows hovered nearby as we spoke, catching the scent of the charred and salted grain we were offered as a snack. Shivraj is a bonded laborer like Baldev, but a little better off. He is also older at forty-five, and has built up a few possessions. But he still carries a debt that he can't get free of:

> *I've always lived here, so did my father and grandfather. We've always been here and we've always worked for the same master. When my father died I had to take over his debt; that was almost thirty years ago. When he died he owed the master 1,200 rupees, a lot of money!*

Have you ever been out of debt?

> *No, never, neither were my father or grandfather. But it goes up and down. I started with the 1,200 rupees my father owed, but I had to bor-row more to get started. About twenty years ago was the largest debt I've ever had; it reached 2,500 rupees. I was young then and not so careful. We also had to borrow for family occasions like when my son got married. Two or three years ago I got it down to under 200 rupees [$6]. It was almost to the point that I could pay it off, but we couldn't make it to the next harvest. I had to borrow to get the fertilizer and seed for planting, so now I owe about 1,400 rupees [$39]. About 500 rupees of that is what I owe the government to pay the water charges for irrigating my plot. I should be able to pay that back from my harvest. In fact I have to find a way to pay that, because if I don't they won't let me have any more water for my crop. But the way things are going it looks like after I pay that I'll need to borrow from my master to buy fertilizer for this year. My master charges me interest on the money I borrow to buy fertilizer and what I owe him for having his tractor plough my field. I have to pay him*

5 rupees every month for every 100 rupees I borrow. At this rate it can take me two or three seasons to pay off the debt for one planting, but by then I've built up more debt for the next season, and the total debt keeps growing. We really haven't been able to keep up since my son left three years ago.

What happened? Why did your son leave?

He just disappeared, I don't know why. He left his wife and daughter, that's this little girl, and just took off. We were worried sick, we looked everywhere, but we could never find him. He was about twenty years old then, and when he and I worked together we could make enough to get ahead of the debt; but since he left I've had to support his wife and baby as well.

At this point Shivraj stopped and looked thoughtfully at us as if trying to decide about something. In a few moments he called to his wife in the house and asked her to bring something out. When she came she brought a letter, creased and soiled; remaining turned away from us, she handed it to Shivraj. Two days before, after not hearing anything for three years, they had received this letter from their son. Shivraj and his wife are both illiterate, and one of their neighbors had tried to read it to them, but the neighbor couldn't make out all the words. Shivraj felt ashamed of his son's desertion, but he was desperate to know where he was, so he asked if my Indian colleague, Pramod Singh, could read the letter for him. His son had gone to a "letter writer" since he was illiterate as well. Pramod read the letter. In it the son said that he was well and working with some traveling entertainers, that he hoped to send some money some day, and that he was sorry. That was all, no return address, though Pramod could see that it had been mailed from a town in another state. Shivraj was disappointed:

I wish we could find out how to contact him. We want him to come home, we're worried about him. Maybe he ran off because of the debt. Sometimes I think that he didn't want to stay and work for the master like I do. But what kind of life does he have now? Travelers like that, they're bad people. And what about his wife and daughter?

We talked a bit more about his son, and the place the letter had come from. We could see no way to contact him without a return address, and Shivraj became resigned that even my educated colleague couldn't solve this problem.

Shivraj seemed to have a very clear grasp of his predicament, of the exact amounts he owed and how the interest compounded his debts. He was reasonably successful in growing crops and he managed to get two crops a year from his plot using irrigation. In this way they could have a more varied diet than most families. It seemed to me that he would be exactly the sort of man that the government programs could help. So I asked him had he ever thought of applying for government help to get out of bondage.

Oh no! That's a big mistake, that can only make things worse! I guess you don't know what happened to my brother Munsi. He lives here in Bandi too, over on the other side of the lake. See, there are different schemes that are supposed to rehabilitate farmers like us. But now the landlords make a deal with the local officials and they get all the money. Munsi's master came to him all friendly and said, "I'm having some troubles; if you don't help me I won't be able to keep giving you the grain every day—please, can you help me? If you help me now, someday I'll help you." So Munsi agreed to help. His master got some forms from the government for a scheme that loans money to laborers to help them set up on their own. He filled them in and he got Munsi to put his thumbprint on the paper, and since he's the master, he could prove that Munsi was a bonded laborer and was eligible for the money. Well, the master got 35,000 rupees [almost $1,000] as a loan in Munsi's name and then we heard that he had put it in an interest-bearing account in the bank in the city in the name of the master's son. Now Munsi is really trapped. The master has got all this money and he says that someday he'll give Munsi some. Meanwhile it's Munsi that owes the money to the government. Every time government workers come to the village Munsi begins to weep and runs out to hide in the fields! He's afraid that they will send him to jail, and where can he get 35,000 rupees? He has to do anything his master says now or *he will get into trouble with the government. It's no good telling the officials, because they did all this with Munsi's master and got a cut of the money. Anyway, now they get to report that another laborer has been rehabilitated. I've got enough problems without getting that kind of help!*

Corruption often touches the programs that aim to free bonded workers. The schemes originating in the capital commonly are enforced at the local level by officials who work hand in glove with the local landlords. As we'll see later, several studies have shown that rehabilitation programs can be a curse as well as a blessing. But sometimes they do succeed. There seem to be two key factors to success: the honesty of the government workers and the appropriateness of the scheme to the real-life circumstances of the bonded laborer. To fight their way out of bondage the laborers have to work hard, but they already know how to do that. Given a chance, they can turn their lives around. I could see this clearly when I met a remarkable woman named Leela.

LEELA Leela is about thirty years old and came as something of a surprise to me when we met. Unlike the other women in the village, she neither covered her face nor walked away when we came to her house. Instead, she asked us to sit on the benches outside her door and spoke to us very directly, looking us in the eye. There was a confidence in her that we had not seen in anyone in the village, male or female, except the landlord. On the wall of her house was a sign in Hindi; I asked her what it said.

This is the name of our organization; it is called the "Ladies' Self-help Organization." Some women came from the government a few years ago and showed us how to start it. I went around and got my neighbors to join in; we have about twenty-two women who belong now.

What do you do in this organization?

When we first started, the government ladies talked to us about health and how to keep from getting sick and how to keep the children healthy.

One woman also helped us to learn to read and write. I already knew how to read and write a little bit in Hindi, so with this teaching I got to practice reading and writing again and I began to improve. Then we had an election and I was elected to be the "chairperson" [the word she used means something like "leading representative"]. Soon we began to have "trainings." For example, we learned how to grow different spices, how to gather them at the right times, and how to bundle them up and dry them and make them ready to sell. Now we can have our own spices and sell some as well for money. After a year or so there was another scheme. This one made a big change for us. In this scheme every woman in the organization was given a milk goat. The goats weren't free, they cost 800 rupees [$22] each, but we didn't have to pay right away. Goats usually have two kids, so when our goats had their kids, we raised them up and then sold one to pay back the scheme for the milk goat they gave us. Now we each had two goats and we could have our own milk.

Then the government sent a doctor to this area. He helped us a lot and I began to get training from the government women as a midwife. Then I started to help the doctor when he went to deliver babies. We had never had a doctor before and it was a big improvement. It was a lot of work but I got in the practice of being a midwife. After some time the doctor tried to get me a job working for the government in this way. We waited a long time, but finally they said no, I couldn't be paid. They didn't have enough money to pay a local midwife. I still helped the doctor so I could learn more. Then after some time he gave me two oxen for the work I had done to help him. They are worth about 1,000 rupees [$28] each. This really changed our lives.

How did these oxen change things?

You see, with the oxen we—that is, my husband and I—could farm by ourselves. We don't own any land, but with the oxen we can do sharecropping. Now we've got about ten acres that we sharecrop with the landlord. Since we have our own oxen we can do our own ploughing. Right now we're putting all ten acres into soy beans. It is hard work; we have to plough the fields at least three times to make them ready. Then there is the planting and the weeding all through the time the beans are growing.

The deal with the landlord for the sharecropping is fifty-fifty. We split the cost of the seed and fertilizer and irrigation. Then after harvest the landlord gets half the crop. We might get as much as 150 kilos of soy beans per acre, so we can make some money there even after the expenses. Of course, the oxen take some upkeep; we spend more than 1,000 rupees a year on them, but we can also hire them out sometimes. At the same time we are still working for our old master. My husband and I both work in his fields and we get the daily amount of grain for the work we do and he lets us use a plot for growing food. Between the sharecropping and the work we have to do for our master we have to work all the time, but with the extra money from sharecropping we get more to eat and the children can go to school. We have five children, two boys and three girls; now the boys and the middle girl all go to school. We can just afford their books and all. It is still hard to make ends meet what with five kids. With seven of us the food we grow on the plot our master lets us use doesn't last the whole year. It begins to run out in the late winter; this is the slack time for other work as well, and since there is no work for us to do the master cuts back on the grain he gives us. Late winter and early spring can be very hard; sometimes I can get some extra work but everyone is looking for work then as well. Later in the year I can cook for some weddings, but it is only in the peak times like harvest when we know we'll get enough work.

According to the Indian government Leela and her husband are "semi-attached." It is a curiously bureaucratic term, but the government's difficulties in enforcing the law against debt bondage have led it to resort to the same tricks of terminology we've seen in other countries. After the first campaign in the late 1970s to free bonded laborers, a process called "rehabilitation" in India, the efforts have slowed. As more and more of the responsibility for rehabilitation has been given to local officials, corruption and bureaucratic indifference have taken over. Local officials were initially granted funds and support for rehabilitation, but they are now penalized if they "discover" large numbers of bonded laborers. The judiciary comes down hard when cases of bondage are uncovered. They rightly ask why the local officials have allowed this bondage to continue for so long, and what has happened to the funding allocated for rehabilitation. A court case will often lead to an investigation by central government inspectors. To avoid being charged with failing to enforce the laws against bondage, local officials simply ignore the bonded labor that exists. Many states report that debt bondage has been completely eradicated inside their boundaries, though a visit tells a radically different story. According to the recent official reports, bonded labor had ceased to exist in Bandi, though no one had thought to tell Baldev and the others in the village. To help this concealment, bonded labor is officially transformed into "attached" labor, a more innocuous term since "attachment" is not against the law. Baldev and Shivraj are "attached" because they can work only for their master. Leela and her husband are "semi-attached": although they still work on the master's land in return for the food allocation, they also sharecrop and thus have some income and work outside the koliya system. Heaven knows how Munsi should be labeled. Officially he's been rehabilitated, but in reality his bondage has taken on the new dimension of direct state complicity. Munsi has been doubly enslaved in a way that required both imagination and gall. These were attributes we found in many of the area's landlords.

THE LANDLORDS I had hoped to go deeply into the life of a landlord, to try to know his history and his way of thinking, the nature of his relationship with his bonded laborers, and his views on the future, but it was not to be. True, landlords would talk to us, but they controlled the conversations and they had thoroughly worked out their explanations and justifications. Some were remarkably frank. Take the landlord who also held the position of deputy labor commissioner for the district, who explained:

> *Of course I have bonded laborers: I'm a landlord. I keep them and their families and they work for me. When they aren't in the fields I have them doing the household work, washing clothes, cooking, cleaning, making repairs, everything. After all, they are from the Kohl caste; that's what*

they do, work for Vasyas like me. I give them food and a little land to work. They've also borrowed money [he wouldn't say how much] so I have to make sure that they stay on my land until it is paid back. They will work on my farm until it is all paid back, I don't care how old they get—you can't just give money away!

Anyway, they're doing fine. Look, with the grain I give them and the land, they are getting a lot more than the official farm labor rate of 67 rupees a day. I don't mind giving them so much because since I am a Labor Department official, I don't have to pay any bribes to anyone. If I wasn't, I would have to pay the police just to keep my own laborers. After all, there is nothing wrong in keeping bonded labor. They benefit from the system and so do I; even if agriculture is completely mechanized I'll still keep my bonded laborers. You see, the way we do it I am like a father to these workers. It is a father-son relationship: I protect them and guide them. Sometimes I have to discipline them as well, just as a father would. It wasn't easy keeping my laborers when the new law came in, but since I was in charge of rehabilitation for my village I was never bothered much about it. Now, officially, our village is completely rehabilitated and I spend much more time trying to convince people that the old system is better and we need to change the law. The bonded system was about security for the workers; it would be better to keep it and just make sure that the grain payment and land value equals the minimum wage rate, which it does.

When Pramod began to press him on this, pointing out that in his position he was supposed to stop bondage not promote it, he threw us out.

I felt like I was back in Alabama again: "Slavery is good," "It provides security for *these people*," "You know they can't take care of themselves," "Why, I'm like a father to them . . . ." Not surprisingly, his numbers didn't add up either. While it is true that the official minimum daily wage for farm laborers is 67 rupees ($1.85), in Bandi no free worker is ever paid more than 30 rupees (83 cents). But even that amount was more than twice what the bonded laborers were getting. The value of the grain given to the families was between 5 and 10 rupees a day. The value of their crop for both eating and selling might add another 8 rupees a day. In other words, the whole family is paid the equivalent of perhaps $3.50 for a sixty-hour week, or less than 6 cents an hour. At that rate, even with small acreages and low sale prices, the landlords can make a nice profit. A human family only costs them a little more than twice as much to keep as does a pair of oxen, and the humans can be put to many more tasks. Bonded labor makes up a small fraction of the running costs of a landlord's farm.

Most of the landlords were happy to talk about the economics of farming. As long as we kept asking detailed questions about the cost of seed, or the benefits of phosphate versus urea fertilizers on rice yields, they would even get out their account books to help us record the information. They seemed eager to have the whole story of their farming told, to make it clear that bonded labor was just a small part of the big picture. They wanted to be seen as up-to-date agriculturists who just happened to be helping a few families of ignorant laborers hold on to their jobs. But bonded labor was in fact the key to their profitability. Most of the costs the landlords faced were relatively fixed: the expenses for seed, fertilizer, irrigation, land tax, tractor rental, and fuel varied slightly from year to year, but always upward. Similarly, the price they could get for their produce varied little. Only by keeping their labor costs to the absolute minimum through bondage could they make strong profits. One landlord who kept two bonded laborer families and farmed about fifty acres was able to make a profit of 56 percent in an average year. If he had paid the local daily wage rate of 30 rupees to his laborers, that profit would have fallen to 36 percent. If he had paid the national minimum rate of 67 rupees, he would have made less than 1 percent profit on his farm each year.

These profits, though not as large as those found in the new slavery, make possible a lifestyle far removed from that of Baldev and Markhi. The landlord, who lived in the center of Bandi, had a brick-built house of eight or nine rooms, with a large veranda circling it. Inside was running water, electricity, and bottled gas for cooking. Behind it was a large walled garden for vegetables and flowers, and surrounding it were the barns and sheds that housed his livestock and equipment. The landlord probably has a bicycle, maybe a motorcycle, and possibly a car or a tractor. The landlord's family eats a healthy variety of food, including luxuries like soft drinks and sweets. If a member of his family gets sick he can pay the doctor and buy medicine. The profit he makes from agriculture alone is equivalent to ten times the income of his bonded laborers, and like most landlords he has other businesses. Landlords normally own the local shop or the mill, and of course are moneylenders. The landlord's sons usually receive higher education and take jobs in local government or business in the city. Though a landlord's total income is not large by Western standards, here it is the difference between living in the modern world and living, like Baldev and Markhi, in the Dark Ages. Yet for all the benefits they enjoy on the backs of their bonded laborers, most landlords know that their situation is precarious.

A Tractor Ride to the Future

The back of the Indian five-rupee note shows a field of rich soil just as the sun is dipping behind some tree-lined hills in the distance. In the center of the picture is a man driving a tractor toward the sunset and pulling a single-bladed plough that turns the dark earth. It is a vision of the mechanized future of agriculture, and it is the dream of peasant farmers everywhere. For the upper-caste landlords this picture marks the end of their old way of life. Only the biggest landlords have holdings large enough to justify the cost of complete mechanization; for the others, viability is dependent on bondage. Yet the smaller landlords have to compete with mechanization as it brings larger fields into production and increases output. As the size of the harvests increases, the price of grain falls. The more that Indian agriculture is mechanized, the less profit the landlords will make using the old system of bonded labor. There is no slack in the cost of a bonded laborer: any further reduction and the worker starves and can't work. That profits would entirely disappear if the minimum wage rate were paid to farmworkers shows how the custom of centuries of bondage must either disappear or evolve into a different kind of exploitation. It is no wonder that landlords are trying to shore up the system against change and rehabilitation.

Over and over the landlords we interviewed explained that bondage was really just a kind of "father-son" relationship. It was as if they had been issued a press pack from the slaveholder central office. They had a number of arguments: they presented themselves as a form of social security for the disadvantaged and unskilled, they pointed to the generations of traditional "cooperation" between their caste and the workers, and they spoke darkly of the sad fate that rural peasants met in the cities. They all said, "Everyone does it—all the landlords around here have bonded laborers." Yes, there might be some problems and bad treatment, but the landlords knew who caused this: it was the fault of the nouveau riche middle castes who were buying into farming. It was the same checklist of excuses used by plantation owners in the American South before the Civil War.[4]

The nouveau riche middle castes represent a special, twofold threat to the landlords. Active in business, some families of the middle castes are amassing large fortunes. In India land has always been the ultimate measure of wealth, and they are buying farmland when it becomes available. The upper-caste landlords are extremely reluctant to let land out of their grip, and they feel great cultural pressure to hold on to this traditional base of their power and well-being—but money talks. The nouveau riche can bring shocking change to the rural areas, especially because they break the united front that the landlords have always maintained before the lower-caste workers. These new middle-caste landowners are suspicious of their upper-caste neighbors and see them as competitors, even enemies, rather than as people who share the same interests. If they could, the middle castes would drive the upper castes off the land, and they are willing to use the bonded laborers as a weapon. More likely to use modern farming techniques, they will take the side of the bonded laborers in any dispute as a way of weakening the old upper-caste landlords. The middle castes may also use the bonded laborers to threaten the landlords' political power.

Landlords also feel threatened because their control of bonded labor faces another challenge, this time in the political arena. After the assassination of Rajiv Gandhi in 1991, several political changes took place, though they were not necessarily linked to his death. First there was a crackdown on official corruption, which is continuing. Corruption is still commonplace, but in some areas it is threatened, and that affects the cozy control that the upper castes have had over government at all levels. More important was the influence of a handful of honest officials in the voter registration administration. In spite of tremendous resistance from the upper castes, they mounted a nationwide campaign to register all potential voters. It resulted in a dramatic upsurge in the registration of people from the lower castes and tribal groups. Voting rates for these groups reached as high as 75 percent in the last elections, up from single figures in the past. The Congress Party, which had pretty much ruled India since independence and which best represented the upper castes, was suddenly out on its ear. In Uttar Pradesh the state is now governed by parties controlled by the middle castes, which make up the largest part of the population. This government is unlikely to close its eyes to labor abuses by upper-caste landed gentry. As India marked fifty years of independence in August 1997, its prime minister, Inder Kujmal Gujral, made an anticorruption campaign the centerpiece of the celebrations. In this climate of shifting power and the urge to reform, the rehabilitation program sputters along.

There's No Rehabilitation with a Dead Ox

India's rehabilitation of bonded labor is the most successful failure of all such programs in the world. Subverted, maligned, embezzled, coopted, underfunded, overregulated, paralyzingly bureaucratic, farcically enforced, and tragically accomplished it might be, but unlike most attempts to tackle slavery in the world, it sometimes actually works. Here is an example drawn from a district official's report:

> As reported by the Assistant Collector of Guntar District 16, large scale bonded labour was exposed by a journalist in Guntar District. The administration moved quite swiftly to the site—about 150 kilometers from District headquarters—and got 321 bonded labourers identified and released. All of these persons were working in the slate quarries. Most of them were from the Salim district [of the state] of Tamil Nadu. When they were brought here, they were given an advance of 1000 to 2000 rupees. This formed the basis of their debt bondage and they were kept under threat in the quarries. All of the bonded labourers were released and sent to their native places. They were provided with only the ad hoc grant of 500 rupees.[5]

The plan is simple in outline: when government workers or aid workers identify bonded labor, there is a set procedure for registering them. When they have been registered their debts are canceled and they are free to leave their masters. To enable them to walk away from bondage a grant of 6,250 rupees is made to each family, often in land or livestock, but with 500 rupees given immediately to make sure they can feed themselves while they take stock and prepare for freedom. (Note that in the case above the local officials gave out only the 500 rupees, preferring to let these migrant workers return immediately to their home state.) The law setting up the program also establishes vigilance committees that search out bonded laborers, get them registered, organize their payments and rehabilitation, and protect them from retribution or intimidation by the landlords. Half of the cost of the program comes from central government and half from the state government.

This was the plan, and when it works it works fairly well. It is the modern Indian equivalent of the forty acres and a mule that American slaves were praying for (but never received) at the end of the U.S. Civil War. With a little help from a vigilance committee, the grant should pay for a she-buffalo or an ox and cover the expense of reclaiming and leveling a plot of land with some left over. Alternatively, the money can be used to set up the family in a business, buying the equipment needed for a cottage industry. A typical example would be the case of Lakheram, a bonded farm laborer in Uttar Pradesh, taken from government records:

> Lakheram worked as a bonded laborer for a Brahmin landlord after taking a loan of 2000 rupees for his own wedding. He worked the Brahmin's fields for about ten years until his release in the rehabilitation program. He was given a buffalo under the government assistance program worth about 4000 rupees. He was also given a piece of land and now works about two acres, cultivating rice and beans for his family's use. He currently shares his brother's house, which is a single room hut holding twelve people altogether. Lakheram feels happy to be free of bondage. He has been able to buy some utensils and clothes. His goal is to build a house of his own.[6]

Some states have improved on the basic program. In Andhra Pradesh, other state funds were used to buy and prepare land by sinking wells before it was granted to the freed laborers. This allowed their rehabilitation grant to go much further. In the state of Bihar the grant was doubled from state funds. Bihar also set up a separate project to rehabilitate bonded children from the carpet industry. This included residential schools providing free education, with free books, school uniforms, and meals, as well as craft training. In Karnataka state, a land reform act lets the government give bonded laborers ownership of the plots they were allowed to use by their masters. In Uttar Pradesh activists working with vigilance committees track down and release women from city brothels and return them to their home villages. And in Orissa, low-level government jobs have been set aside for freed laborers.

So why don't the landlords just get more bonded laborers to replace the ones they've lost? Occasionally they do, but this kind of traditional agricultural bondage relies on its local nature. Centuries of custom put lower-caste laborers at the beck and call of upper-caste landlords. When that relationship is broken, it is very difficult for the landlords to find people from other areas, people with different customs and histories, who will happily slip into the historic roles of master and slave. What is more, there is little room for them in most rural communities. Freed laborers normally stay on in their houses, often gaining possession of their garden plots as well. Unless a landlord wants to sacrifice farmland to building houses for new bonded workers, he is stuck with the new free farm laborers. And if he does put up housing for imported workers with whom he has no long-term relations, how does he know they will stick by their debts, or not report for rehabilitation as soon as they have houses and gardens? It is possible to pull the feudal serf out of bondage; it is almost impossible to push one back into it.

A parallel situation occurred in the United States after the Civil War. Some plantation owners in the Mississippi Delta drove the freed slaves off their land and replaced them with boatloads of Chinese laborers. The Chinese were in debt bondage for the cost of their transportation to America, and the plantation owners planned to keep them that way. They fully expected these quiet and obedient Chinese to be long-term replacements for their African slaves. It never happened. The first generation of Chinese worked on the farms, taking the place of the slaves, but their experience of directing all of the family's earning power toward a single goal brought most of their children out of debt. The second generation opened shops and cottage industries and never looked back. The Delta Chinese, as they are known today, add a prosperous dimension to modern Mississippi. The old plantation owners were blindsided by their false sense of superiority and by a group of people who just weren't going to go along with their own enslavement.

This also points to why people who manage to get out of bondage will stay out. To be sure, some slip back into debt, or are tricked or forced back into debt. But the longer they stay out of bondage, the more likely they are to avoid sliding back into it. The rehabilitation programs can make a big difference here. Some activists organize public meetings where the freed laborers are told about their rights and what they can expect in rehabilitation. This knowledge, once acquired, is like a vaccination against bondage. And given sufficient and appropriate resources for independence, most laborers are capable of holding their own. They are used to hard work and squeezing a living out of little.

Great things can happen if a family can achieve freedom and economic independence, but often the family never makes it that far. Just about everything that could go wrong with the rehabilitation program has gone wrong. Every kind of fraud and cheating imaginable, and some beyond imagining, has sucked away its funds like so many leeches. In one district of Uttar Pradesh, land was allocated to freed laborers, but incomplete land records allowed part of it to be claimed and taken by landlords. The remaining land, according to an official report, "was in a spot where even monkeys could not have access."[7] The same laborers were to receive milk cows or oxen, but the job of supplying them was given to a dishonest contractor who delivered some cows that were dead and others so ill that they had to be carried away on the shoulders of the laborers. Highland sheep awarded to laborers in the lowlands have died of the heat, and lowland animals have gone to highland farmers and died of the cold. Many laborers with no experience in animal husbandry were given livestock with sad results; for example, one district gave each freed laborer a dozen chickens, without providing any advice about how to care for them. Some laborers received "small-business" equipment—perhaps a sewing machine, or tools for bicycle repair—which sometimes has been both appropriate and successful. But other equipment grants were farcical, as when two farm laborers were given a drum and bugle and told to become musicians.

Bad as it is, the provision of land and livestock has not been abused as seriously as the giving of cash grants. All across India tens of thousands of "ghost" bonded laborers have appeared, concocted by district officials in league with landlords who have collected millions of rupees for their "rehabilitation." In some places the local officials work with the landlords and the grants are paid directly against existing debts (instead of these debts simply being canceled). As a result, a freed laborer might receive only 400 or 500 of the 6,250 rupees he or she is due, and is soon facing debt and bondage again. Rocky, useless land has been sold at inflated prices by landlords to district officials; they distribute it to laborers who then have to abandon their land when it cannot be made to grow food. Banks, shopkeepers, and local officials have all added "processing charges" or "acceptance fees" to the grants, skimming off more millions of rupees. For the unscrupulous, the rehabilitation of bonded labor has been a bonanza.

Much of the rehabilitation program has been a fiasco—yet it remains just about the only scheme in the world that *does* free laborers in bondage. In Uttar Pradesh alone, 26,000 bonded laborers were freed between 1979 and 1989. Most of the problems with the program can be traced back to two faults in its implementation. First, only a few of the vigilance committees that were to be set up to watch and guide rehabilitation were ever constituted. Without oversight the opportunities for cheating and graft were plentiful. Second, virtually no landlord has ever been prosecuted for abusing bonded laborers. The law allows masters to be charged and punished, but it simply doesn't happen. The reformers had assumed that it was not necessary to fine every landlord who had bonded laborers so long as there was no interference with rehabilitation, but the almost total lack of judicial backup has meant that some landlords feel free to threaten and coerce laborers back into bondage.

The importance of these two factors is seen in districts where the vigilance committees are active and work closely with the judiciary. There, the rehabilitations are generally successful. In one part of Uttar Pradesh, the vigilance committee used its purchasing power to supply ten sheep and a dozen chickens to each family, and included instructions for their care. Then each family was allowed to choose from a number of optional rehabilitation schemes the one most appropriate to their circumstances—farming, cottage industry, livestock, even small-scale transport, or some combination. A study two years later found 95 percent reporting adequate earnings to support their families. Laborers often find themselves free and economically independent without any knowledge of how to stay that way. They need help to get established and to learn the way of their new lives. Bondage can be compared to living in a prison or a mental institution; those who get out have to learn about living in the "real world." Like some ex-convicts, some ex-slaves may never manage it, but their chances are increased with every bit of help they receive in the crucial first days of freedom.

The Indian National Academy of Administration, which trains government workers, made an extensive study of bonded labor and rehabilitation in 1989–90.[8] They examined hundreds of local schemes and saw what had worked and what had failed. The basic law was fine, they said, when it was fully carried out, but some refinements were needed:

Freed laborers should have a say in the type of rehabilitation they receive.

Rehabilitation should be organized so that freedom is immediately followed by training and support.

The land given to freed laborers should be capable of producing food, and the laborer should be given a clear and ironclad deed to the property.

There should be some funds set aside for low-interest loans and emergency grants in the first few years of freedom.

The follow-up support should include helping laborers to set up small credit unions.

Some low-level government jobs should be set aside for freed laborers.

More education should be available to the children of freed laborers.

More control of the rehabilitation process should pass to the central government.

Small grants should be made available to pay for funeral and wedding expenses, since these are often what force laborers to borrow from landlords.

These are commonsense suggestions derived from actual examples of successful rehabilitations. They don't require vast sums of money or going against local customs. Add these provisions to the existing law and make sure there are sufficient resources, and even more of those in bondage should find their way to freedom. Of course, the success of the program requires that the officials leading it be honest.

Honesty is something of an imponderable in government. How do you guarantee it? Government officials, especially in poor developing countries, are constantly tempted. Around the world slavery grows out of official dishonesty and greed. In Thailand it was difficult to find honest officials; they couldn't last in a system of government soaked through with corruption from top to bottom. Corruption is a big issue in India, but that in itself indicates that corruption is seen as a problem. A free press has something to do with keeping government honest; so does a tradition of service among the educated elite. When democracy works well, politicians have to be more careful—and even a handful of honest bureaucrats can be the downfall of a corrupt political machine. All these factors can promote honest government in India. If they can be strengthened, bondage will decline even more rapidly.

Another important factor is the influence of activist groups and charities, always called NGOs (nongovernmental organizations) in the developing world. While some NGOs might fall apart, and the terrible pressures of government antagonism plus inadequate and irregular funding can often make this happen, most hold to their mission. The best of the NGOs like Free the Slaves or the Red Cross, are respected throughout the world. An excellent feature of the Indian rehabilitation law is that NGOs are encouraged to take part. This means that activists can help identify bonded laborers and free them. Since the law allows bonded laborers to go to court against their masters, a lawyer, paid for by an NGO, can make tremendous headway in identifying and freeing workers. Western aid agencies and charities working with rehabilitation programs can see their funds go into long-term solutions rather than short-term fixes.

It is important to remember the relative power of our Western dollars, pounds, kroner, and euros. The 6,250 rupees that can completely transform the lives of a family in bondage equals $133 at the August 2004 exchange rate. The same amount would easily serve as the seed money for a small credit union that could free a whole village from being trapped in debt. In the next chapter we'll examine ways to *do* something about slavery, seeing what works and what doesn't. We must look back to Siri and Bilal and Baldev and Leela, and ask: How do we break these chains?

7

WHAT CAN BE DONE?

WHEN I BEGAN TO STUDY SLAVERY I BECAME convinced that we really didn't understand what was going on. But as I traveled around the world meeting slaves, both the patterns of new slavery and the changes in old slavery and feudalism emerged and became clearer. Three key factors helped create the new slavery and change the old slavery. The first is the population explosion that flooded the world's labor markets with millions of poor and vulnerable people. The second is the revolution of economic globalization and modernized agriculture, which has dispossessed poor farmers and made them vulnerable to enslavement. In the new world economy capital flies wherever labor is cheapest, and the financial links of slavery can stretch around the world. The third factor is the chaos of greed, violence, and corruption created by this economic change in many developing countries, change that is destroying the social rules and traditional bonds of responsibility that might have protected potential slaves. The emergence of the new slavery in Thailand and Brazil, in particular, clearly shows how these factors have interacted.

Population growth, economic change, and corruption affect slavery and bondage differently in different places. In Mauritania the old slavery still exists, but economic change has brought slaves into the city and altered their lives and work. In India and Pakistan hybrid forms of bondage have emerged that mix the worst parts of feudalism and modern capitalism. The three factors are clearly interrelated. William Greider has written about this new global economy and the revolution it has brought to the world. He wasn't addressing slavery, but he could have been: "The great paradox of this economic revolution is that its new technologies enable people and nations to take sudden leaps into modernity, while at the same time they promote the renewal of once-forbidden barbarisms. Amid the newness of things, exploitation of the weak by the strong also flourishes."[1] Slavery is exactly the sort of barbarism he describes, and this points up the very novelty of the changes buffeting the developing world. This novelty becomes a problem when we want to increase public awareness of slavery.

Everyone *knows* what slavery is—yet almost no one knows. The old slavery is so much a part of human history and of our shared understanding of the world that for most people slavery simply means one person legally owning another person. And as everyone *knows*, that sort of slavery was abolished long ago. It is something about which we might feel guilty or angry (an ugly episode in human history) and also a little smug and superior (since it is all in the past now, and *we're* more civilized than that). This is a terrible ignorance that leads us to overlook suffering and death. We couldn't be more wrong if we believed that because the Black Death ended in the Middle Ages, we don't have to worry about epidemics anymore. In fact, new diseases are evolving all the time; slavery is also evolving and changing, erupting whenever the conditions are right.

Today, all over the world, the conditions *are* right for slavery. Although it is against the law almost everywhere, although the world is smaller and less of it is hidden than ever before, slavery grows. In this book we've seen it growing, and we've seen the conditions that lead to slavery. When we let slaves speak we find that their lives have many things in common. All the slaves we have met are being economically exploited; only their profitability makes them interesting to the slave-holders. And all of them are being held under the threat of violence. Sometimes that violence dominates the entire relationship, as is the case with Siri in the brothel in Thailand. At other times it fades into the background, as in Mauritania, but it never disappears. These two essential ingredients of slavery—profitability and violence—combine with the three factors listed above that drive the evolution of new forms of slavery. They also point out the areas where we must focus our attention if we are to stop slavery.

"Cheap and Expendable Commodities"—Population

The Industrial Revolution in Europe and North America brought a population boom and enormous social change. As Greider has noted, "Some human beings were set free, while other lives were turned into cheap and expendable commodities."[2] The same thing is happening in the developing world today. In the ballooning populations, rapid economic change is bringing some people into the modern world of good medicine and technology, "Western" lifestyles, and a new sense of self and achievement. Other people are being consumed, often from childhood, by the industries driving this change. The sheer volume of people in the developing world compared to the number of new industrial jobs means that many of them are, as the English worker says when he's been fired, "redundant."

Slowing the population explosion and softening its effects do not directly address slavery or its eradication. But it is important to remember that the very strategies that work best to stop overpopulation also go to the heart of why slavery exists. The only proven cure for overpopulation is to eliminate extremes of poverty. The best contraceptives in the world—education and social protection against poverty in old age and illness—are also the best guard against enslavement. When families have a sudden need for cash, perhaps to buy medicine, they become vulnerable to enslavement. Lacking education they are prey to bogus contracts and dishonest accounting. In the long term, wiping out slavery requires helping the world's poor to gain greater control over their lives.

The Business of Slavery Is Business— The Globalized Economy

There is an important link between population and economic growth. Sometimes economic growth is presented as a tide that raises all boats, the idea being that industrializing the economy of Thailand or Brazil will improve the lives of everyone, rich and poor. This is certainly not true in the short term. Professor Lae Dilokvidhyarat, an economist in Thailand, observes, "Some people gain greater benefit from development . . . but the weaker people pay more than they get in return, much more."[3] We all understand what it means to pay out more than we get in return: if that goes on very long the result is debt and destitution, conditions that can lead to enslavement. Given the penetration of multinational companies into developing countries, that debt might mean a slave is ultimately serving a global business.

Today economic links can tie the slave in the field or the brothel to the highest reaches of international corporations. How these links join up is the central mystery of the new slavery, and one that desperately needs investigation. Such links between slaves and world business are hardly new. In the nineteenth century the booming British cloth industry was forced to acknowledge that slave labor supplied most of its raw material—cotton. Some British textile workers tried to resist working with slave cotton, yet many felt they had no choice but to work with whatever materials the boss provided. Other workers felt the whole question was none of their business. There was no moral leadership from the owners; they said they *had* to buy the cheapest cotton in the market to compete. And the government of the time, while benefiting from the tax on the industry, followed a strict hands-off policy, arguing that "the market" made the best decisions. Many companies, investors, and workers face a similar dilemma today. What would you do if you discovered that your job depended on slave labor? When we look into the mystery of the way slavery is linked into the world economy, we'd better be prepared for a few nasty surprises.

Major economic changes of the last ten years have pushed global business into greater contact with oppressed, even enslaved, workers. International trade agreements (especially the General Agreement on Tariffs and Trade and the North American Free Trade Agreement) have broken down barriers to trade and capital movement between countries. The overarching and compelling logic of always using the cheapest raw materials worked by the cheapest labor now drives corporations across borders. "Capital has wings," New York financier Robert A. Johnson explains. "Capital can deal with twenty labor markets at once and pick and choose among them. Labor is fixed in one place. So power has shifted."[4] As international business now seeks to buy labor at the lowest cost, often through subcontractors, some of these contractors achieve the *lowest* cost by using slave labor. Meanwhile, the companies ask themselves: Why pay $20 an hour for a factory worker in Europe when one will work for $1 an hour or less in India? Why buy sugar from U.S. farmers when it is much cheaper from the Dominican Republic (where enslaved Haitians do the harvesting)? Building materials such as bricks are so cheap in Pakistan—why not build there? There are tremendous opportunities in land and cattle in Brazil, and the subcontractors provide labor *so* cheaply! As long as one doesn't look too closely, the bargains are there for the taking. The businessperson can just say: "My job is to get the best deal, I can't worry about local problems."

Major companies around the world have been repeating that phrase. But the late 1990s controversy in the United States over child labor in sweatshops making clothes and shoes for household names like Nike and the Gap has helped change this attitude dramatically. When an educated public brings pressure to bear, businesspeople *can* learn to worry about local problems. In India, for example, there are between 65 and

100 million children ages fourteen and younger who work more than eight hours a day.[5] They fill the sweatshops and do many other kinds of work. Worse, about 15 million of these children are not child laborers but child slaves. And enslaved children are even more hidden; trapped in debt bondage, they tend not to work in sweatshops producing for large-scale export but in smaller-scale, more isolated businesses. Unlike the owners of factories making soccer balls, their masters have little fear of exposure or public pressure.

In the new slavery, responsibility is easily avoided. One of the basic facts about the old slavery was that the slave and the master were intimately bound together. But in slavery today we can see that the distance between "master" and slave is growing wider and wider. In Mauritania, the clearest example of the old slavery, slaves still live in their master's household, often taking his family name. In the modernized feudalism of Pakistan and India, the masters have taken a step away from their slaves and have introduced a layer of managers. In the fully developed new slavery of Thailand or Brazil there are elaborate chains of contracts and control. These become so complicated that it is hard to say who exactly "owns" the slave. But just because we can't finger the slaveholder doesn't mean that slavery has ceased to exist, any more than a murder doesn't exist because the killer can't be found. The new slavery is a crime with millions of victims but very few identifiable criminals—and that makes its eradication very difficult.

For the most part, these criminals are "respectable" businesspeople. The interlocking web of contracts and subcontracts enables local investors to get excellent returns on businesses without necessarily knowing exactly how the money is made. The investment club that owns a Thai brothel puts its management into the hands of a professional manager (pimp) and bookkeeper. The brothel wouldn't exist without the club's capital and the profits flow back to those investors, but they may never know how the girls came to be there. The new slavery diffuses slaveholding, making it harder to see. It is no wonder that the laws against the old slavery don't seem to be enforceable anymore.

This disappearance of slave*owners* is a problem, but not an insurmountable one. All sorts of crime are evolving rapidly. Enormous sophistication is the hallmark of both high-level drug finance and computer fraud, for example. But law enforcement continues to catch up, becoming more sophisticated as well. With slavery, this is going to take a little longer; because most people don't even realize the crime is being committed, there is little public pressure to draw on. In the developed countries very few people actually suffer slavery, and in the rest of the world the slaves are silenced. The laws themselves will have to be rewritten to extend responsibility and culpability. New or changed laws should address *conspiracy* to enslave or *profiting* from slavery, in the same way as laws against homicide punish *conspiracy* to murder and don't restrict guilt to the person who pulls the trigger. The physical distance between slave and master is increasing, so laws must be crafted to guarantee that increased distance doesn't mean decreased responsibility.

If responsibility for slaveholding is extended to those who profit from it, we have to confront a shocking ethical problem. Those who profit from slavery might include anyone—even you or me. Your pension fund or mutual fund may be buying stock (which is, after all, part ownership) in companies that own companies that subcontract slave labor. How far up the economic ladder are we going to go? How many links have to stand between a slave and an "owner" before the latter's responsibility ends? Or does it? Is ignorance an excuse? If your job were to depend on the availability of slave-produced raw materials, where would you stand? Some of those nineteenth-century British textile workers protested profiting from slavery—they lost their jobs and went hungry. What about the manufacturers or wholesalers who turn a blind eye to the slave-made products they buy and sell? For years carpets made by slave children have been sold in the best department stores (and many still are). Certainly the overseas buyers know, but does the board of directors? Will company directors take measures to ensure that they are not involved in slavery? And will legal responsibility be individual or corporate? Is there greater justice in charging the individual who knowingly supplies slave-made goods to a retail chain, or in making the retail chain pay a big fine for selling them? Or should both be held liable?

We must accept that there are several layers of responsibility. We have to decide how much responsibility we, as citizens and human beings, carry for the eradication of slavery. William Greider points out:

> The deepest meaning of the global industrial revolution is that people no longer have free choice in the matter of identity. Ready or not, they are already of the world. As producers or consumers, as workers or merchants or investors, they are now bound to distant others through the complex strands of commerce and finance reorganizing the globe as a unified marketplace. The prosperity of South Carolina or Scotland is deeply linked to Stuttgart's or Kuala Lumpur's. The true social values of Californians or Swedes will be determined by what is tolerated in the factories of Thailand or Bangladesh.[6]

If we have not indirectly participated in slavery through investment, we almost certainly have through consumption. Slave-produced goods and services flow into the global market, making up a tiny but significant part of what we buy. But the sheer volume of our consumption overwhelms our ability to make responsible choices. We don't have time to research the living conditions of the people who produce everything we buy. And if we should choose to ask these questions, how would we go about it? Should the local supermarket be responsible for investigating labor relations around the world, or for getting you the best food at the lowest price? Then we also have to consider what happens when we get answers we don't like. For example, Haitian men, women, and children have been enslaved in the Dominican Republic to harvest sugar, sugar exported to the United States and other countries. Will we stop eating chocolate or drinking soft drinks until we can be sure no slavery went into their production? Are we ready to pay $5 for a candy bar if that is what it takes to ensure that the producers are not

enslaved and get a decent wage? When we can work out how to research the market and discover where and how slave-made goods enter
our lives, there will be an even bigger question to face: How much are
you willing to pay to end slavery?

Putting Our Money Where Our Mouth Is

Let's be realistic: most people are willing to pay *something* to end slavery, but they're not willing to make a great sacrifice. The good news
is that if enough people feel that way, a small sacrifice is all that will
be needed. There are now about 27 million people in slavery: though
the number is large, taken country by country the problem shrinks.
What is more, no miracle is required—just the enforcement of existing laws and agreements, the development of a few new ones, and the
provision of help to get these people and families on their feet. Making that happen will not be easy. For local workers and researchers,
going up against vicious and violent slaveholders is a scary prospect.
But we have to remember that violence is the tool, not the aim, of slavery. Slaveholders will violently defend their lucrative businesses, but
they will walk away from the slaves and the business if it stops making
money. Putting the pressure on its profits is a key strategy for ending
slavery.

There are already pilot programs showing the effectiveness of tar-
geting profits. One of the worst industries in India for the abuse of
child slaves has been rug and carpet making. If you have an oriental rug
on your floor right now, there is a good chance that it was woven by
slave children. For many years campaigners in India tried to free and
rehabilitate these bonded laborers with only partial success. But a few
years ago the Rugmark Campaign set out to put the pressure not on the
makers but on the buyers of carpets. Working from a tiny office with
little funds, these activists proposed that people should look for a special tag on handmade rugs that guaranteed that they were not made

by slaves. To earn the Rugmark, producers had to agree to only three things: not to exploit children, to cooperate with independent monitoring, and to turn over 1 percent of the carpet wholesale price to a welfare fund for child workers. Special effort was put into building up a sophisticated monitoring team that can detect fake labels, knows carpet making inside and out, and can't be corrupted. Today the German, U.S., and Canadian governments have recognized the Rugmark. The biggest mail order company in the world, the Otto Versand Group, plus major retailers in the United States, Germany, and Holland, now import only Rugmarked carpets. In Europe the market share of "slave-free" carpets is 30 percent and growing. Of course there is a long way to go: some British retailers, including Liberty and John Lewis, have refused to stock Rugmark carpets, and southern and eastern Europe are only now being introduced to Rugmark, but the campaign continues to strengthen.

Most important is its impact on the lives of bonded child laborers. The 1 percent contribution from the producers has now built and staffed six Rugmark schools in India, which serve a total of 1,400 students. The campaign itself has drawn the attention of other organizations, and so the German government and UNICEF (the United Nations Children's Fund) now fund other schools in the areas that were once the recruiting grounds for the carpet belt. Helped to stay in school, the children aren't lured away to bondage. Confronted with buyers from the retail chains who insist on "slave-free" goods, the worst of the slaveholders leave the business and the other producers do what is necessary to earn the Rugmark. It is a tremendous example of positive consumer power.

This campaign shows that when Western consumers and retailers learn about the links between slavery and the products they want, they are willing to change their buying habits. But how do we extend this consumer power to other kinds of slavery? The Rugmark succeeded in part because a rug is a specific and tangible product that comes to the consumer looking just as it did when it left the loom of the child slave. But the charcoal from a Brazilian forest supplies steel mills and factories, not Western consumers. The bricks made in Pakistan are bought by local builders or sometimes the government. And the "product" of enslaved Thai prostitutes is not something we find at the supermarket. Yet it is the nature of the global economy that all of these "enterprises" are linked to other parts of the economy. Since they are linked, there has to be some point where pressure can be applied. Finding these links and bringing pressure to bear is the great challenge of fighting the new slavery. The connections are sometimes intricate and obscure, but they must be uncovered. Consider the flow of charcoal into steel production in Brazil, steel that is shipped to make car parts in Mexico, parts that are then assembled into new cars in the United States, before being sold in Canada. It is complicated, but the people involved in these businesses trace these supply chains every day; a reasonably intelligent researcher could certainly do the same.

Here is an area where the antislavery campaign can learn from the environmental movement. People concerned with the environment often must similarly trace the links between polluters in one country and parent companies in another. Like slavery, some of the worst kinds of eco-crime are hidden, as in the trade in the skins and horns of endangered species. Several years ago a number of environmental organizations realized that they needed detectives, special eco-detectives, to search out these links and expose the criminals. From this start the Environmental Investigation Agency (EIA) was born. Chances are that you have never heard of the EIA, a small charity based in London that takes on the hard and sometimes clandestine work of digging up the dirt on eco-criminals. Members of the investigative staff are specialists, good with hidden cameras, used to living rough, and exacting in their search for truth. Many of the blockbuster stories broken by the big environmental organizations were actually uncovered by the EIA.[7]

The complexity of the global economy and the international character of the new slavery demand the same sort of investigation. Many people think that this sort of work is already being done by the United Nations, but that is not the case. Only in the most severe situations, such as the collapse of the former Yugoslavia, is the UN authorized to carry out work *inside* countries. Reports from in-country informants flow to the UN from the International Labor Organization, but the UN does not normally take action or impose sanctions; it only discusses and announces the results of those discussions. In the face of persistent denials of slavery by national representatives, the UN can only persist in asking questions. In spite of the important work it does around the world, the UN is supported by its member states and will bend over backward at times to avoid upsetting them. The UN also operates on a philosophy of inclusion at all costs, on the assumption that it is better to have countries that violate human rights inside the UN and talking than outside the UN and answering to no one. To keep countries within the fold, the UN works hard to avoid confrontation. Like it or not, the UN can never be truly independent in its operation—that independence necessarily is left to the activist organizations of the voluntary sector.

To solve the puzzle of how slavery is linked to our lives, we need to draw on good researchers, good economists, and good businesspeople: researchers to follow the flow of raw materials and products from the hands of slaves to their ultimate consumer, economists to explore the nature of slave-based businesses and work out viable alternatives, and experienced businesspeople to help the businesses all along the product chain find the best way to end their participation in slavery. And all that research and information would be useless without educators and communicators to help consumers make careful and conscious buying decisions that support the rehabilitation of slaves. I believe that when people know that their purchasing and investing can actually help free slaves, they will do the right thing. Unfortunately, today most of us are in ignorance about slave-made goods or how our pensions or stocks and shares may be investments in slavery. But before we look at the organizations that might help end our ignorance, we must examine closely the third key factor that makes slavery possible—government corruption.

Absolute Power, Absolute Chaos—Corruption and Violence

When we try to understand corrupt government it is worth considering for a moment one of the most inhuman and deadly governments in recent history—Hitler's Germany. Many people have the mistaken impression that the Nazi administration worked with terrible efficiency. In fact, behind the rigidly goose-stepping armies was a government of chaos and random cruelty. The historian Ian Kershaw has shown how the Nazis and their führer worship produced "the biggest confusion in government that has ever existed in a civilized state." When the center of government was taken up with random acts of racism and cruelty, the extensions of government, such as the police, ran wild. In Germany, Kershaw explains, "most of the police remained in their posts when the Nazi regime began; but they did not have to carry on as usual—they were now off the leash."[8] The only orders they had from the central government were to suppress all enemies of the state, especially Jews, and to achieve that suppression anything was allowed. In the case of Nazi Germany, as in Burma today, one mechanism of suppression was slave labor.

In much of the developing world, governments are equally chaotic. Their core motive, however, is not Nazi anti-Semitism but greed. Globalization means that values dominating the Western economies have been injected into developing countries. The idea that profit is its own justification, that success conveys respectability, drives new businesses, which therefore ignore the human cost. State activities that were previously nonprofit (everything from law enforcement to famine relief) are being turned into profit-making businesses. As politicians and businesspeople share the new revenue, corruption sets in. When rulers begin to chase the vast potential wealth of the global economy, the order of the state breaks down. As Greider explains, under such conditions "law always suffers. The bonds of social consent have been torn asunder and people find themselves free to make their own rules. That leads to another recurring feature of economic revolution—corruption."[9] Every country contains some corruption, but it is the special power of rapid economic change to dramatically increase both its intensity and scale. Existing power structures are overturned and a battle breaks out to fill the power vacuum. Economies that had been stable, though perhaps poor, are replaced by haphazard development and exploitation. And, as we have seen, in the absence of law, greed can overwhelm human rights.

Every country manifests some degree of corruption. The crucial question is: Which is stronger, the corruption or the bonds of social consent? You can ask the same questions of every government in the world: Do the people in power, from presidents down to police, work according to the rules or for their own enrichment? Are public relationships shaped by common aims or by exploitation? My Russian friend told me how shocked he was by police behavior in America: "They stopped my car, but didn't demand money!" The point is simple: when the police go rotten, anything can go rotten. When law enforcement—and the violent potential of gun and jail behind the law—is selective and profit-seeking, the law has effectively ceased to exist. In the heat of greed, any law against slavery can effectively vanish.

Around the world there are police who participate in slavery. We've seen how they act as slave-catchers and brutal enforcers in Thailand, Pakistan, and Brazil. Yet in many countries the police are working hard to end slavery. In either case they rely on their trump card: their monopoly on legal violence. Everywhere slavery has been studied we see that a critical factor allowing slavery to exist is the unrestricted use of violence by slaveholders. For the slaveholders to capture and hold slaves, they must be able to control them through violence. For slaveholders to use violence freely, the enforcement of law must be perverted and its protection denied to slaves. When police and government are corrupt they sell the right to use violence (or sell violence itself as a service). In effect they are selling a license for hunting slaves.

This violence can take many forms—often horrific, because slaves are relatively cheap in today's economy. Since no slave represents a large investment, there is little to be lost in killing or injuring one. Even in India, where the ancient feudal system smooths over conflict, violence is just below the surface. It is only in Mauritania, where the last vestiges of the old slavery continue, that masters temper their violence to protect their investment. Of course, because slaves are exploited for their labor, physical violence that would harm their ability to work is usually a last resort. There is more profit in breaking minds than in breaking bodies. The infliction of psychological terror and mental destruction of the kind that caused some concentration camp inmates to serve the Nazis without resistance is a common thread running through all forms of the new slavery.

When I sat with Siri in the brothel in Thailand and looked into the flat deadness of her eyes, listened to the hopelessness in her voice, and saw the destruction of her personality and her will to escape, I glimpsed the horror of a life captured and destroyed to feed the greed of the slaveholder. It is not easy to crush a human mind, but with enough brutality, time, and indifference to suffering it can be done. Around the world it *is* being done. The slaveholders provide the brutality, the corrupt police and governments ensure that slavery is practiced with impunity, and the overarching materialism of our global economy justifies a general indifference. To close the circle and make the link with global economic change we have to remember once again that while violence is the tool by which slavery is achieved, the aim of slavery is profit. Unlike a century ago, no modern slaveholders delude themselves that they are somehow "civilizing" their slaves, or lifting them toward religious salvation. In the lean, mean global economy slavery is stripped of its moral justifications: slaves equal profits. Part of that income pays for the violence needed to ensure that the profits keep coming.

But what can we do to end the violence and corruption that support slavery? Clearly, this is no easy task and, like the struggle against crime, it may be never-ending, but it *can* be done. There are several ways to go about it. One effective path is followed by groups like Anti-Slavery International, Free the Slaves, and Amnesty International. Watching and listening, studying and monitoring, they investigate abuses of human rights by corrupt regimes. They are dedicated to in-depth, factual, and responsible reporting of abuses. They then make it their business to carry those reports both to the public and to international bodies. Because they maintain a reputation for trustworthy research, their announcements carry weight, and exposure by these organizations can bring sanctions from other countries and the public. The current military dictatorship in Burma, which enslaves its own citizens, has faced censure in the media and in the United Nations and the European Union after reports from these groups. Naming and shaming constitute an important first step.

In the countries where slavery exists there are also local groups that fearlessly expose, name, and shame slaveholders; these include the Pastoral Land Commission (CPT) in Brazil, SOS Slaves in Mauritania, and the Human Rights Commission in Pakistan. Without their research, undertaken at great personal risk, the vast extent of slavery around the world would be concealed. CPT workers have been killed for asking too many questions in Brazil, human rights workers in Pakistan like Shakil Pathan have been attacked, and on the day I sat down to write this I had word from Mauritania that the head of SOS Slaves, Boubacar ould Massaoud, had once again been arrested and imprisoned, this time for talking to a French journalist. One of the most important things we can do to combat slavery is to help protect these local campaigners. We must ensure that their groups are tightly connected to bodies like Free the Slaves and to make certain that FTS has broad public support. When the human rights workers in rural Thailand know that international organizations are watching out for them—and, more important, when slaveholders, corrupt police, and governments know that they are being watched from abroad—that knowledge brings power and protection to those fighting slavery.

The fight against slavery also needs to draw on the experiences of other successful campaigns. Let me give two examples. In Britain today there are antiracist groups that monitor the police and legal system to make sure that black people receive fair treatment. These nongovernmental, voluntary groups inspect jails, provide legal help, investigate allegations of police violence, and campaign and lobby against racist treatment by the state. If a black person dies in police custody, the government knows that the group will demand a full investigation and report. Racists who might be tempted to abuse their position of power know that they could become the focus of attention and legal action. The CPT in Brazil and SOS Slaves in Mauritania (when they are allowed to operate) perform much the same function with regard to slavery. But this type of local antislavery group needs to be fostered and protected in all the countries where the state is not enforcing the laws against slavery.

The anti-apartheid movement provides my second example. When the apartheid system of racist oppression ruled South Africa, anti-apartheid groups around the world kept up the pressure that hastened its downfall. These groups made an enormous difference in three ways. First, they (like Anti-Slavery International and Free the Slaves) worked to keep the abuses of the apartheid system in the public eye, focusing again and again on the violence needed to prop up the racist government. By the late 1980s, was there anyone in the first world unaware of the imprisonment of Nelson Mandela? Second, they mounted campaigns to bring financial pressure on the apartheid regime, boycotting goods and calling for disinvestment from South Africa. The apartheid system really cracked when big American investment houses and universities began to pull out, hurting the regime financially. Third, they supported the local groups in South Africa through political lobbying, with legal aid, and with money. When a local activist was arrested, letters would flood in from around the world. As the groups lobbied governments to isolate the apartheid regime, these three ways of fighting apartheid had a powerful impact. All of them can be adopted and used effectively by antislavery campaigners.

The economic sanctions that the anti-apartheid movement brought to bear against South Africa bring us back to the questions of financial links. Today the World Trade Organization (WTO) and the International Monetary Fund (IMF) oversee governments, businesses, and industries around the world. They both wield enormous power by issuing trade credits, which could be linked to human rights guarantees. But human rights and the use of slavery are so low on their agenda as to be invisible. Greider puts it well:

> The terms of trade are usually thought of as commercial agreements, but they are also an implicit statement of moral values. In its present terms, the global system values property over human life. When a nation like China steals the property of capital, pirating copyrights, films or technology, other countries will take action to stop it and be willing to impose sanctions and penalty tariffs on the offending nation's trade. When human lives are stolen . . . nothing happens to the offenders since, according to the free market's sense of conscience, there is no crime.[10]

We are back to the terms of the abolition campaigns of the nineteenth century: if we are going to stop slavery we must convince the world that human rights need even more protection than property rights. The freedom of human beings must have priority over the free market in goods. This seems such a fundamental truth that it is hard to imagine that anyone would disagree. But where are the international laws to protect slaves and punish governments that allow enslavement? Governments and businesses are more likely to suffer international penalties today for counterfeiting a Britney Spears CD than for using slave labor.

In 1997 at the International Court of Justice in The Hague, Bosnian Serb military leaders were charged with genocide and other war crimes.

In the same year the WTO threatened Britain with fines and penalties for refusing to import American beef treated with steroids. Also in 1997 the United Nations maintained economic sanctions against Iraq while its inspection teams searched the country for biological and chemical weapons. But what country has been sanctioned by the UN for slavery? Where are the UN inspection teams charged with searching out slave labor? Where are the penalties from the WTO for exporting slave-made goods? Who speaks for slaves in the International Court of Justice? Viewed objectively the situation is bizarre: block the free movement of dead cows between countries and be penalized; buy and sell live humans across national borders and no one cares. The tremendous power of the IMF and the WTO has to be brought to bear on slavery.[11]

To bring an end to slavery, we have to take a very dispassionate look at slaves as a commodity. Just as we must explore how slave-made goods fit into the international economy, so we must come to understand how slaves flow from place to place and into the hands of slaveholders. Slavery will never be stopped if freed slaves can be easily replaced with new slaves. Say the words "slave trade" and most people picture wooden ships leaving Africa for the New World, but the trade has been evolving and changing. The modern version uses false passports and airline tickets. It packs slaves into trucks and bribes border guards. It covers its tracks with false work contracts and fraudulent visas. It does with people what organized crime does with heroin, and often more successfully. Within countries and across borders we must follow the slaves and plug the loopholes. The U.S. Drug Enforcement Agency leads other countries in spending billions of dollars to stem the flow of drugs. What budget contains funds to counter the flow of slaves?

There is an important historical precedent. In the nineteenth century Britain's foreign policy included an active program against the slave trade. Fleets of warships were sent to the west coast of Africa to intercept slavers and to free slaves. Slave ships were confiscated and destroyed, and rewards were paid to informants who tipped off the patrols. The slave trade became both dangerous and bad business. We still have the capability to intercept slaves today. In the last few years, both the United States and Great Britain have sent fleets of warships and whole armies to overthrow the Iraqi government at a cost of billions of dollars. When the political will is there, governments find the needed money and muscle.

At airports and border crossings around the world there should be officials searching for slaves. Investigators should be tracing the flow of slaves and confiscating cars, trucks, boats, and aircraft. Sting operations should be trying to buy slaves and busting the dealers. Almost all of the skills of existing law enforcement can be brought to bear against slavery. Even the flow of slaves inside countries such as Brazil and Thailand can be stopped. The treaties are already in place that allow the U.S. Drug Enforcement Agency to work with local law enforcement, giving them funds, training, and equipment to stop the production and flow of drugs. Where are the same sort of treaties to stop the flow of slaves? It is worth remembering that almost all countries have signed a treaty promising to "take all effective measures to prevent ships and aircraft authorized to fly their flags from conveying slaves and to punish persons guilty of such acts."[12]

A nonprofit group called Global Survival Network, based in Washington, D.C., has studied the enslavement and shipment of young women from Russia and Ukraine to countries far and wide, including Israel and Japan. Their report stated that "undercover interviews with gangsters, pimps and corrupt officials found that local police forces—often those best able to prevent trafficking—are least interested in helping." According to Gillian Caldwell of the Network, "In Tokyo a sympathetic senator arranged a meeting for us with senior police officials to discuss the growing prevalence of trafficking women from Russia into Japan. The police insisted it wasn't a problem, and they didn't even want the concrete information we could have provided. That didn't surprise local relief agencies, who cited instances in which police had actually sold trafficked women back to the criminal networks which had enslaved them."[13]

National laws on trafficking are vague, and cooperation between countries is rare. Punishments are slight, and criminal gangs find it easier to transport women than drugs. Notice that the crime itself tends to be called "trafficking" rather than by its true name—the slave trade. For all the lip service and good intentions, it is clear that most Western governments are more concerned about the pirating of computer software or the importing of counterfeit designer watches than about the modern slave trade. In the nineteenth century, business and governments supported the slave trade because it was very profitable. In an ironic twist, businesses and governments today aren't interested in stopping the slave trade because it *doesn't* threaten profits. The presence of a few hundred Russian girls in Japanese brothels doesn't affect the balance of payments. The most vocal complaints get the attention of governments and the UN—and the loudest voices belong to the big corporations, not the human rights groups. So the international laws against the theft of software or copyright are highly developed, richly resourced, and strictly enforced. The laws against the slave trade are vague, crippled by neglect, and ignored. But we cannot put all the blame on the governments and the UN. They simply mirror the concerns that are brought to them. They reflect the preoccupations of their constituents.

Forty Acres, a Mule, and Psychotherapy

The constituents of the United Nations with the greatest power to direct policy and action are the most economically powerful countries, including the United States, Great Britain, Germany, China, and Japan. They also have the biggest say in the World Trade Organization, guarding the profits of their multinational corporations. But there is another set of constituents without any powerful friends: the slaves. Who speaks for them? Who guards their interests in the world economy and the world's capital cities? If they had to rely solely on the UN, the world's slaves would have little chance of freedom. Groups like Anti-Slavery International work hard, but they are like water dripping on the great boulders of the UN and national governments. Most slaves have to look to themselves for salvation. In the fight to eradicate slavery, we must consider the action of slaves freeing themselves.

Here is an absolute truth—the human and economic relationships of modern slavery are complex. It would be so much easier to understand and combat slavery if there were very clear good guys and bad guys, if all slaveholders were cruel and all slaves yearned for freedom, if the solution to all slavery were simply to set slaves free. But being free means more than just walking away from bondage. Freedom is a condition both physical and mental, and liberation is a bitter victory if it leads only to starvation or reenslavement. Ultimately, slaves have to find their own way into true freedom. The physical and psychological dependence they often feel toward their masters can make this a long process. If we expect an abused child in our country to need years of therapy and guidance to overcome his or her trauma, we can hardly expect abused slaves to enter free society immediately as full citizens. It is true that many ex-slaves are phenomenally resilient, but those who have suffered the most, such as freed slave-prostitutes in Thailand, may need a lifetime of care. Their suffering can scar them permanently and strain all their human relationships. Some of the well-known writers of this century, such as Maya Angelou and Toni Morrison, have explored how the trauma of slavery is passed down even through subsequent free generations. In the struggle to survive not just slavery but liberation, there is one striking parallel between the old slavery of the United States and the new slavery of today: when slavery came to an end in 1865 the slaves were (and are today) just tossed aside. If slavery is to end, we must learn how ex-slaves can best secure their own freedom.

There are only a few models we can turn to. Some are like Pureza Lopes Loyola, a poor Brazilian woman who has made liberation her cause. She began her crusade when her own son disappeared while working on a rural estate in northern Brazil. Selling most of her possessions, she traveled thousands of miles searching out the isolated and heavily guarded ranches where hundreds of workers were held in bondage. Helped by the Pastoral Land Commission (CPT) she began to file official complaints, some of which led to legal action and the release of bonded laborers. In May 1996 she finally located her son, who had indeed been enslaved on one of the ranches. Pureza Lopes Loyola brought a fearlessness and determination to the task and helped shame the Brazilian government into at least promising new laws. She was never enslaved, and her search was possible because she was free to travel; but buoyed up by her faith, she has led many slaves to freedom and given them the courage to speak out and denounce their captors. Despite many death threats she persists in her crusade, pursuing politicians, journalists, businesspeople, and ranch owners. In 1997 she was awarded the Anti-Slavery Award in London; her success shows what can be accomplished by even one activist at the local level.

If it weren't for El Hor and SOS Slaves in Mauritania, both of which are staffed, in part, by ex-slaves, we would be ignorant of much of the slavery there. These courageous organizations press for freedom, for equal treatment, and for the return of slave children to their parents. Their work barely has an effect on the vast extent of slavery in Mauritania, and when they gain some success they are likely to be arrested and locked up. But even though their reports are censored and suppressed and they themselves are constantly watched and followed, they nevertheless symbolize hope. When I spoke to slaves in the capital of Mauritania they had all heard of El Hor. They didn't understand about political lobbying or fighting cases in the courts, but they knew there were people working to free them—and it meant the world to them.

And recall the remarkable woman we met in India, Leela. Here is a bonded laborer, the daughter and wife of bonded laborers, helping to lead the families of her village up out of slavery. The key ingredients in this transformation are education, hard work, and very small capital inputs. Of course, "very small" is a relative measure. The milk goat the government provided to each of the women of Leela's self-help organization cost 800 rupees, a sum beyond their ability to save, but 800 rupees is about $20. What the women brought to the arrangement was the ability to work hard with very little. Sums as small as $100 are large enough to establish ex-slaves in independent businesses. The Indian government rehabilitation grant comes to around $160 and will, in a village, buy livestock and secure land and housing. But rehabilitation means more than just freedom plus a pair of goats.

One of the best places to see the right kind of rehabilitation is in India, in the programs set up by the South Asian Coalition on Child Servitude (SACCS). Following the teachings of Mahatma Gandhi, they focus on the poorest of the poor—often bonded farmworkers like those we met in Bandi—and work to enable them to set their own goals. Recognizing that minds must become free as well as bodies, SACCS provides education in human rights to bonded laborers. Human rights expert Richard Pierre Claude explains:

> In 1991 SACCS established a vocational rehabilitation center for freed persons to "help them become self-supportive and build their self-confidence and extricate them from their traumatic spell." Called *Mukti Ashram* (a retreat for liberation), the training center works with 60 trainees at a time supplying three months of vocational and literacy training, as well as human rights education. The Ashram also runs two-week orientation courses for selected ex-trainees on how to liberate bonded laborers, including children. Thus, by 1995, Mukti Ashram had graduated 1,000 trained activists who work to combat bonded labor[;] . . . most of them have become economically independent in their native villages besides helping the community to unite and struggle for their rights.[14]

It is an effective response to enslavement that dramatically improves the chances of staying free for those living in the areas where SACCS operates.

For many freed slaves, liberation brings new problems. A lifetime of dependence cannot be swept away in an instant. A person denied autonomy, who has never had to make choices, can be paralyzed when faced with making decisions. If we can learn anything from the lives of freed slaves, it is that liberation is a *process*, not an event. If we are serious about stopping slavery we have to be committed to supporting freed slaves in a process that can take years. We must think very carefully about what slaves need to achieve true freedom and consider how to help slaves as people. There is a growing body of knowledge about how to treat both the physical and mental injuries suffered by victims of torture. Psychologists are currently studying how to counter the trauma of war in children. But what do we know of the psychology of slavery? How do we heal the trauma of captivity? If Siri were ever released from her brothel in Thailand, what would be the prognosis for her mental health? If we are to end slavery, we will have to become experts in repairing the damage slavery brings to both mind and body. We will have to look carefully at the lessons of the Mukti Ashram.

We will also have to become experts in slaves as economic beings. Slaves usually have few skills and do jobs that are not worth much on the free market. But if they are freed and can't support themselves, how will they avoid being enslaved again? Small children are dependent on their parents, who often expect them to do simple tasks around the house. Slaves are kept in a state of permanent dependence and are generally prevented from learning all but the simplest tasks. We would never dream of dropping an eight-year-old into the job market to compete for his or her livelihood, but this has happened to thousands of freed slaves. Governments in the United States and Great Britain are spending millions to find ways to help single mothers get training, come off welfare, and enter the job market; thousands of people, from policy analysts to social workers, are involved. But for the 27 million slaves around the world, only a handful of people work to understand and build new economic routes from slavery to self-sufficiency. The economic process of becoming self-supporting parallels the growth to psychological independence. They are bound together, and we will have to learn exactly how to nurture them in tandem.

On subjects from psychology to small-scale economics to large-scale law enforcement, we need much more research and development. Almost no work has been done on understanding how best to sustain ex-slaves in their freedom. That said, the little that has been done suggests several ways to help people to stay free: giving them access to credit, letting them make their own decisions about what work they will do, overcoming corruption in the rehabilitation programs, guaranteeing the presence and oversight of powerful people on the side of ex-slaves, and providing that greatest of liberators, education. We know that very small credit unions have revolutionized the lives of many of the poorest of the poor in India and Bangladesh, and that their default rates on loans are lower than those experienced by Western banks.[15] We sometimes think that because in the Western world we have credit cards and mortgages and car loans and monthly payments, credit plays a role only in the big modern economies. Nothing could be further from the truth. Credit mechanisms in the developing world are both complex and virtually unregulated. Credit, debt, and the manipulation of interest and repayment can weave a trap of bondage or provide the lever that lifts a family out of slavery.

We also have the advice of the Indian Academy of Administration, which studied a number of both successful and unsuccessful "rehabilitations" and highlighted the importance of letting the ex-slaves guide their own transformation. But where there is slavery, there is corruption, and corruption can poison the rehabilitation process. The Rugmark program counters corruption with its own independent inspectors. When rehabilitation work has been successful in India, it has been because the vigilance committees are honest and hardworking. Ways have to be found to bring power to bear on the side of freed slaves. This doesn't have to be police or even government power—those officials, in fact, may be the main points of opposition—nor does it need to be overwhelming or violent power. Often the presence of aid workers or human rights observers from the cities is sufficient.

There is room here for a whole new job category: the freedom worker, much like those trained at the Mukti Ashram. Ideally, a local independent advisor would be placed with freed slaves for a year or two. He or she would not arrive with a plan for "development," but would enable ex-slaves to arrive at their own plans and then help in carrying them out. Such a worker would have to be teacher, counselor, advocate, co-worker, and friend. The Indian experience shows that advice and support are crucial to successful rehabilitation. The key to preventing reenslavement is education. When people can recognize the trap of bondage, know their rights as citizens, understand the strength of their community, and find new ways to earn their living, they are less vulnerable to slavery. Many Western charities tug at the heartstrings of the public with pleas to "sponsor" a poor child in a developing country. Research shows this is probably not the most effective way to help such children out of poverty—but perhaps it could help freed slaves. Where are their sponsors? Who will pay for freedom workers in developing countries? At the moment, with governments ducking their responsibilities, we have to look to the tiny organizations that have refused to give up and refused to pretend slavery doesn't exist.

The New Abolitionists

Sadly, the agencies and organizations in the developed world that will find and train freedom workers, trace the economic links of slave business, educate the public about the realities of modern slavery, and press governments to uphold their own laws are caught in a vicious circle of ignorance and lack of support. The main groups working against slavery are Free the Slaves, in America, and Anti-Slavery International (ASI), in Britain. ASI is the world's oldest human rights organization. Both groups work hard to expose and combat slavery and child labor. But Free the Slaves and ASI together have fewer than 15,000 supporters and members. They are mice fighting a herd of elephants. Compared to organizations such as Greenpeace or Amnesty International, which have millions of supporters worldwide, they are tiny. Why?

They are trapped by public ignorance: most people believe that slavery ended in the nineteenth century. To convince them otherwise requires a big publicity push, but to mount such an effort they need to be big organizations with lots of resources. And to be big organizations they need thousands of supporters who *know* slavery didn't end in the nineteenth century. Without massive support they can't undertake massive recruitment. It is hard to pull oneself up by the bootstraps, but that is exactly what the antislavery movement has to do. A number of other organizations address slavery as a part of their larger work; the Catholic Agency for Overseas Development (CAFOD), Oxfam, Human Rights Watch, and UNICEF have all tackled slavery from their own perspectives. What has been missing is a unified attack.

Before that unified attack can be launched two things have to happen. First, organizations that oppose slavery have to *focus* on slavery. For many groups, slavery is a peripheral problem linked to others. In the first pages of this book I stressed that slavery should not be confused with anything else: it is not prison labor, it is not all forms of child labor, it is not just being very poor and having few choices. All these things are terrible and need to be addressed, but they are not slavery. Slavery in a real, not metaphorical, form is growing and evolving. Human rights organizations must treat slavery as a separate and distinct type of human rights abuse. We have to *name* the problem as slavery, rather than roll it up into a mishmash of other problems. Only if we are very clear that slavery is the object of our research and campaigning can the work against slavery move ahead. Slavery is a complex and dynamic problem that has to be understood in its own right.

Part of the problem with naming slavery is precisely that: *slavery* is a very strong word. But the second thing that organizations must do is to use hard language and step even harder on some toes. Some organizations, and the UN in particular, are very timid about saying, "In country X there is slavery." As we've seen, in countries where slavery exists governments try to conceal it within bureaucratic language. Indian farmers are no longer "bonded labor" but "attached workers." With a wave of a pen, all the slaves in Mauritania became "ex-slaves." They might be called "contract labor" in the charcoal fields of Brazil or "employees" in the brothels of Thailand, but these people are slaves. And with millions of slaves in the world, we simply cannot allow the word *slavery* to become so diluted in meaning that it has no power to identify and condemn real slavery. One of the great achievements of Amnesty International is that it has never pulled its punches: torture is always called *torture*, and the reality of political repression has become clear to many more people. Slavery, too, must be shown in all its horror as well as its complexity. When the public stops asking, "What do you mean by slavery?" and "You mean slavery still exists?" (questions I have to answer several times a week), then slaves will be on their way to freedom.

We are seeing the beginning of a new abolitionist movement, facing challenges as difficult and entrenched as those faced in the early nineteenth century. One of those challenges is that we don't *want* to believe that slavery exists. Many people in developed countries feel good about the fact that slavery was abolished "back then" and are shocked and disappointed that it will have to be abolished all over again. In fact, the work to be done today doesn't diminish the achievements of the nineteenth-century abolitionists one bit. They fought to stop legal slavery, and they won that fight. We must stop illegal slavery.

If we are going to win, one of the first things we have to do is admit our own ignorance. Slaveholders, businesspeople, even governments hide slavery behind smoke screens of words and definitions. We have to penetrate this smoke and know slavery for what it is, recognizing that it is not a "third world" issue but a global reality—a reality in which we are already involved and implicated. In our own families, we have to admit that slavery touches us. Churches were the core of the original abolitionist movement. All along the Mason-Dixon line in America, church groups helped run the underground railway that brought slaves north to freedom. Today many churches are dedicated to protecting and preserving families. Yet what is more destructive to the life of a family than slavery? Think of Mauritanian slaveholders taking children from their mothers, or the sale of daughters in Thailand: slavery is unquestionably an abomination that denies the sanctity of life and crushes the young and vulnerable. Are we really ready to watch happily while our children kick soccer balls made by child slaves? Anyone who has children wants the best for them, but can the best be bought at the price of someone else's child?

It is a huge fight. On one side are people making a great deal of money from slavery. On the other is a handful of activists who have to spend more time fighting ignorance than fighting the slaveholders themselves. At every level, from family to job to church to political party, those who believe that slavery must stop have to join together. The people in slavery in the developing world will do almost anything to get free, but they can't do it alone. They will share with us their knowledge and strength, but we must share with them our resources and power. Otherwise, what we like to call the "free world" will continue to feed on slavery.

Hollow Mockery and Brass-Fronted Impudence

In 1852, preparing for the big Fourth of July celebrations, the city fathers of Rochester, New York, thought to ask one of their more famous citizens, Frederick Douglass, to give the keynote speech. Douglass was an escaped slave from the southern states who had become a leader in the fight for abolition. Perhaps the city fathers expected Douglass to be grateful to be living in freedom, or to favorably compare America's great tradition of liberty to the rule of European kings and tyrants. They were in for a surprise. When the whole town assembled for the celebration on Independence Day, Douglass mounted the platform and spoke:

> What to the American slave is your Fourth of July? . . . a day that reveals to him more than all other days, the gross injustice and cruelty to which he is a constant victim . . . your celebration is a sham; your boasted liberty an unholy license; your national greatness, swelling vanity; . . . your denunciation of tyrants, brass-fronted impudence; your shouts of liberty and equality, hollow mockery; your prayers and hymns, your sermons and thanksgivings, your religious parade are . . . bombast, fraud, deception, impiety and hypocrisy.[16]

I suspect that Douglass wasn't invited to the barbecue that followed. He poured into the ears of his audience biting ridicule and sarcasm, beneath which lay a single, simple question: If there are still slaves, how can you be proud of your freedom?

We have to answer the same question today. Whether we like it or not, we are now a global people. We must ask ourselves: Are we willing to live in a world with slaves? If not, we are obligated to take responsibility for things that are connected to us, even when far away. Unless we work to understand the links that tie us to slavery and then take action to break those links, we are puppets, subject to forces we can't or won't control. Not to take action is simply to give up and let other people jerk the strings that tie us to slavery. Of course, there are many kinds of exploitation in the world, many kinds of injustice and violence that merit our concern. But slavery is exploitation, violence, and injustice all rolled together in their most potent combination. If there is one fundamental violation of our humanity we cannot allow, it is slavery. If there is one basic truth that virtually every human being can agree on, it is that slavery must end. What good is our economic and political power, if we can't use it to free slaves? If we can't choose to stop slavery, how can we say that we are free?

CODA
Three Things You Can Do to Stop Slavery

We can eradicate slavery. The laws are in place, international agencies like the UN are ready, but nothing will happen until the public demands action. When every person that doesn't want to live in a world with slavery takes these three steps, slavery will end.

Step 1. Learn—If you have just read this book, you've already taken this step. Now share this book with a friend, your church, your class, and order one for your library. Remember that every penny of the royalties goes to anti-slavery work. Then keep educating yourself about how slavery infiltrates our world and our lives. There is a constantly updated flow of information at www.freethe slaves.net and www.antislavery.org.

Step 2. Join with others who want to end slavery—Around the world *Free the Slaves* and *Anti-Slavery International* are working to end slavery. We do this through supporting local organizations that liberate people who've been enslaved; through helping businesses and consumers stop buying into slavery; and through persuading national governments to enforce anti-slavery laws. There are millions of people just like you who want slavery to end today. To make your voice heard, join *Free the Slaves* in the USA, or its sister organization *Anti-Slavery International* in Europe. To do so simply contact them at: www. freetheslaves.net and www.antislavery.org. Or you can write or call at:

Free the Slaves	*Anti-Slavery International*
1326 14th Street NW	Thomas Clarkson House
Washington DC, 20005, USA	Broomgrove Road,
Phone: 202 588 1865	London, SW9 9TL, England.
	Phone: 020 7501 8920

Step 3. Act!—When you have joined *Free the Slaves* two things will happen: First, you'll be alerted to effective and timely actions you can take against slavery. Second, you'll be able to add your thoughts, energies, and commitment to ending slavery. Young people and older people, all types of skills, every mind and every heart is needed.

You'll also be asked to make a donation. It is truly needed. If you add up all the money spent in the world to fight slavery every year, it wouldn't equal the cost of one new army tank. When you consider that the cost of freeing most slaves, through activism and law enforcement, may be as little as $20, this disparity is obscene. As the (unpaid) Director of *Free the Slaves*, I've met dozens of ex-slaves who are starting new lives because local activists were funded to rescue and support them. As you know from reading this book, I've also met hundreds of slaves around the world who haven't been reached by the under-funded local organizations struggling against slavery. I will never accept that slavery should continue to be their fate.

And while you're at it, here are four more things you can do right away:

1. *Don't put this book on the shelf*—give it to someone else to read. Ignorance about slavery is one of the main reasons why it still grows. Take it to your club or church group where books are borrowed and discussed.

2. *Ask hard questions of charities*—if you currently support any charity that works in the developing world, be it child sponsorship, missionary work, or medical relief, ask them: What are you doing to stop slavery or to stop people being vulnerable to slavery and trafficking? And if they're not doing anything, tell them what you know about slavery and help lead them to action.

3. *Ask hard questions of politicians*—some of the most powerful weapons against slavery are the "sticks and carrots" of economic sanctions, trade, and support of developed countries. A law passed in the US Congress all but stopped child slavery in Dominican sugar fields overnight. When politicians want your vote, ask them what they are doing to stop slavery.

4. *Ask hard questions of your pension fund and your investments*—can your pen-sion fund or mutual fund assure you that they are not investing your money in companies that are linked to slave labor? What criteria besides profit guide their choice of investment? If they can't or won't give you a straight answer, move your money. There are ethical funds that avoid investing in companies that might be linked to slavery so that you don't have to profit from slavery.

Consider this gift to your children

- *Imagine* that after 6,000 years of slavery we commit ourselves to achieving its eradication.
- *Imagine* that your generation will be the one that is looked back on in his-tory as 'the generation that ended slavery'.
- *Imagine* that your children, and your grandchildren, will grow up in a world where slavery is just seen as an ugly blot on our history.
- *Imagine* a world where every person is born in freedom and lives in liberty.

OK, enough imagining, let's make it happen!

APPENDIX 1

A NOTE ON RESEARCH METHODS

Academic texts often place a section on research methodology just after a re-view of the literature and just before a chapter titled "Results." I chose not to follow that structure in order to better let the case studies I have presented speak for themselves. That said, I hope that this note will help clarify the methods I used to collect the information reported in this book and allay any concerns about the safety of my informants.

Up until now, most studies of slavery have been carried out by journalists or human rights campaigners. They have done wonderful work, and I have quoted and referred to such work repeatedly in this book. But they would usually be the first to admit that they often lack an overarching conceptual framework, as well as the time and space needed to go deeply into the social and economic re-lationships that underpin slavery. Journalists and activists have largely concen-trated on exposing and denouncing specific human rights violations, as well they should. But looking at specific violations of law doesn't get at the full reality of slavery. I think Richard A. Falk got it right when he wrote, "In essence, the pro-tection of human rights is an outcome of struggle between opposed social forces and cannot be understood primarily as an exercise in law-creation or rational persuasion."[1] What is generally lacking is the deeper research I have tried to do, getting up close to the details of an individual slave's life and work.

Five countries were chosen for these case studies according to a number of criteria. I was looking for countries that had a significant amount of slavery and those countries in which distinct economic activities using slave labor could be identified. I was interested in choosing countries that demonstrated different types of slavery, which varied between old and new forms. Access was another criterion (Burma, for example, is currently all but inaccessible), as was my desire to find at least one country in the New World. Because large numbers of people in Pakistan and India have been identified as bonded laborers, I felt that those two countries had to be included. Within each country I looked for one area of economic activity that could be effectively studied. Prostitution in Thailand was chosen because of the expertise of my fellow researcher there, Dr. Rachel Harrison, and because I felt the reader might have some knowledge of the topic from stories in the media. Water delivery in Mauritania was chosen after we began our work there because the water carriers' mobile style of work made them more accessible to us. Some earlier work had been done on charcoal making in Brazil, and I used that information to build up a research plan there. The same is true of brickmaking in Pakistan, though as I have found that the business is in decline, in retrospect I might have done better to select another area of work. The ancient and continuing use of bonded labor in Indian agriculture made it an obvious target, but again, perhaps not the best choice; it might have been more appropriate to concentrate on the small manufacturing businesses in India, which more obviously feed into the global economy. No one should assume that I have made a definitive statement about slavery in any of these countries, about these specific economic enterprises, or about the social relationships that tie them together. And by no means is this research exhaustive; there are many other countries that could be, and should be, studied. North Africa and the Gulf states, other countries of Southeast Asia and South America, and the shipment of slaves into virtually all countries of the developed world—especially western Europe, the United States, and Japan—all need large-scale and in-depth investigation.

I decided to use case studies for two key reasons. First, I followed the advice of Robert K. Yin, an authority on this research technique: "Case studies are the preferred strategy when how or why questions are being posed, when the investigator has little control over events and when the focus is on a contemporary phenomenon within some real-life context."[2] The research had to be exploratory because contemporary slavery is almost completely neglected in the social sciences. It is an area that is wide open for research, but also one in which earlier studies offer little guidance. Qualitative techniques are normally used to open new areas of interest, and in researching a topic that involves a kind of crime—and possibly holds some danger for researcher and research subjects—

I believe the less intrusive case study is the most appropriate methodology. Second, I chose this technique because it was my aim to make some comparisons among the five countries in which I gathered information. To the best of my knowledge, this is the first time that the same set of guiding research questions has been asked of situations of slavery in more than one place (a complete set of my research questions ends this appendix). I am convinced that the global nature of contemporary slavery requires such an approach. It was my aim in each country to gather all possible information on slavery there, as well as large amounts of background information on national history, culture, and economics, which would then be fleshed out and illustrated through the case studies of a specific economic activity.

It would have been impossible to carry out these tasks without the help of the research colleagues who worked with me in each country. It took almost two years to identify and recruit for each of the five countries researchers with the depth of knowledge, experience, research skills, and languages that I needed: Dr. Rachel Harrison and Gampol Nirawan in Thailand, N'Gadi N'di in Mauritania, Luciano Padrão in Brazil, Haris Gazdar in Pakistan, and Pramod Singh and Dr. Praveen Jha in India. I have to say that I was tremendously fortunate; each one of these researchers proved to be an even better colleague than I had hoped. Each one of them provided me with a large amount of information and guidance long before I visited his or her country. Each one opened my eyes to a new culture, and demonstrated great sensitivity when we met with enslaved people. In each country I worked with my researchers to find and interview slaves and slaveholders. Sometimes I would do the interviewing, with the researcher acting as translator; at other times the researcher would do the interviewing. In all countries we were careful to translate our questions ahead of time to ensure that what we asked made sense to the respondents.

In every country we put the safety of the slaves first. All of our respondents were asked if they would agree to talk to with us and assured of their anonymity. If someone was nervous or frightened, we moved on. Slaves have enough problems without being hassled by researchers! I appreciate that people might feel especially concerned about the young women we interviewed in the brothels in Thailand, about a male researcher approaching young women forced into prostitution, and about their safety. We were keenly aware of these problems as well. I should be clear that my fellow researcher in Thailand was a woman who has many years' experience in interviewing and working with sex workers. We visited brothels under the guidance and with the introduction of local HIV/

AIDS workers who are accepted and trusted by the young women. When we did have a chance to have longer conversations with Siri and another young woman, we were accompanied by Siri's mother as well. Much of this information was collected as we visited a rural Buddhist temple and then sat down together to a long lunch at a riverside restaurant. Their names, and the names of all slaves in this book (with the exception of those taken from other published works), have been changed. I will admit that I was not always completely truthful with slaveholders. In Pakistan, for example, we introduced ourselves to brick kiln owners as researchers studying small businesses and the way that such businesses fit into the national economy: this was true, just not the whole truth. In India I found that having grown up in a rural area went a long way in gaining the cooperation of the landlords. By asking them about crop yields, growing seasons, rotation techniques, fuel and seed costs, fertilizer types and expense, and the histories of their animals, I found they would soon branch into the area I hadn't brought up: labor, and bonded labor in particular. For me, the research was an overwhelming learning experience, one that added new depth to my more than twenty years of experience in social research.

What follows is the set of guiding questions that I tried to answer in each of the five countries I studied. Not all of the questions applied to each place, but we attempted to find equivalents between countries. Of course, having now completed the research there are some questions I might omit and new ones that I would add. You will note that there are a large number of questions about the precise details of the businesses that I studied. I completed the research with much more information on these topics than has been included in this book. I was persuaded by my editors that this detail was beyond the interest of most readers, and stepping back from the material I know this to be true—but if anyone would like to start their own brick kiln I can give them some pointers.

Slavery Research Questions

DEMOGRAPHICS For each unit (that is, a farm, a brothel, a brickworks, or whatever is the local and specific unit of "production"):

1. *Size*

   How many slaves/ unfree laborers are held in the unit
   (kiln/factory/brothel/farm, etc.)?

How does this unit compare with others of its type (same "business") in the same geographical area in terms of total number of "employees" and the amount of business/production?

Is it big, small, or average when compared to other such units?

What is the range of sizes of such units within the same geographical area?

Are such units known to be different in size in other geographical areas?

2. *Scale of Enslavement*

What proportion of the local workforce in that sector is enslaved/unfree?

What proportion overall in the workforce in that particular village/region?

What is the population of the nearest geographical unit (village/town/district)?

What is the best estimate of the number of enslaved/unfree laborers within that geographical unit?

3. *Gender and Age Breakdown*

What proportion of the unfree laborers in each unit are male/female?

What proportion are children; what is the age breakdown?

Is the work they are doing specifically categorized for men or women?

Is there segregation of tasks? (That is, if the ultimate "product" requires several steps of stages in its production, are these jobs segregated to different groups—men, women, or children?)

Are the slaves/unfree laborers held as individuals, or as families?

4. *Ethnic Differences*

What ethnic backgrounds are the slaves?

Are the slaves from a different ethnic group than the slaveholders?

Are there ethnic differences between the slaves and others involved in slavery (e.g., the community around the unit) or users of products of slavery (e.g., brothel users)?

Is there a history of domination by one of these groups over another?

5. *Religious Differences*

Are there religious differences between slave and slaveholder and/or between slave and the consumer of slave products?

What is the nature of the religiosity of all the people in the context? That is, what is the religious context within the village/city/country—a predominant religion? regular practice? institution of religious law?

6. *Location of Slavery*

Are the units using slave labor mainly in rural or urban settings, or do they appear equally in both?

Are they geographically or otherwise isolated?

Do they tend to exist in places where "modern" norms and ideas do not prevail?

Do local people know of the existence of slavery in their area?

Does the local/national government know?

7. *Effect of the Work on Slaves*

How does enslavement affect their life expectancy?

Does the production process bring any specific health dangers?

At what age are slaves normally not able to continue the work, and what happens to them then?

8. *The Slaveholders*

Who are they: age, sex, education level, class/caste background?

How do they fit into the society/community? What is their role?

How are they perceived by other members of the community?

How long have they lived in this community?

Do they have other jobs/enterprises?

Is slaveholding an inherited occupation?

Why are they slaveholders when others of similar background are not?

If they were not slaveholders, what would they be likely to be doing?

How do/would they explain their holding of these laborers?

FORMS AND PROCESSES

1. *Economics of Slavery*

How much capital is needed to establish this form of production?

Details on overheads:

> What is the cost of a slave?
>
> What costs are there in addition to the purchase price/loan?
>
> What are the subsistence costs of a slave?
>
> What rents are paid by the slaveholders?
>
> What other expenses do they have connected to labor?
>
> What is the cost of any necessary raw materials?
>
> What is the cost of the legitimating mechanism that conceals the illegality of slaveholding?
>
> What kinds of permits, bribes, and so forth are needed to start and maintain production/operation?
>
> What other workers are needed and how much are they paid?

What is the cost of "free labor" if hired to do the same work?

What is their estimated total turnover?

What profit does the owner make?

What competition does the owner face?

Is the market for the product or service increasing or decreasing?

Do they pay any taxes and/or bribes?

What is the potential for mechanization to replace slaves?

Is the production unit part of the formal or informal economy?

If the item is also produced mechanically rather than by slaves, does the mechanized production serve a different market?

Is mechanized production becoming more economical?

What are the obstacles to mechanization?

2. *Profit on Investment*

How does the profit from slave production compare with profit from paid labor production? Are there other ways that the slaveholders could invest their capital?

If so, would they invest their capital elsewhere if given the choice?

Do they have the choice?

How committed are the slaveholders to enterprise using slave labor?

Could they easily and profitably shift to other forms of investment—or is their stake in slaveholding too high?

3. *Economic Indicators (for the local area/region/nation)*

   What are local wage rates and what is the local cost of living?

   What are the absolute and relative poverty levels?

   What does it cost to keep a person alive?

   What is the rate of inflation?

   How has the local economy been changing?

   What is the unemployment rate?

4. *Work and Production Processes*

   What is a full description of the work being done?

   Within this area of production, which element of the work is done by slave labor?

   Is the work seasonal?

   Is it the top end of the product range or the lower end? (That is, is it a "high-quality," "high-cost" product or a "low-quality," "low-cost" product when compared to the corresponding product of nonslaves in the same market?)

   Is the slave-produced item part of a bigger product? (That is, is the product a "finished" product ready for sale/use, or will it require further processing before sale/use; if a service rather than a product, is it a "final" service or part of a larger/longer service?)

   Is the market for the product local, national, or international?

   How many processes/stops does the item go through before reaching its end use?

5. *Consumer Choices*

   Who is the end consumer of the product?

   How does the slave-produced item compare with the product from other sources?

   If the consumer chose not to use slave-produced items, what would be another source of the item, and what would be the price difference?

6. *Process of Enslavement*

   Is the process of enslavement debt, trickery, use of contracts, violence? Or a combination of these?

What would be a typical story of enslavement in this situation?

Is there a legitimating social, cultural, or legal mechanism? If so, what is it?

Is it possible to copy/transcribe any "contract" or debt bond?

What is the first point of contact between potential slave and slaver?

How is the potential slave approached?

What are the factors that might push or pull a person into enslavement—social, family, economic, cultural? (What is the slaver offering that draws the person into the relationship?)

What are the aspects of potential slaves' lives that are pushing them toward enslavement?

What makes them vulnerable to enslavement?

What alternatives exist to enslavement for the slaves?

How would they survive if not enslaved?

How do they seal the bargain?

At what point is the agreement irrevocable?

Is it really irrevocable or is that just the perception of the slave?

Once enslaved, are they likely to be retained by the person who enslaved them, or will they be sold?

Is the slaver a procurer, a middleperson, or the person who uses the slaves?

What is the process until they end up in the place they're likely to stay?

Once they're there, are they likely to be later sold or traded to others?

What makes them attractive slaves—what attributes do they need to have?

Are they enslaved with a view to filling a particular job?

Might they be moved to other work at some stage?

7. *The Relationship*

How does the enslaved person see the situation he or she is in?

Does that perspective change at different points in the relationship?

What is the social relationship between the slave and the slaveholder? (That is, how is it perceived by each of them and how is it perceived by the people around them?)

Do the people who enslave try to justify enslavement—to themselves, the community, the government? If so, how?

What is the nature of control over the slave? How is violence used or threatened?

What social or psychological violence might be used to control the slave?

What social norms, beyond the threat of violence, bind the slave and the slaveholder?

What is the role of government or official acquiescence or participation in enslavement?

Is the slave/slaveholder relationship "enforced" by local "law enforcement"?

Is there any possibility of manumission? If so, how can that process take place?

If you've been a slave, does it affect what you can do afterward?

If you stop being a slave, are you socially marked or otherwise affected?

8. *Children of Slaves*

What happens to any children of slaves?

What control do slaves have over their offspring?

Are children a help or hindrance to the slave?

Do they increase or decrease the value of the slave to the slaveholder?

Do slaves control their reproduction at all?

9. *Necessary Preconditions*

Can it be said that violence and its threat are not the monopoly of the state in this local area/region/country? (That is, are people with power or weapons able to use them without a high chance of state intervention, and specifically to use them to capture and/or hold slaves?)

Are there social norms that validate or allow enslavement (at least for the slaver and those with whom immediate trading of slave-produced goods or services takes place)?

What is the legitimating mechanism that allows the concealment of slavery, which is officially illegal?

EXCERPTS FROM INTERNATIONAL CONVENTIONS ON SLAVERY

The source for all documents quoted below is Centre for Human Rights Geneva, *Universal Instruments*, vol. 1 of *Human Rights: A Compilation of International Instruments* (New York: United Nations, 1994).

Slavery Convention of the League of Nations (1926)

Article 1   For the purpose of the present Convention, the following definitions are agreed upon:

(1) Slavery is the status or condition of a person over whom any or all of the powers attaching to the right of ownership are exercised.

(2) The slave trade includes all acts involved in the capture, acquisition or disposal of a person with intent to reduce him to slavery; all acts involved in the acquisition of a slave with a view to selling or exchanging him; all acts of disposal by sale or exchange of a slave acquired with a view to being sold or exchanged, and, in general, every act of trade or transport in slaves.

Article 2   The High Contracting Parties undertake, each in respect of the territories placed under its sovereignty, jurisdiction, protection, suzerainty or tutelage, so far as they have not already taken the necessary steps:

(a) To prevent and suppress the slave trade;

(b) To bring about, progressively and as soon as possible, the complete abolition of slavery in all its forms.

Article 3   The High Contracting Parties undertake to adopt all appropriate measures with a view to preventing and suppressing the embarkation, disembarkation and transport of slaves in their territorial waters and upon all vessels flying their respective flags.

(The 1926 Convention was adopted with slight amendments by the United Nations in 1953.)

The Universal Declaration of Human Rights (1948)

Article 1   All human beings are born free and equal in dignity and rights.

Article 4   No one shall be held in slavery or servitude; slavery and the slave trade shall be prohibited in all their forms.

Article 13(1)   Everyone has the right to freedom of movement and residence within the borders of each state.

Article 23(1)   Everyone has the right to the free choice of employment, to just and favourable conditions of work and to protection against unemployment.

Supplementary Convention on the Abolition of Slavery, the Slave Trade, and Institutions and Practices Similar to Slavery (1956)

SECTION 1—INSTITUTIONS AND PRACTICES SIMILAR TO SLAVERY

Article 1   Each of the States Parties to this Convention shall take all practicable and necessary legislative and other measures to bring about progressively and as soon as possible the complete abolition or abandonment of the following institutions and practices, where they still exist and whether or not they are covered by the definition of slavery contained in article 1 of the Slavery Convention signed at Geneva on 25 September 1926:

(a) Debt bondage, that is to say, the status or condition arising from a pledge by a debtor of his personal services or of those of a person under his control as security for a debt, if the value of those services as reasonably assessed is not applied towards the liquidation of the debt or the length and nature of those services are not respectively limited and defined;

(b) Serfdom, that is to say, the condition or status of a tenant who is by law, custom or agreement bound to live and labour on land belonging to another person and to render some determinate service to such other person, whether for reward or not, and is not free to change his status;

(c) Any institution or practice whereby:

    (i) A woman, without the right to refuse, is promised or given in marriage on payment of a consideration in money or in kind to her parents, guardian, family or any other person or group; or

    (ii) The husband of a woman, his family, or his clan, has the right to transfer her to another person for value received or otherwise; or

    (iii) A woman on the death of her husband is liable to be inherited by another person;

(d) Any institution or practice whereby a child or young person under the age of 18 years, is delivered by either or both of his natural parents or by his guardian to another person, whether for reward or not, with a view to the exploitation of the child or young person or of his labour.

Article 2   With a view to bringing to an end the institutions and practices mentioned in article 1 (c) of this Convention, the States Parties undertake to prescribe, where appropriate, suitable minimum ages of marriage, to encourage the use of facilities whereby the consent of both parties to a marriage may be freely expressed in the presence of a competent civil or religious authority, and to encourage the registration of marriages.

SECTION II—THE SLAVE TRADE

Article 3

    1. The act of conveying or attempting to convey slaves from one country to another by whatever means of transport, or of being accessory thereto, shall be a criminal offence under the laws of the States Parties to this Convention and persons convicted thereof shall be liable to very severe penalties.

    2. (a) The States Parties shall take all effective measures to prevent ships and aircraft authorised to fly their flags from conveying slaves and to punish persons guilty of such acts or of using national flags for that purpose.

    (b) The States Parties shall take all effective measures to ensure that their ports, airfields and coasts are not used for the conveyance of slaves.

    3. The States Parties to this Convention shall exchange information in order to ensure the practical co-ordination of the measures taken by them in combating the slave trade and shall inform each other of every case of the slave trade, and of every attempt to commit this criminal offence, which comes to their notice.

Article 4   Any slave who takes refuge on board any vessel of a State Party to this Convention shall *ipso facto* be free.

SECTION III—SLAVERY AND INSTITUTIONS AND PRACTICES SIMILAR TO SLAVERY

Article 5   In a country where the abolition or abandonment of slavery, or of the institutions or practices mentioned in article 1 of this Convention, is not yet complete, the act of mutilating, branding or otherwise marking a slave or a person of servile status in order to indicate his status, or as a punishment, or for any other reason, or of being accessory thereto, shall be a criminal offence under the laws of the States Parties to this Convention and persons convicted thereof shall be liable to punishment.

Article 6

  1. The act of enslaving another person or of inducing another person to give himself or a person dependent upon him into slavery, or of attempting these acts, or being accessory thereto, or being a party to a conspiracy to accomplish any such acts, shall be a criminal offence under the laws of the States Parties to this Convention and persons convicted thereof shall be liable to punishment.

  2. Subject to the provisions of the introductory paragraph of article 1 of this Convention, the provisions of paragraph 1 of the present article shall also apply to the act of inducing another person to place himself or a person dependent upon him into the servile status resulting from any of the institutions or practices mentioned in article 1, to any attempt to perform such acts, to being accessory thereto, and to being a party to a conspiracy to accomplish such acts.

SECTION IV—DEFINITIONS

Article 7   For the purposes of the present Convention:

  (a) "Slavery" means, as defined in the Slavery Convention of 1926, the status or condition of a person over whom any or all of the powers attaching to the right of ownership are exercised, and "slave" means a person in such condition or status:

  (b) "A person of servile status" means a person in the condition or status resulting from any of the institutions or practices mentioned in article 1 of this Convention;

  (c) "Slave trade" means and includes all acts involved in the capture, acquisition or disposal of a person with intent to reduce him to slavery; all acts involved in the acquisition of a slave with a view to selling or exchanging him; all acts of disposal by sale or exchange of a person acquired with a view to being sold or exchanged; and, in general, every act of trade or transport in slaves by whatever means of conveyance.

NOTES

Chapter 1. The New Slavery

1. Quoted by Alison Sutton in *Slavery in Brazil: A Link in the Chain of Modernisation* (London: Anti-Slavery International, 1994), p. 102.

2. From a letter given to SEICOM (Secretaria de Industria, Comercio e Mineracao do Estado do Para) researchers, published in 1992 in Rita Maria Rodrigues, *As Mulheres do Ouro: A Forca de Trabalho Feminino nos Garimpos do Tapajos* (The women of gold: Female labor force in the Garimpos of Tapajos) (Belem: SEICOM, 1992), quoted by Sutton in *Slavery in Brazil*, p. 97.

3. Quoted by Sue Branford, "Brazilian Congress Tells of Half-Million Child Prostitutes," *Guardian*, 29 June 1993, p. 12.

4. The word *slave* comes from the word *Slav* (as in "Slavic peoples"), arriving in Middle English from Old French *esclave* and medieval Latin *sclavus, sclava* "Slavonic (captive)." It comes from Roman times when Germans supplied the slave markets of Europe with captured Slavs. See Milton Meltzer, *Slavery: A World History* (New York: De Capo Press, 1993), pp. 1–6. Within sociology Orlando Patterson (*Slavery and Social Death* [Cambridge, Mass.: Harvard University Press, 1982]) has posited a definition of slavery, which he applies to examples of historical slavery, that centers on the "social death" of the slave: "slavery is the permanent, violent domination of natally alienated and generally dishonored persons" (p. 13). It is a definition that has some power in helping us to understand the slavery of the past, but I feel it is less useful in

considering the slavery of the present. More useful as a guide to carrying out research into contemporary slavery is his division, derived from David V. I. Bell (*Power, Influence, and Authority* [New York: Oxford University Press, 1975], p. 26), of the power relation of slavery into three facets: "The first is social and involves the use or threat of violence in the control of one person by another. The second is the psychological facet of influence, the capacity to persuade another person to change the way he perceives his interests and his circumstances. And the third is the cultural facet of authority, 'the means of transforming force into right and obedience into duty' which, according to Jean Jacques Rousseau, the powerful find necessary to 'ensure them continual mastership'" (p. 2). The coercive power of the slaveholder and the relationship of that power to the coercive power of the state are crucial to slavery. One might think that Karl Marx would have defined slavery from an economic perspective, but in fact he called it a "relation of domination" (*Grundrisse: Foundations of the Critique of Political Economy*, trans. Martin Nicolaus [Harmondsworth: Penguin, 1973], pp. 325–26). And although many commentators have assigned slavery to a Marxian precapitalist twilight, Marx himself saw it as contemporary reality needing careful social and economic analysis. My own definition of a slave would be *a person held by violence or the threat of violence for economic exploitation*. I appreciate that this is general in the extreme, but I believe that any useful definition must be kept general so as to encompass the wide variations of form that slavery takes.

5. See, for example, Benjamin Quarles, *The Negro in the American Revolution* (Chapel Hill: published for the Institute of Early American History and Culture, Williamsburg, Va., by University of North Carolina Press, 1961); David Brion Davis, *The Problem of Slavery in the Age of Revolution, 1770–1823* (Ithaca: Cornell University Press, 1975).

6. An excellent review of the early history of slavery may be found in Meltzer, *Slavery*.

7. William Greider, *One World, Ready or Not: The Manic Logic of Global Capitalism* (New York: Simon and Schuster, 1997), p. 37.

8. There is a very large literature on the economic history of slavery in the United States; see, for example, Roger L. Ransom, *Conflict and Compromise: The Political Economy of Slavery, Emancipation, and the American Civil War* (Cambridge: Cambridge University Press, 1989).

9. See Eugene Genovese, *Roll, Jordan, Roll: The World the Slaves Made* (New York: Vintage, 1976), pp. 416, 420.

10. See Ted C. Fishman, "The Joys of Global Investment," *Harpers*, February 1997, pp. 35–44.

11. For more on restavecs, see Jean Robert Cadet, *Restevec: Haitian Slave Child to Middle Class American* (Austin: U. of Texas Press, 1998); or "Restavec: Child Labor in Haiti," a report by the Minnesota Lawyers International Human Rights Committee (University of Minnesota, August 1990).

12. *The Forgotten Slaves: Report on a Mission to Investigate the Girl-Child Slaves of West Africa* (Melbourne: Anti-Slavery Society of Australia, 1996). Also see Howard W. French, "The Ritual Slaves of Ghana: Young and Female," *New York Times*, 20 January 1997, pp. A1, A5.

13. *The Game's Up* (London: Children's Society, 1996); see also Maggie O'Kane, "Death of Innocence," *Guardian*, 12 February 1996, sec. G2, pp. 2–3.

14. Steven Greenhouse, "Three Plead Guilty to Enslaving Migrant Workers in South Carolina," *New York Times*, 8 May 1997, sec. A, p. 20; Carey Goldberg, "Sex Slavery, Thailand to New York," *New York Times*, 11 September 1995, sec. B, p. 1. See also Ky Henderson, "The New Slavery," *Human Rights* 24, no. 4 (fall 1997); available http://www.abanet.org/irr/hr/kyslave.html (12 October 1998).

15. Great Britain Department of Trade and Industry, *Overseas Trade Statistics of the United Kingdom* (London: H. M. Stationery Office, 1997); Economist Intelligence Unit, *Country Forecast Brazil, Third Quarter 1997*, ed. Graham Stock (London: EIU, 1997).

16. See Roger L. Ransom, "The Economics of Slavery," in his *Conflict and Compromise*, pp. 41–81.

17. Roger Plant, *Sugar and Modern Slavery: A Tale of Two Countries* (London: Zed Books, 1987); see also Mary Jane Camejo, *A Troubled Year: Haitians in the Dominican Republic*, an Americas Watch report (New York: Americas Watch and the National Coalition for Haitian Refugees, 1992).

18. Arthur Leathley, "Party to Debate Claims That Britain Is a 'Slave Haven,'" *Times* (London), 23 September 1996, p. 8; "Girls in the Slave Trade," *Guardian*, 26 February 1996, sec. G2, p. 6.

19. Bridget Anderson, *Britain's Secret Slaves: An Investigation into the Plight of Overseas Domestic Workers* (London: Anti-Slavery International, 1993), p. 47.

20. Ibid., p. 68.

21. See Genovese, *Roll, Jordan, Roll*, pp. 30–48.

22. For the relevant United Nations conventions, see Slavery Convention,

25 September 1926, 46 Stat. 2183, 60 L.N.T.S. 253; Protocol of Amendment to the Slavery Convention, 7 December 1953, 212 U.N.T.S. 17; Supplementary Convention on the Abolition of Slavery, the Slave Trade, and Institutions and Practices Similar to Slavery, 7 September 1956, 18 U.S.T. 3201, T.I.A.S. No. 6418, 266 U.N.T.S. 3; ILO Convention (No. 29) Concerning Forced or Compulsory Labour, 10 June 1930, 39 U.N.T.S. 55; ILO Convention (No. 105) Concerning the Abolition of Forced Labour, 25 June 1957, 320 U.N.T.S. 291. Appendix 2 provides excerpts of the relevant UN conventions on slavery and debt bondage.

Chapter 2. Thailand

1. Siri is, of course, a pseudonym; the names of all respondents have been changed for their protection. See appendix 1 for a description of my research methods and how respondents were protected. I spoke with them in December 1996.

2. I. B. Horner, *Women under Primitive Buddhism* (London: Routledge, 1930), p. 43.

3. "Caught in Modern Slavery: Tourism and Child Prostitution in Thailand," Country Report Summary prepared by Sudarat Sereewat-Srisang for the Ecumenical Consultation held in Chiang Mai in May 1990.

4. Foreign exchange rates are in constant flux. Unless otherwise noted, dollar equivalences for all currencies reflect the rate at the time of the research.

5. From interviews done by Human Rights Watch with freed child prostitutes in shelters in Thailand, reported in Jasmine Caye, *Preliminary Survey on Regional Child Trafficking for Prostitution in Thailand* (Bangkok: Center for the Protection of Children's Rights [CPCR], 1996), p. 25.

6. Thais told me that it would be very surprising if a well-off man or a politician did not have at least one mistress. When I was last in Thailand there was much public mirth over the clash of wife and mistress outside the hospital room of a high government official who had suffered a heart attack, as each in turn barricaded the door.

7. See Mark VanLandingham, Chanpen Saengtienchai, John Knodel, and Anthony Pramualratana, *Friends, Wives, and Extramarital Sex in Thailand* (Bangkok: Institute of Population Studies, Chulalongkorn University, 1995), pp. 9–25.

8. Ibid., p. 53.

9. See ibid., p. 34: "Several women [interviewed] were willing to put up with

their husband's commercial sex patronage because they saw it as an alternative to his taking a minor wife or mistress, which was viewed as a much more serious threat to the financial and emotional security of the marriage."

10. Quoted in ibid., p. 18.

11. See Pasuk Phongpaichit and Chris Baker, *Thailand's Boom* (Chiang Mai: Silkworm Books, 1996), pp. 51–54.

12. Government will and resources accomplished a dramatic drop in HIV infection, but increasing condom use requires being able to choose to use condoms. Enslaved prostitutes do not have that choice.

13. Personal communication, December 1996.

14. R. D. Laing, *The Politics of Experience* (Harmondsworth: Penguin, 1967), p. 95.

15. Chuan Leekpai is quoted in "PM Gives Himself 3-Month Deadline to Curb Child Sex," *Nation*, 14 November 1992, p. 3.

16. Growing police involvement was discussed both by government AIDS workers interviewed and by *A Modern Form of Slavery: Trafficking of Burmese Women and Girls into Brothels in Thailand*, Asia Watch/Women's Rights Project (New York: Human Rights Watch, 1993), pp. 84–96.

17. Thailand's leading newspapers played an important role in keeping this case in the public eye. See esp. "Mystery Surrounds the Death of a Prostitute in Songkhla," *Bangkok Post*, 8 November 1992; "Police Have Strong Evidence in Prostitute Murder Case," *Bangkok Post*, 2 December 1992, p. 5.

18. "20 Songkhla Policemen Transferred," *Nation*, 9 March 1993, p. 8.

19. *A Modern Form of Slavery*, p. 3.

20. "Ranong Brothel Raids Net 148 Burmese Girls," *Nation*, 16 July 1993, p. 12.

21. *A Modern Form of Slavery*, p. 112.

22. See *International Report on Trafficking in Women (Asia-Pacific Region)* (Bangkok: Global Alliance Against Traffic in Women [GAATW], 1996); Sudarat Sereewat, *Prostitution: Thai-European Connection* (Geneva: Commission on the Churches' Participation in Development, World Council of Churches, n.d.). Women's rights and antitrafficking organizations in Thailand have also published a number of personal accounts of women enslaved as prostitutes and sold overseas. These pamphlets are disseminated widely in the hope of making young women more aware of the threat of enslavement. Good examples are Siriporn Skrobanek, *The Diary of Prang* (Bangkok: Foundation for Women, 1994); and White Ink (pseud.), *Our Lives, Our Stories* (Bangkok: Foundation

for Women, 1995). They follow the lives of women "exported," the first to Germany and the second to Japan.

23. Carey Goldberg, "Sex Slavery, Thailand to New York," *New York Times,* 11 September 1995, sec. B, p. 1.

24. Quoted in ibid.

25. "Chavalit Wants All Brothels Closed," *Bangkok Post,* 7 November 1992, p. 1.

26. Report of the Coordination Center for the Prevention and Suppression of Child Prostitutes and Child Labor Abuse, Crime Suppression Division (of the Thai National Police), Bangkok, 1995.

27. Colonel Surasak was interviewed by researchers from Asia Watch and quoted in *A Modern Form of Slavery,* p. 84.

28. See: www.un.or.th/traffickingproject

29. Quoted in Thanh-Dam Truong, *Sex, Morality, and Money: Prostitution and Tourism in Southeast Asia* (London: Zed Books, 1990), p. 179.

30. Center for the Protection of Children's Rights, "Case Study Report on Commercial Sexual Exploitation of Children in Thailand" (Bangkok, November 2003), p. 37.

31. Quoted in S. D. Bamber, K. J. Hewison, and J. Underwood, "A History of Sexually Transmitted Diseases in Thailand: Policy and Politics," *Genitourinary Medicine* 69, no. 2 (1993): 150–51.

32. The brochures are quoted in Truong, *Sex, Morality, and Money,* p. 178.

33. Phongpaichit and Baker, *Thailand's Boom,* p. 237.

Chapter 3. Mauritania

1. The cases of Temrazgint mint M'Bareck and Fatma mint Souleymane are taken from *Note D'Information Sur L'Esclavage en Mauritanie* (Nouakchott: SOS Esclaves, 1995), pp. 13–14.

2. David Hecht, "Where African Slavery Still Exists in the Eyes of Many," *Christian Science Monitor,* 13 February 1997, p. 6.

3. This and the other examples in this paragraph, drawn from Chapter 70 of the Koran, are noted in John Mercer, *Slavery in Mauritania Today* (London: Anti-Slavery International, 1981); quotations from pp. 29–30.

4. The Ministry of the Interior censors all newspaper copy before it is published, and the Press Law allows the minister of the interior to stop publication entirely. Given the low level of literacy, radio is probably the most important

medium for reaching the public. All radio and television stations, as well as two of the main newspapers, are owned and operated by the government.

5. Fred Saint-James, "50 Millions d'esclaves dans le monde," *Paris Match*, 11 April 1986, pp. 3–9, 88; quotation, 7.

6. From Richard Trillo and Jim Hudgens, "Mauritania," in *West Africa: The Rough Guide*, 2nd ed. (London: Penguin, 1995), p. 92.

7. World Bank Operational Manual, OP3.10, Annex C, August 2003.

8. *L'Esclavage en Mauritanie*, pp. 5–6.

9. Reported in "Slavery in Mauritania," statement by Boubacar Messaoud, president of SOS Esclaves to the Working Group on Contemporary Forms of Slavery, Sub-Commission on Prevention of Discrimination and Protection of Minorities, United Nations Economic and Social Council Commission on Human Rights, Geneva, 21 June 1996.

10. Temrazgint mint M'Bareck, interviewed on 12 July 1995 and reported in *L'Esclavage en Mauritanie*, p. 14.

11. Trillo and Hudgens, "Mauritania," p. 112.

12. "Human Rights Report for Mauritania" (Washington, D.C.: Department of State, 1999), p. 14.

Chapter 4. Brazil

1. Alison Sutton, *Slavery in Brazil: A Link in the Chain of Modernisation* (London: Anti-Slavery International, 1994), p. 34.

2. David Cleary, Dilwyn Jenkins, Oliver Marshall, and Jim Hine, *Brazil: The Rough Guide* (London: Penguin, 1997), p. 133.

3. The woman quoted was interviewed by Alison Sutton in Piauí, April 1992; see Sutton, *Slavery in Brazil*, p. 34.

4. José de Souza Martins, "Escravidão Hoje no Brasil," *Folha de São Paulo*, 13 May 1986, p. 7.

5. By 1996 approximately 10,000 people, including women and children, were being held in about 200 charcoal camps in Mato Grosso. (It is important to remember that I concentrated my research on three counties in the state of Mato Grosso do Sul: the 10,000 people held there were just a fraction of all those held in bondage throughout Brazil.)

6. "Working Conditions That Amount to Slavery," *Correspondent*, BBC2, 23 August 1995 (the reporter from Brazil was Julien Pettifor); Diana Jean Schemo,

"Of Modern Bondage—Special Report: Brazilians Chained to Job, and Desperate," *New York Times*, 10 August 1995, pp. A1, A6.

7. State secretary for agriculture in Mato Grosso do Sul, Ribas do Rio Pardo, reported in the local press, March 1992; quoted in Sutton, *Slavery in Brazil*, p. 73.

8. Sutton, *Slavery in Brazil*, p. 144.

Chapter 5. Pakistan

1. Cassandra Balchin, "Slavery in Pakistan, I—How the Other Half Dies," *Nation*, 5 September 1988, p. 1.

2. Farhad Karim, *Contemporary Forms of Slavery in Pakistan* (London: Human Rights Watch, 1995), p. 38.

3. Quoted in Cassandra Balchin, "Slavery in Pakistan, II—Exploitation All the Way," *Nation*, 6 September 1988, p. 24.

4. Ibid.

5. Quoted in Cassandra Balchin, "Slavery in Pakistan, III—Official Apathy," *Nation*, 8 September 1988, p. 1.

6. See Human Rights Commission of Pakistan, *State of Human Rights in Pakistan 1996* (Lahore: HRCP, 1996), p. 84.

7. Ibid., p. 85.

8. Ibid., p. 77.

9. Ibid., p. 123.

10. Ibid., p. 54.

11. Information on the Supreme Court and related cases are taken from *All Pakistan Legal Decisions*, vol. 42, 1990, "Darshan Masih v. State (Muhammad Afzal Zullah, J.)" PLD 1990 Supreme Court 513; and *All Pakistan Legal Decisions*, vol. 44, 1992 (6), "Central Statutes."

12. Human Rights Commission of Pakistan, *State of Human Rights in Pakistan, 1994* (Lahore: HRCP, 1994), p. 120.

Chapter 6. India

1. A study by Purola Block found that "these girls were taken into prostitution by their own husbands, fathers, and brothers . . . to earn freedom for the men of the family from the local money-lenders. Ironically, in several cases, men got into debt while buying their wives and later these very brides were sent into prostitution to earn their husbands' release"; quoted in "Incidence of Bonded

Labour in Uttar Pradesh," *Incidence of Bonded Labour in India*, vol. 1, *Area, Nature, and Extent* (Mussoorie: Lal Bahadur Shastri, National Academy of Administration, 1990), sec. 23, p. 10. The report continues: "This tradition is so old and wide spread that no social stigma is attached to such prostitutes on their return."

2. This incident was reported in several sources: see the *Indian Express*, 3 October 1985; A. Dingwaney, *Bonded Labour in India* (New Delhi: Rural Labour Cell, 1991); and "Incidence of Bonded Labour in Uttar Pradesh."

3. The official minimum wage for farm labor is currently 76 rupees per day; actual wages in the village of Bandi may fall to half that. The value of grain given to a bonded laborer like Baldev is 6 rupees per day.

4. See Eugene D. Genovese, *Roll, Jordon, Roll: The World the Slaves Made* (New York: Random House, 1976), pp. 49–86.

5. Reported in "Migrant Bonded Labour," in *Incidence of Bonded Labour in India*, vol. 3, *Summary of the Report and Issues for Consideration*, sec. 7, p. 10.

6. IAS [Indian Administration Service] Probationers, *Study Reports on Bonded Labour* (Mussoorie: National Academy of Administration, 1989–90), 6:83.

7. "Uttar Pradesh," in *Incidence of Bonded Labour in India*, vol. 4, *Study Reports*, sec. 17, p. 235.

8. This is the five-volume *Incidence of Bonded Labour in India*.

Chapter 7. What Can Be Done?

1. William Greider, *One World, Ready or Not: The Manic Logic of Global Capitalism* (New York: Simon and Schuster, 1997), p. 12.

2. Ibid., p. 342.

3. Quoted in ibid., p. 355.

4. Quoted in ibid., p. 24.

5. Human Rights Watch, *The Small Hands of Slavery: Bonded Child Labour in India* (New York: Human Rights Watch, 1996), pp. 14–16.

6. Greider, *One World, Ready or Not*, p. 333.

7. The EIA was the first to expose the billion-dollar trade in elephant ivory, the world's largest stockpile of rhino horn, and the illegal trade in CFC gases, among other stories. For more on the EIA, see www.eia-international.org (accessed 8 January 2004).

8. Ian Kershaw, speaking in "The Nazis," *BBC Timewatch*, BBC2, 20 October 1997.

9. Greider, *One World, Ready or Not*, p. 35.

10. Ibid., p. 359.

11. At present slavery is far down the list of UN priorities as well; it is being dealt with by a Working Group of a Sub-Commission of a Commission of the Economic and Social Council, which answers to the General Assembly (and is usually lost in the shuffle).

12. The 1956 Supplementary Convention on the Abolition of Slavery; see appendix 2 for more of the relevant excerpts.

13. Caldwell is quoted in Michael Specter, "Traffickers' New Cargo: Naive Slavic Women," *New York Times*, 11 January 1998, p. 6.

14. Richard Pierre Claude, personal communication, 22 October 1997. I am grateful to Professor Claude for providing this information.

15. See Susan Johnson and Ben Rogaly, *Microfinance and Poverty Reduction*, an Oxfam Development Guideline (Oxford: Oxfam, 1997).

16. Frederick Douglass, "What to the Slave Is the Fourth of July?" in *The Frederick Douglass Papers*, ed. John A. Blassingame et al. (New Haven: Yale University Press, 1979), 2:359.

Appendix 1. A Note on Research Methods

1. Richard A. Falk, "Theoretical Foundations of Human Rights," in *Human Rights and State Sovereignty* (New York: Holmes and Meier, 1981), p. 34.

2. Robert K. Yin, *Case Study Research: Design and Methods*, 2nd ed. (Thousand Oaks, Calif.: Sage, 1994), p. 1.

ACKNOWLEDGMENTS

Many people played a role in carrying out the research for this book, helping me to write it, or supporting the work in other ways. Crucial to the success of the research were my co-workers in the countries I visited: Dr. Rachel Harrison and Gampol Nirawan in Thailand, N'Gadi N'di in Mauritania, Luciano Padrão in Brazil, Haris Gazdar in Pakistan, and Pramod Singh and Dr. Praveen Jha in India. At the beginning of the project Sophie Sarre and Marjorie Farquharson helped me to ransack several libraries. Maureen Alexander-Sinclair gave me important tips on cracking the Anti-Slavery International archives.

At the University of Surrey Roehampton I had tremendous support from my colleagues, especially Professor Graham Fennell, Professor Martin Albrow, Dr. Christopher Jackman, Linda Wilson, and the Social Research Unit. I enjoyed partial financial support from the Faculty of Social Sciences through Dean David Woodman. Vicky Wood helped with translations from and to French. At ASI Mike Dottridge, David Ould, Mariam Ouattara, and Rose McCausland gave me the benefit of their experience and contacts, their insight and commitment.

Anitra Brown and Christopher Rowley, dear friends and much better writers than I'll ever be, gave me important guidance about finding my voice and getting it down on paper. They also fed me tidbits of information from around the world. Members of my family were also pressed into reading early drafts and provided critical help: I'm grateful to Mary Bales, Barbara Baumann, Janet Anna, and Sandy and Kami Cott. One could not hope for a more enthusiastic and supportive editor than Doug Abrams Arava at the University of California

Press, and the external readers of the first draft made many helpful suggestions, especially Professor Richard Pierre Claude. Sue Heinemann and Alice Falk did sterling work editing the text. Lysiane Pilois, at Key Travel, wonderfully managed the tangled arrangements for traveling around the world. After a hard day at the word processor, Sally Arvanitis and Vicki Friend always gave me a warm welcome with my carrot cake and coffee at LooLoo's cafe.

From Streatham Friends Meeting came moral support that opened the way in the most adverse circumstances and filled me with confidence and light. My best friend (and wife), Ginny Baumann, is responsible for much of the clarity in this book (the fuzziness is all mine), for the lack of split infinitives, and for the speed with which it was produced. I doubt it ever would have come about without her help. Our son, Gabriel, was born a few months before I began the fieldwork. In times of discouragement, his joy buoyed me up. Of course, most important in making this book were the men, women, and children around the world who suffered my questions and my camera, who patiently explained to me the nature of their lives.

INDEX

abolition, 258–62; in Brazil, 123–24; in India, 196; in Mauritania, 81, 88, 94, 108–9, 112; in Pakistan, 191; working for, 263–64. *See also* freedom

activism, 43, 148, 231, 247–48, 258–62; for children, 43, 78, 241; in Mauritania, 82, 90, 109, 116, 120, 247–48, 254; in Thailand, 43, 78–79

Afghan workers, in Pakistan, 164–65

Africa, 9, 12, 21–22

Afro-Mauritanians, 91, 113, 116; persecution of, 89–90, 93, 94

agriculture: debt bondage and, 9, 16, 17–18, 23; in India, 196–98, 201–2, 205–23; modernization and, 221–22, 232; in Pakistan, 154

Ahmadi Muslims, Pakistan, 177

AIDS/HIV, 36, 49, 54–55, 59–60, 76

All-Pakistan Brick Kiln Owners' Association, 162–63

Amazon, 4, 30–31

American South, 222; India parallels to, 226; Mauritania parallels to, 113–14, 119; old slavery in, 6, 10–11, 15–16, 24–25; segregation in, 6–7; slave codes in, 30

Amnesty International, 230, 247, 259, 260

ancient Egypt, slavery in, 12, 197

ancient Greece, slavery in, 12

Anderson, Bridget, 27–28

Angelou, Maya, 253

antiracist groups, British, 248

Anti-Slavery Award, 254

Anti-Slavery International (ASI), 7, 28, 247–48, 253, 258–59; addresses for, 263

antislavery organizations: in Mauritania, 90, 102–3, 109, 116, 120, 247–48, 254. *See also* activism; Anti-Slavery International; human rights

Antitrafficking Law (1928; Thailand), 72

apartheid, 248–49

Arabization, in Mauritania, 93–94, 113

ASI. *See* Anti-Slavery International

Baldev and Markhi (India), 205–11

Bandi village (India), 204–21

Bangladesh, bonded labor in, 9

barbarism, modern, 233

BBC, 144, 147

Bhutto Benazir, 191

Bilal, Mauritania, 100–103

blood ties, Pakistani, 172

bondage: history of, 197; length of, 15, 19; types of, in India, 198–99, 200

bonded labor, 23, 33; in Bangladesh, 9; in India, 9, 16–18, 219–23, 266, 286–87n1; in Nepal, 9; in Pakistan, 9, 191, 230, 233, 266. *See also* debt bondage

291

Bonded Labour Abolition Act (Pakistan), 191

Brazil, 121–48; abolition, 123–24; charcoal making in, 4, 23, 125–34, 147, 242, 266, 285n5; economy, 124–25; European settlement of, 123; foreign debt and, 124; government of, 125, 148; multinational corporations in, 125; new slavery in, 25, 31, 33, 232; old slavery in, 24–25

bribery, 54. See also corruption

brick kilns, in Pakistan, 152–54, 157, 161–64, 174

Brick Kiln Workers Union (Pakistan), 163

brickmaking, in Pakistan, 149–54, 185–93, 266

Brickworkers Union (Pakistan), 187–92

Britain: antiracist groups in, 248; antislavery enforcement in, 123, 250–51; domestic slaves in, 3, 26–28; Immigration Acts, 28; nineteenth-century textile industry in, 235, 238; prostitution in, 22

Britain's Secret Slaves (Anderson), 27–28

brothels, 5; income of, 49, 54–57; in Thailand, 34–37, 40, 53–59, 73

Buddhism, in Thailand, 38–39, 62–63

Burma, 37, 247, 266; Thai prostitution and, 66–68; war slavery and, 21

business: slavery and, 142–43, 147, 238–39, 243

Cabral, Pedro Alvares, 123

CAFOD. See Catholic Agency for Overseas Development

Caldwell, Gillian, 251

capitalism, 13–14, 233

Caribbean, 3–4, 21, 25

carpet industry, child slavery in, 238, 240–41

case studies, 265–67; in Brazil (charcoal workers), 127–28, 135–39; in Britain (Laxmi Swami), 27–28; in France (Seba), 1–3; in India, 205–11 (Baldev and Markhi), 211–15 (Shivraj and Munsi), 215–17 (Leela), 225; in Mauritania (Bilal), 100–103; in Pakistan (brickworkers), 149–50, 157, 179–82; in Thailand (Siri), 34–37, 41–42, 63

caste: India, 202, 206, 218–19, 222–23; Pakistan, 172–73, 184

Catholic Agency for Overseas Development (CAFOD), 259

CCEM. See French Committee against Modern Slavery

Center for the Protection of Children's Rights (Thailand), 43, 78

Centre for Human Rights (Geneva), 275

change: in developing countries, 234; economic, 12, 232, 236, 245; social, 12–13, 77–78, 121–22

charcoal camps, in Brazil, 129–34, 147, 285n5

charcoal making, in Brazil, 4, 23, 125–31, 242, 266

chattel slavery, 19–20

child labor: in Brazilian charcoal camps, 143–46; in carpet making, 225, 238, 240–41; in India, 198–99, 200, 209; in Mauritania, 112; in Pakistan brickmaking, 150–52, 154, 188

children: activism for, 43, 78, 241; in debt bondage, 150–52, 154, 188, 237; enslaved, 237, 238, 241, 254, 261, 274; as household slaves, 3, 21; in Mauritania, 86–87, 97, 111; in Pakistan, 184–85; in Rugmark Campaign, 241; in sex slavery, 39, 43, 73–74, 78–79. See also child labor

Christians, in Pakistan, 152, 162–64, 173, 177

churches, abolition role of, 261

civil order, breakdown of, 29–30

Claude, Richard Pierre, 255

cold war, end of, 13–14

commercial sex, in Thailand, 43–48, 51, 53–57, 71, 75–79

compensation, in Mauritania, 113–14

Congress Party (India), 223

construction projects, Indian bonded labor in, 203–4

consumers: power of, 241; slave-produced goods and, 23–24, 239, 272

contracts: debt bondage and, 18–20; fraudulent, 17, 26–27, 31

corruption, 232; governmental, 12–14, 29–31, 32–33, 63–64, 244–47; police, 29–30, 179, 245–46, 251–52; in rehabilitation programs, 214–15, 219, 230, 257–58

CPT. See Pastoral Land Commission

credit, developing countries and, 257

Daddah, President Mokhtar ould, 92–93

debt bondage, 9, 19–20; agriculture and, 16–18, 23, 154, 196–98, 201–2, 205–23; in Brazil, 128–29; children in, 150–